Journey on the James

JOURNEY ON THE JAMES

Three Weeks through the Heart of Virginia

Earl Swift

UNIVERSITY PRESS OF VIRGINIA

Charlottesville and London

THE UNIVERSITY PRESS OF VIRGINIA
© 2001 by Earl Swift
All rights reserved
Printed in the United States of America
First published 2001

♾ The paper used in this publication meets the minimum requirements of the American
National Standard for Information Sciences—Permanence of Paper for Printed Library
Materials, ANSI Z39.48 1984.

Library of Congress Cataloging-in-Publication Data

Swift, Earl, 1958–
    Journey on the James : three weeks through the heart of Virginia / Earl Swift.
      p.   cm.
    ISBN 0-8139-2021-3 (alk. paper)
    1. James River (Va.)—Description and travel.   2. James River Valley (Va.)—
Description and travel.   3. James River Valley (Va.)—History, Local.   4. Swift,
Earl, 1958– —Journeys—Virginia—James River.   5. Canoes and canoeing—
Virginia—James River.   I. Title.

F232.J2 S9   2001
975.5'4—dc21   00-047307

FOR *SAYLOR*

CONTENTS

Journey on the James

THE INFANT JACKSON RIVER
TRICKLES TOWARD HIGHTOWN,
BEGINNING A 430-ODD-MILE DOWNHILL
RUN TO HAMPTON ROADS.

DAY ONE

On which the journey's protagonists wander hypothermic and disoriented on Lantz Mountain, birthplace of the James

🐜 Five minutes into the journey, and already I'm lost.

I'm trudging through dew-soaked grass on Jacob Hevener's farm in the Alleghenies of western Virginia. My quarry, the beginning of a mighty river, is reputed to be somewhere on this windswept ridge out back of Hevener's farmhouse.

Only my third-generation photocopy of a twenty-one-year-old government topo map doesn't do this mountainside justice. On paper the river's black on treeless white, a narrow but plain line that wanders an inch or so across a couple of contour lines, then dead-ends next to a tiny, hollow square—a barn. What actually greets me is a foot-wide cleft furred with tall grass, crisscrossed by barbed wire and electric fence, studded with cowpies and swallowed by thickets of live oak. It vanishes behind hummocks too low to earn the map's attention, jogs out of sight beyond folds in the slope. Dozens of rivulets spill into the stream, and at some forks both are so tiny it's a coin-flip to pick which is the tributary, which the main branch.

"Damn," I sigh. I march through the grass skirting a small farm pond and reach a barbed-wire fence. I climb two of its rusted strands, one hand on an ancient, rough-cut post, the other resting gingerly between a pair of menacing barbs on its top wire, the entire fence wobbling beneath me. Holding my breath, I throw a leg over the top and promptly catch my knee on a barb. It grabs my skin and doesn't let go.

Six minutes into the journey, and already I may have tetanus.

"You OK?" Ian Martin hollers from twenty yards away. He's my partner in this venture, the expedition's photographer and crew chief—not only its chief, but all of its Indians, as well—and he's struggling to adjust his camera bag's straps so that he can get over the fence without ripping out his entrails.

"I'll get back to you on that," I tell him, and carefully lift my other leg over the top. The barb is still snagged on my knee. I give it a hard jerk, it pops free with a twang, and a thick, dark drop of blood quickly forms a dome over the hole in my leg. "Watch out for those barbs," I warn. "You might have to drag me out of here if I get lockjaw." I limp down the fence, take his camera bag from him, and watch as he scales the wires.

"Where to?" he asks.

I study the map. "It's got to be pretty much straight ahead, maybe slightly to the right," I say. "But it's hard to tell. The scale of this thing isn't much help."

"There've gotta be snakes all over here," Ian mutters. I follow his gaze into the shade of the live oaks, where resting cattle have worn shallow, bare-dirt bowls in the ground. Just beyond the nearest is what looks to be the stream, down to a few inches wide, barely visible in the gloom. Ian's right: it looks like a postcard sent by vacationing timber rattlers.

But beginning the trip means reaching the beginning, and we must begin the trip. I stride into the oaks and pick up a stout fallen branch, and whack it on the ground as we climb uphill, eyes peeled for movement. Ian splits off after a couple minutes, following another trace that we spot fifty yards away through the trees, and for a while we keep track of each other with occasional shouts. "You see anything?"

"No."

"Me neither."

Then, through the oaks' low branches, I catch a glimpse of weathered planking on a high knoll off to my right. I hike out of the trees, start scrambling up the knoll's close-cropped flank. "Ian!" I yell. "Over here!"

The barn is a forlorn thing, roof fuzzed with rust, boards warped and worn by a century of long highland winters. We cross its yard, weave among ancient farm machinery rusting between clumps of purple thistle, a wedge of old wagon wheel, a piece of shotgun-sprayed sheet metal. The barn's door is blocked by an X of lumber nailed across its mouth. Inside, the floor is ankle-deep in manure, and hay dangles from cracks in the ceiling. Crickets chirp in the gloom.

A gust, cold for early September, sweeps over the knoll. The tin roof quivers, a flap of loose metal clangs. I zip my jacket tight around my neck. It seems abandoned, this place, forgotten. But we've driven across the wide Piedmont, climbed switchbacking two-lane highways, crossed a chain of smoky ridgelines to reach this pasture and barn in Virginia's northwest corner. For my map, sparse on details though it is, shows that this slouching old building holds a remarkable place on the American landscape. Rain falling on one side of its roof drains northward, into an inches-wide brook that downstream sheds its qualifiers—"South Fork," "South Branch"—to become the Potomac. Rain on its far side wriggles down the sloping pasture we've just climbed to meet a dribble of water, gin-clear and icy, that leaks from the rock beneath.

The source of the Jackson River.

Parent to the James.

From this trickle grows a river that offered sustenance to Indian and early colonist, carried pioneers to the new lands of the West, bloomed red with the blood spilled in three wars. No other feature of American topography has so witnessed the country's history. The continent's first permanent English settlement, Jamestown, rose on the river's bank. George Washington explored it, fought on it, and hatched plans for a grand canal system along its shore. On the run from the Redcoats, Thomas Jefferson may have holed up in a cave in its bluffs.

The first fights between settlers and Indians broke out here, and grew into great battles. The nation's first mines, factories, hospitals, farms, and forts rose on its edges. African-American adventurers poled *batteaux* through the Blue Ridge on its fast, foaming waters, and Patrick Henry demanded liberty or death within earshot of its falls. When the Civil War came, the James was a battleground, and captured Union troops endured an outdoor POW camp on one of its islands. Just beyond its mouth, the federal ironclad *Monitor* and the *Confederate* Virginia traded point-blank blows in the world's first modern sea battle. And the James remained at the center of American life throughout the twentieth century: its shipyards helped win two world wars and turned out America's greatest ocean liners and aircraft carriers, and below Jamestown it widens into one of the world's greatest natural harbors and the busiest port on the East Coast.

Ian and I circle the barn, running our hands over boards roughened by ice and wind and curled like ski tips, and turn to gaze on the streams flanking this little bulge in the mountainside. They veer apart just below, the Potomac curving northward, the Jackson meandering behind Hevener's place before abruptly cutting south. I know, in the abstract, where it goes from there; I've lived near the James's mouth for most of my adult life, have dragged a fingertip along the length of its blue course on road maps, have braided its path on scores of travels across Virginia. I've admired its massiveness while crossing its mouth, just as New Yorkers might pay the Hudson a moment's mind on the George Washington Bridge. But the James has always been, at best, passing scenery to me; and at worst, a messy, powerful interloper in my well-ordered, landlubbing life.

So I have embarked on a voyage of discovery: I have come to Highland

County, and this farm at a tiny crossroads hamlet called Hightown, to find the James's beginning, and from here to travel its length. I'll hike the riverbank until the stream's big enough to navigate by inner tube, tube it until it's deep enough to support a canoe, then paddle it through mountains and Piedmont and coastal plain to its mouth at Hampton Roads.

It is an adventure fraught with the possibility of failure. The Jackson and James tumble through rocky gorges on their descent through the mountains, spill over a host of dams, on occasion churn through tremendous rapids. I'll be alone in a fourteen-and-a-half-foot plastic boat. I haven't canoed since I was a Boy Scout.

Ian, meanwhile, will parallel my route in his station wagon. The arrangement will separate us for hours at a time, so that if I get into trouble, he won't be able to help. And he may have problems of his own: Ian's car is a fourteen-year-old Volvo with 275,000 miles on it.

The seeds of our odyssey were sown one afternoon in early 1998, as I stared at a computer screen.

I was at work. I had no office; my entire domain consisted of my balky green-on-black monitor, a grimy keyboard, and my desk: standard black powdercoated steel; skinny center drawer intended for pens and paper clips but stuffed with photos and old bills and a desiccated stamp pad and Coffee Mate packets and keys that opened locks and doors I couldn't identify; top right drawer of wholly impractical middling size, layered in more such crap and an empty stapler, a dozen cassettes, and a cheap Walkman; and file drawer, stuffed with old letters and newspaper clippings and an emergency change of clothes. A matching hutch gave me room for a dictionary, a thesaurus, several reference books, two phone directories, a bulging folder of maps, and a half-dozen framed pictures of my chubby-cheeked, smiling daughter. My desk was ringed by others just like it, arranged so that I couldn't make eye contact with anyone sitting at them. Outside that ring was another, and another beyond that, and another group circled still farther out.

Being a cog in a gearworks usually didn't bother me much. I wrote stories for a newspaper, found a lot of satisfaction in turning them out; and though the newsroom's sea of desks might strike an outsider as bleak and nameless, it made for an egalitarian work environment, one in which the bosses sat at desks exactly like my own. But on this particular afternoon, I was awash in ennui. I felt trapped in a routine of regular stories cranked out on regularly spaced deadlines. I felt stifled by my yuppie reliance on electronics, climate control, off-street parking. I was sick of the music on the worn cassette tapes in my drawer. I hated my clothes.

It was one of those episodes of restlessness and self-loathing that some people cure with vacations, others with shopping sprees, still others with work-place violence. None seemed a solution in my case. What I needed was a break from my everyday existence. A challenge I wasn't sure I could pull off. A little brinkmanship. I eyed my colleagues in quiet orbit around me, foreheads creased in concentration as they stared at their screens. Yeah, I thought, an adventure. I needed to get my blood moving. To depend on my wits and muscle for a while. To exchange the mundane worries that jumbled my life—insurance pay-ments, office politics, day-care arrangements—for more primal anxieties. Brain-stem stuff, like: Do I have enough water? Where will I sleep? And: Holy Christ, is that a snake?

Then something happened that made me feel a game piece in some cos-mic chess match. I was called into a conference with my boss, Dennis Hartig, *The Virginian-Pilot's* managing editor, a big cheese. I don't remember what he wanted to see me about, but I clearly recall the conversation taking an unex-pected turn. "You know what I think would be a great story?" he suddenly asked. "You know what story I'd love to see *you* do someday?"

I braced myself. Such talk, with any editor, rarely ends happily. "No," I al-most whispered. "What?"

And apropos of nothing we'd ever discussed before, Dennis said: "A series on canoeing the whole length of the James River." He clapped his hands, stood up from his chair, practically yelled: "Wouldn't that be *great*?"

So here I am, in the company of the only *Pilot* photographer willing to spend three weeks sitting in his car, watching someone else splash downriver through the Virginia backcountry. I didn't know Ian well before we set out on the six-hour drive to Highland County yesterday. I now know that he inter-sects with the world around him with wide eyes and heartfelt profanity. That he harbors a penchant for the Swedes: his apartment looks like an IKEA spread; he owns a thousand-dollar Swedish mattress carved from some oddball foam rubber that sucks you into its depths and clenches you fast as you sleep; he drives two ancient Volvos, both of which he has completely disassembled and reassembled.

And that he, like me, overpacks. From the barn we can see his station wagon down on the two-laner outside Hevener's farmhouse, visibly sagging under the weight of all we've crammed into its hatch: stacks of clothes; three hundred dollars in freeze-dried meals, instant coffee, peanut butter and beer; two isobu-tane stoves; two nylon backpacking tents; our sleeping bags; sleeping pads, flash-lights, lanterns and assorted small camping tools; a two-wheeled cart that straps to the canoe; my eight-foot, two-bladed kayaking paddle; a life vest; knap-sacks; six gallons of bottled water; a deflated truck inner tube and a bicycle pump with which to inflate it; a whitewater helmet; two plastic ice chests; Ian's pillow, a $120 Swedish model that matches his mattress; our briefcases, bloated with maps, reference books, and notes; two laptop computers; and a big plastic suitcase containing a $15,000 digital camera kit that Ian will use to take his pictures and zip them via computer to the newspaper. I find myself looking at the car and wondering what it measures in cubits.

Jacob Hevener was weighing cattle with other locals when we pulled up outside his thousand-acre spread this morning. He broke away from the business long enough to point out his rambling, green-roofed farmhouse, and to tell us we'd find the Jackson just beyond it. "Go on up there and look around," he said, "and I'll be done here in twenty, thirty minutes."

Passing his front door, we decided to ring the bell to alert Hevener's wife, Carol, that we'd be on the property. She eyed me doubtfully when she saw my shorts. "You'll have to put some long britches on," she said. "It was forty-six degrees this morning." The thought had occurred to me, as well: chilly gusts were creating oceanic waves in the acres of tall grass around us. I didn't tell Mrs. Hevener that I packed for this trip in ninety-degree weather back in Norfolk. I didn't tell her that I hadn't expected the temperature to drop fifty degrees on the drive westward. I didn't tell her that despite packing for every conceivable need— we'll even be able to drink cappuccino in camp—I have not brought a single pair of long pants.

Now I'm eager to leave the barn, to get moving, to regain some feeling in my legs. "Well," I say, turning to Ian, "what do you say we try to find the beginning of this river? We've got to be close."

"OK," he says. "Where to?"

I point vaguely up Lantz Mountain. "Somewhere over there."

We head down the knoll's lumpy flank as I study the map and struggle to jibe our surroundings with their printed facsimile. In the wrinkle enfolding the infant Jackson we find the water six inches wide and gurgling fast, and hike uphill against the flow. The stream narrows to five inches. Four. Two.

Finally, at a rock pile around the base of a haggard-looking walnut tree, it ends. The water seeping from the earth here is a half-inch wide, no more, and it pulses slowly over a tiny, inch-tall waterfall to begin its downhill journey. I glance across the knoll, see its far side descend to the Potomac, and realize that this knob of land—this sliver of perhaps 150 yards—is all that keeps the northern half of Virginia from being an island.

Then I crouch down at the rock pile's edge and hold my finger under the trickle, and try to imagine the same river five miles wide and five fathoms deep at its mouth.

On our way down the mountain Ian realizes he's misplaced a camera lens. We hunt around the scrub near the barbed-wire fence, figuring he may have dropped it in the traverse, but turn up nothing. Ian barks a string of obscenities. "I can't do without that thing," he announces. "I've got to find it."

"Maybe you dropped it up at the barn," I suggest.

"We could have a look."

"Tell you what," I say. "*You* have a look. I'll head back to the farm and talk to Mr. Hevener." He stalks off into the live oaks. "Watch out for snakes!" I holler after him. He promptly picks up a fallen tree limb and starts beating the ground with it.

Below me, Hightown glows white under a clear, bright sky. I hike downhill through knee-high grass along the stream's jogging cut, and soon the ground flattens, and the Jackson trickles into Hevener's round pond, loiters a while, and spills down a streambed on the other side. From there it cuts southeast, veering away from the farmhouse. I part with the river and stroll up past the house, glancing back toward the barn. There's no sign of Ian. I cross the farmhouse's side yard and spot Jacob Hevener across the two-laner out front—U.S. Route 250, the descendant of an old turnpike, and probably not a lot busier today than it was when new, in 1838. Hevener has troubling news. We've visited the wrong barn.

Sure enough, he says, the Jackson does climb up to where we found its end. And the Potomac might well be the stream I saw on the far side of the knoll, as my government map says it is. But the barn known throughout the county for draining into both the James and Potomac isn't the decrepit wreck I've just explored; it's the much better-looking tractor barn in front of which we now stand, just across the road from his house. We stroll that way for a closer look, sit on the tailgate of a minivan parked a few yards from the barn's open bays. The southern half of its roof, he explains, drains across the road and down a gently sloping field to the Jackson; the northern side finds the Potomac somewhere beyond view in a field out back.

I'm inclined to believe Hevener, who has lived on the land for seventy-four years, was Hightown's postmaster for thirty, and is the sixth generation of his family to farm here. In fact, when I browsed last night in the library in Monterey, the Highland County seat, I ran across a map of the county drawn by Thomas Campbell, Highland's surveyor from 1848 to 1858, and right where Hightown is now the map read simply "Jacob Hevener."

Heveners were among the county's early settlers, among the legion of German immigrants who poured into the Shenandoah Valley and the mountains around it in the eighteenth century. The first of them is mentioned in county records way back in 1794. "There was Jacob Senior," Hevener says. "Jacob Junior. Then there's George Washington—he's my great-grandfather, George Washington Hevener. Then George William Hevener. Then my father, Richard Washington Hevener."

But as much as I trust the present-day Hevener's knowledge of the land, I can read a topo map, too. "Look at this," I say, opening my packet of charts to show him the tiny square marking the uphill barn, the dashed-line river traces dead-ending on either side.

"That might be," he allows. "I'm sure your map is right. But this is *the* barn."

I'm mulling this silently when Ian appears in the field beyond the farmhouse and crosses the road, smiling, hollering "I found it!" We slouch outside the tractor barn for a few minutes, enjoying the sunshine, trying to stay in the lee of the minivan as the wind continues to swoop down off Lantz Mountain, listening to Hevener talk of his life on the farm, and as postmaster, and as proprietor of the Hevener Store, the biggest building in the cluster of houses, old commercial buildings, and cattle sheds that constitute Hightown proper. The store closed in 1994, Hevener says, but he still owns it, and it looks now as it did when the surrounding farms depended on the place for their groceries. He suggests we take a look, so with his pet beagle, Bee Gee, we stroll the empty highway's centerline.

The building is a steep-roofed frame place, tall, its gable facing the main road, its entrance shaded by a broad plank porch. Inside, Hevener treats Ian and me to Coca-Colas in glass bottles. We drink them while touring the museum he's made of the place: the store's glass cases and display shelves are filled with miniature cars, carefully crafted and authentically detailed. I wander under the stamped-tin ceiling to a back wall, where I find a wind-up phone and, tacked to the plaster beside it, a list of often-called neighbors, their names written on paper turned the color of toffee, their phone extensions a series of dashes and dots rather than numbers. Hevener demonstrates the contraption for us, giving the little crank on the phone's side a couple long spins, then a short. Dash-dash-dot. The machine's innards whine like a tin friction toy. Might seem primitive, Hevener says, but provided you took a little care in your cranking, it was about as reliable as push buttons.

Taking advantage of our shelter, we reopen the maps and have our host walk us through what to expect along the river below the farmhouse. A few fences, he says. Otherwise, rolling hills and cattle. He offers to call his neighbors downstream, let them know we'll be passing through. We say goodbye, and leave Hevener and Bee Gee to lock up.

Back behind the farmhouse, I stop by a small fenced cemetery where five generations of Heveners are buried. I climb the rails to sit on top. Jacob Sr., a small headstone reads. Born in 1773, died in 1860. The name of his wife, Catherine, is on another. Henry Hevener, born in 1824 and dead at 24. Martha Hevener, born in 1832, dead at 29. I turn back toward the Jackson, flowing thinly through the field below. And wonder: Did these pioneers who lived and died on the bank of this tiny stream ever think about where it led? Whom it touched? How it changed?

Then I jump from the fence and head downhill.

It's time to find out for myself.

DAY TWO

On which the expedition follows the infant Jackson through the Alleghenies, and a gantlet of vicious pets

From the Hevener farm the Jackson River, little more than a foot wide and an inch deep, burbles south across rolling pasture. I set off along its banks on trails tamped into the tall grass by processions of cattle, beginning my downstream journey from the river's headwaters to that far-off place where it becomes the James and rolls across Virginia to the sea. I pass limestone outcroppings laid bare by the stream's meanderings; descend into scrubby, breezeless hollows thick with the smell of manure; climb barbed-wire fences that are the only signs of man's presence. Herds of cattle eye me dully from the flanks of nearby hills as I tromp along the stream under an intense sun. Horseflies buzz. Sand-colored grasshoppers flit hard and spiny against my legs. Buzzards wheel overhead.

Then, maybe a mile below the farmhouse, the Jackson's thin ribbon of water corkscrews into a hole in the ground and vanishes. Ahead lies sun-baked, dusty creekbed. I squat beside the hole. It's a foot across, rimmed in saffron-colored rock, and sucks down the gushing water with a thirsty gurgle. It's limestone, like all of the bottomland beside the stream; the ground beneath my feet is probably riddled with caves, and here the Jackson is continuing the process that created them, gnawing an ever-deeper, ever-wider path underground.

I look to the west, beyond the low hills rising beside the riverbed to dragon-backed Lantz Mountain, perhaps a mile away. It is one of dozens of parallel ridges of harder, more resistant sandstone that define the Virginia Appalachians, each of them running northeast to southwest, all of them steep-sided, knobby. I'm in a trench in this corduroy terrain. Beyond Lantz Mountain is another narrow, limestone-floored valley, that of Back Creek, the Jackson's westernmost tributary; then comes another rib, the crest of which marks the state line with West Virginia, and still farther west, another valley. To my east, invisible behind the stream's steep bank, lies Monterey Mountain. Past it is another trench, then a rib, then yet another valley, and so on for thirty straight-line miles. Look at a topo map or a Landsat photo of the region, and the Appalachians here seem a gargantuan set of parallel wrinkles, a bit like those that appear in your skin when you gently pinch your arm. In each of these valleys a stream runs, and eventually, like fingers on a hand, each fuses with the Jackson.

At the moment, however, all this seems a bit academic, because the principal stream has disappeared. I hike fifty yards downstream—or where downstream would be, if there were any water in the bed—but find only a rocky furrow. Up on the hillside to my left I can see the roof of the Volvo, the canoe gleaming in the sun. Ian's evidently parked on the side of the two-lane road that runs through Hightown and parallels the Jackson for its first few miles. Perhaps I'll be able to see the river's continuation from the high ground, I think, and start for the car.

It's a much tougher climb than I expect. I'm wearing shorts and a T-shirt, and carrying only a daypack of water, Clif Bars, and a notebook, but after ten minutes of picking my way up the rocky, vine-covered slope, eyes wide for snakes, I'm sweating and cussing. And it's wasted effort, because the river downstream is invisible behind a bushy knoll.

Ian doesn't hear me coming. When I reach a wire fence at the roadside I see that he's sitting in the driver's seat, listening to a language tape on the stereo and repeating its phrases en Español.

"Ian!"

Nada.

"Ian!" I wave my arms, and the movement catches his eye. He sticks his head out of the car. "Hey."

"Got a problem," I tell him, still wheezing from the climb. "I've lost the river." He smiles and nods, expecting a punch line. "Yeah?"

"Yeah," I say. "I'm serious. The river just disappears into a hole."

"A hole?"

"Maybe you oughta take a look."

He locks up the car, scales the fence, and we weave down the embankment, tripping over the vines every few seconds, avoiding headlong spills through dumb luck alone. Once at the creekbed I lead him upstream to the place where the Jackson spins underground. He stares for several seconds. "Wow," he finally says.

"It's gotta pop back out sooner or later," I offer.

"What *is* this thing?" he asks, crouching next to the hole, staring into its blackness. "Is it a cave?"

"Yeah, I think so. The river probably just sumps out here when it's running low, goes along underground for a ways, then comes back to the surface."

"What's the map say?"

I fish the topo from my pocket. According to the U.S. Geological Survey, the Jackson splashes merrily along in typical mountain-stream style here. It's not supposed to fall into any holes. "It doesn't show it disappearing," I say, "so it doesn't show it coming back."

"Well, I'll walk with you for a while," Ian says. "Let's see what happens."

So we hike the riverbed. A hundred yards downstream, the bed still dry, we reach a chest-high fence that blocks our path. It's barbed wire, and more— at the fence posts the wire isn't simply stapled in place, but looped around what look like miniature plastic thread spools. Our first electric fence. "This was bound to happen," I mutter. "I have a feeling that we're going to be running into a lot of these."

"Man," Ian sighs. "Want to climb back up to the road?"

"Not really."

"Do you think it's turned on?"

"Beats me." I scan the ground at our feet. "Let's find something to throw at it."

Ian finds a long strand of straw, holds it over the top wire, and lets it drop as he hops backward. I'm not sure what we expect to happen—maybe the fence will make a loud zapping as the straw makes contact, or a puff of smoke. Maybe it'll flash. Maybe the straw will instantly burst into flame. But it does nothing at all. The straw slides noiselessly off the wire and dives to the ground. We experiment with a wad of vines, with the same result. "Guess it's turned off," I say. "Why don't you grab it, to make sure."

"No way," Ian says. "If you're so sure it's turned off, why don't *you* grab it?"

"Because I have to hike all day," I tell him. "You just have to sit in the car. If it turns out to be live, you'd have all day to recover."

"Yeah, well, forget that."

At about that point I notice that on its past aboveground jaunts, the Jackson has carved away the soil beneath a short section of the fence. A foot of air separates the riverbed from the bottom wire. If I suck in my gut, I can probably fit. I take off my knapsack and toss it over the fence. "Be careful," Ian says, his voice wavering. I drop onto my back and wriggle head-first under the wire, first pushing myself with my legs, then—when my chest has cleared— dropping my knees flat and walking myself backward on my hands. It proves easy: I come no closer than two inches. Ian lets out a long breath. "Let's hope they all go like that."

"I'm pretty sure it's turned off," I say, brushing myself off and picking up the knapsack. "Check it out."

"I'm going back to the car now."

I wave and head downstream. A few minutes later the Jackson is again glistening beside me, its subterranean side trip complete, and just minutes after that it hooks left and into a culvert under the road. I scramble up the bank, scale the roadside fence and hike the blacktop for a while, watching the stream shimmer across a flat sliver of sun-faded pastureland. Before long the river slips behind a low ridge, and I realize I'll have to abandon the road to keep it in sight. Hiking its bank means crossing private property, so Ian picks me up and we head for the nearest farmhouse, seeking permission.

It's a big white frame place, guarded by a gate on which there's a massive "Beware of Dog" sign. A woman steps off the porch and strolls across the yard to meet me. I explain what I'm doing, and she says that she guesses it would be all right if I walk across her land. "Any electric fences?" I ask.

"Oh, yeah, they're back there," she nods, "but they ought to be turned off."

Ought to be. "You're pretty sure they're off?"

"Yeah," she says, "they're off. Should be."

Should be. I nod toward the sign. "I don't have to worry about the dog?" She shakes her head slowly. "She's tied up," she says. Her tone carries a worrisome touch of uncertainty, as if she means to add, "I think." Then the dog barks. It's a good ways off, behind the house, but its volume—and its diesel tone—is troubling. "That sounds like a big dog," I mumble.

She smiles. "A Doberman and rottweiler mix."

"But she's tied up?" I have a hard time smiling back.

The woman squints at me for a moment, then shrugs. "I have two collars on her," she says. "She keeps breaking them."

I hurry across the meadow below the farmhouse, looking over my shoulder every few seconds. I scale a gate, weave through a grazing herd of cattle, reach an electric fence and, pausing just a second to take a deep breath, grab ahold and pull myself over. I leap the width of the Jackson, climb a second fence, a third. All the while, the dog bellows behind me. Before I know it I've crossed two farms and reached a road crossing. I've made very good time.

A little more than five miles below its head the Jackson cuts through its valley's eastern wall at Vanderpool Gap. The long ridge is crimped there, and in this narrow, steep-sided cleavage is just enough room for a two-lane road and the river to pass. The gap is named for John Vanderpool, the Dutch explorer who discovered it. He reported the presence of the valley through which I've just hiked, but added that the mountains beyond it looked impassable—and indeed, it's easy to see why early settlers found the Appalachians daunting.

They'd spend long days climbing one ridge, sure that it marked the last obstacle before the promised land to the west, only to discover at its crest that another ridge waited just beyond. Throughout the eighteenth century, while cities bloomed at the James's mouth and along its wide, tidal stretch, its upland banks were only sparsely settled. One reason was the terrain Vanderpool traveled: in those roadless days it limited the load a settler could carry to little more than his rifle and an axe—thereby dictating a lifestyle that was rustic and mean even by the standards of the hardiest backwoodsman.

I hike through the gap, the shadows cast by its high walls turning the stream black beside me, conscious that save for the road, the place probably looks a lot like it did when Vanderpool visited. The gap and the valleys it links have not seen farms give way to cities, haven't been built up and torn down and built up again. Time has brought little change. That won't stay the case as I travel downstream. A river's mouth is a port of entry, after all, a station of transients, its population turning over constantly. Its buildings, its style, change with the people living there, so that an acre of ground on the wide, tidal James might have undergone a dozen permutations in the time it took these headwaters to gain settlement. In a way I'll be traveling backwards through time as I hike and paddle downriver, moving from that part of the James last settled, much still in its wild, pre-European state, to marshy tidewater bends where white history runs far deeper.

And in a way the water beside me will make a similar odyssey. The Jackson is young here, cold and clear and just emerged from the earth. As it flows downhill, it will swell with the waters of countless tributaries, with the experience gained on their tumbles from the highlands. By the time the James reaches the oldest European settlements on its banks, it will be old itself, bruised and muddied and miles wide, the sum of a thousand creeks and runs and the journeys they've taken.

I emerge from the gap in a hamlet labeled Vanderpool on my map—a clot of small houses that might have grown into a town if politics hadn't steered an early turnpike around the place. I'm in another valley now, one to the east of the last. The Jackson bends south to run down its middle. I follow.

It's still under six feet wide as it hisses over its stony bed, its level so low that the tops of some fist-sized rocks at its edges are dry. But a few hundred yards below Vanderpool, narrow Town Creek dumps into the river, which widens by a couple of feet, and a little ways farther the Jackson reaches Mackey Spring, a bell-shaped pool. Trout laze amid columns of cold, crystalline water percolating from the spring's floor of rock and sand. The water gushes down a bed of pebbles to the stream, and promptly doubles its size.

It's still far too tiny to float—a dozen feet across but just inches deep. So I walk its edge on U.S. Route 220, my boots squeaking on the asphalt, my back pasty with sweat under my knapsack. Ian leapfrogs me in the car, pulling a quarter-mile ahead, parking on the shoulder to recite Spanish until I've hiked a quarter-mile past him, then driving ahead again. At Mustoe, another speck on the map, we find a couple of houses, a long-closed store and the Victory Chapel, a steep-roofed little church of white clapboard. The door is open, and while Ian lounges on the grass I step inside. The sanctuary is plain but spotless, and I sit in the back pew for several minutes, admiring its hush. Outside we chug a couple of sodas on the riverbank, and scramble down its side to dip our hands into the water's icy rush.

Midday arrives. I hike through a tight stretch of the valley, framed by bluffs sculpted into the vertebrae of some giant subterranean beast. Suddenly the Volvo appears in the road ahead, driving the wrong way. Ian passes me, disappears around a bend, and doubles back a couple minutes later. "I think you better get in the car," he says.

"What's going on?"

"There's a guy working just ahead, on the left side of the road, and he's got an Australian sheep dog with him that looks pretty crazy."

I get in the car. The worker, it turns out, is employed by a trout hatchery that sends a ton of fish to market each Monday. Ian's assessment of his animal is significantly understated: we pull into the hatchery's drive and the dog flings itself at the car, thumping loudly against the doors, then launches itself at our open windows. We roll them up in a hurry, swearing loudly. "That thing's completely nuts," I say, as if Ian hasn't noticed. There's an odd, muffled sound from under the Volvo, and a tremor runs through the floor. "Listen to that," Ian says, eyes wide. "It's actually biting the tires."

True. I peer over the hood's edge to where the sheepdog is valiantly trying to flay the Volvo's right front radial. Ian eases the car forward. This just seems to annoy the thing. It orbits the car as we roll, chomping at each tire in turn, snarling insanely. The only argument against slamming the car in reverse and fleeing the place is that a spring, the Blue Hole, is supposed to be somewhere on the property, and reputed to be quite a sight. So when we reach the worker, I crack my window enough to tell him who we are, what we're doing, and what we want.

Sure, he says, you can have a look at the spring. He points out a tree on the riverbank, beyond the hatchery's long, concrete-lined pools. It's right below that, he says. Just be careful of the electric fence. Then he calls to the dog. It reluctantly abandons its prey, though it keeps barking and growling and tossing foam from its mouth as the fellow chains it up.

We drive as far from the animal as we can, and find ourselves glancing over our shoulders as we struggle with the electric fence. It's a strange contraption; the gate consists of three strands of hot wire hooked to a fence post, each wrapped in a rubber sleeve you grab to unhook it. Even with the rubber, it's a spooky arrangement—the wires remain juiced when unhooked. I watch as Ian opens the gate one wire at a time, laying the unhooked strands in the grass, and we step through the gap. "Wanna just leave it open?" he asks. The dog's still shrieking across the yard. "No," I say. We gingerly rehook the wires.

The Blue Hole is a few yards from the Jackson's edge, round and deep and, as its name suggests, a dark aquamarine. Fish hover close to its surface, dart deeper when they notice our looming figures. "That really is blue," Ian says.

"Yup."

We stand at the spring's edge for a minute or two, eye some cattle on an adjacent pasture. Then we return to the car.

Back on the road, we decide to alter our leapfrogging routine. Ian will no longer drive ahead to wait for me; two near-encounters with hellhounds have me worried that he might flush a lunatic dog out and lure it to the roadside where it would see me, and I'd have to run *toward* the thing to reach the car. Now Ian will lag behind, parking on the roadside until I'm out of sight or a half-mile ahead, whichever comes first, then pulling forward to catch up. But the next several hours are uneventful. I hike on under a cloudless sky, against a cool breeze that sweeps up the valley, crunching steadily on the highway's weedy shoulder. The river veers away from the road, reflects the sunshine from two hundred yards off, swings back to the roadside. Mounds of baled hay slide by. Farmhouses and barns. The chorus from a poultry house reaches me on gusts of wind.

Eventually we come to a spartan grocery at the Jackson's confluence with Bolar Run, a narrow brook that spills from the ridge to the east. Ian and I eat peanut butter sandwiches on the Volvo's hood, talk to a couple of locals who pull up in pickups, and take a quick drive up Bolar Run to Bolar Gap. The stream is said to bubble out of the ground there at the big Bolar Spring, which is in the middle of a settlement called, oddly, Bolar. A century ago the spring's seventy-four-degree water was found to "have a very beneficial effect" on "ailments of the skin and of the internal lining tissues," according to one 1911 account, which also boasted that "people have derived great benefit in cases of eczema and other cutaneous affections, but in nasal catarrh its repute is even higher."

The gap turns out to be skinny, and Bolar a chummy cluster of houses on both sides of the narrow road. Most are big and fine-looking, though in need of some attention. A couple have the porches and roadside placement of boarding houses. The spring's invisible, however: where my map shows it to be, there's a new house going up. We can hear a nail gun firing somewhere inside, but our shouts get no reply, and there's no sign of movement within the walls of new, yellow wood.

The unseen water hole sits smack on the county line, at the northern fringe of a territory famed for its thermal springs. Indians discovered that some of Bath County's bubbling pools ran warm even in harsh highland midwinters, and that a dip left them invigorated. It didn't take white frontiersmen long to pick up on the springs' curious properties, and it didn't take the anemic, the weary, and the city-stressed long to respond to their advertisements. By the early nineteenth century the place was lousy with resorts, each claiming to pack a curative punch exceeding the competition's. Horses, then stages, then trains brought a steady procession of customers seeking respite in mineral water and fresh mountain air. Bath County water was bottled and exported to those who couldn't make the trip.

Today, two of the oldest and best-known resorts survive. A few miles south of Bolar Run, two wooden bathhouses stand just off U.S. 220 at Warm Springs, which has drawn health-seekers since the county's earliest settlement. Six miles farther south is Hot Springs, home of the sprawling Homestead resort of baths and golf courses and amusements for the rich. Neither spring is on the Jackson, but both flow into it.

Ian and I don't have the money, or the inclination, to hang around Hot Springs, but on a side trip to Warm Springs we learn that the men's bathhouse there, an octagonal, jumbled-looking thing, dates to 1761. We stroll inside to find that its floor is almost completely given to a round spring of dark, teal-tinged water. A half-dozen old men are lolling about naked in the pool, complimented by the fact that the building's only light seeps in from the outdoors. We avoid looking at them by gawking at the building's rafters, walls, and ancient dressing rooms. Thomas Jefferson apparently took these waters on several trips to the region, writing that the spring "issues with a very bold stream, sufficient to work a gristmill, and to keep the waters of its bason, which is 30 feet in diameter, at the vital warmth, viz. 96°. of Farenheit's thermometer."

"They relieve rheumatisms," he said of this pool and the one a few yards away, now enclosed by a twenty-sided women's bathhouse built in the early nineteenth century. "Other complaints also of very different natures have been removed or lessened by them." We're looking at a room unchanged from Jefferson's day, I think. Zap us back to an afternoon 180 years ago, and our third president might be one of these old guys displaying his wares.

The attendant invites us to dive in for six bucks, but we pass: the day's traveling isn't done. From the Bolar grocery I set out again on 220, the river off to my left, a 3,200-foot ridge, Little Mountain, rising behind it. There's little sign of life along the highway. Few cars pass. Farmhouses seem unoccupied. Young people in both Highland and Bath counties have forsaken the lives of their ancestors, choosing jobs in the city over farming here, and a good many big spreads are now held by weekenders from Washington, D.C., Baltimore, and Norfolk. The out-of-towners are drawn by the very remoteness that the young natives flee: Highland County doesn't have a traffic light, unless you count a flashing yellow in Monterey, and Bath had more residents in 1900— when it didn't have many—than it has today. Some days, it seems nobody's home across huge patches of these mountains and valleys.

The Jackson zigzags a little as it flows among the lonesome homesteads, but I notice that in the main it runs straight. Studying my map's contour lines, I'm astonished to see that the river's head, back beside the barn, was 3,400 feet above sea level, and that I've now reached the contour for 2,000. In less than thirty overland miles the Jackson has dropped more than a quarter-mile—well over a third of the total tumble that it and its offspring will take on their way to the sea. The river's practically been free-falling out of the mountains. It's had no time for bends.

Late in the afternoon I cross the Route 220 bridge. The Jackson, which swung east of the highway back at Vanderpool, here curves back to the west. Road and river split, 220 running down the east side of steep Rocky Ridge, the water bulleting into a notch between the ridge and long, high, Back Creek Mountain to the west. Ian parks the car and joins me on the span, where we gaze down on the water. It's double its width at Mackey Spring, but still no more than a foot deep. I'll be hiking for a while yet.

But not for much longer today. Walking on the road has left me blistered, achy-kneed, whiny. I'm ready to call it a day. We head for the car, stepping over a roadkill as we go. It takes a moment to identify the flattened carcass, tanned by tire treads and the road's heat, sprigs of fur trembling in the breeze. The paddle-shaped tail gives it away. "Wow," Ian says. "A beaver." We nudge it with our boots. It's as stiff as cardboard, and nearly as weightless. In the midst of its amoebic shape is a pair of long curved teeth, a surprisingly bright orange. "I've seen trees that they've chewed up," I say, "but I'm not sure I've ever actually seen a beaver in the wild before."

"Kinda sad that this is your first."

"Yeah," I admit, "it'd be more satisfying if it were still moving around."

"And alive," Ian suggests.

"Well, yeah."

We leave the beaver where it lies and climb in the car. Our bivouac for the night is a bed-and-breakfast in an antebellum plantation house called Warwickton, on the Jackson some seven or eight miles downstream. Our plan had been to reach it today, but we now decide to backtrack tomorrow morning, pick up the hike where we've left off, and reach the house by lunch. From there—well, from there we'll just see how it goes.

A snaking two-laner off of 220 takes us to a U.S. Forest Service recreation area called Hidden Valley, and we find Warwickton at a dead-end in its center. It's a two-story, Greek revival mansion of red brick, built over three years and finished in 1851. Its front is dominated by a mammoth white portico that stretches across most of its width, supported by four Ionic columns. The Volvo bumps over a low concrete bridge that spans the Jackson, and we climb a gentle drive to a small parking lot beside the mansion. Pam Stidham, half of the couple who keeps the place, is on her knees in the yard, working on a flower bed. She yells that we should head inside, and as we climb the porch we're met by her husband, Ron, a stocky guy in his forties wearing the uniform of a state correctional officer. The uniform is so out of place here that it's almost comic, but as Ron leads us on a tour of the house it's clear that while his paycheck may come courtesy of a state prison, his passion is architecture—and history, and age.

Warwickton was built as the centerpiece of a large plantation, the very sort of place it was used to depict in the 1992 movie "Sommersby." Sold at the turn of the twentieth century, it was converted into a hunt club, then a school, then back to a residence in the late 1940s and early 1950s, when it was used as a summer "cottage" by the W. R. Grace family, of steamship and manufacturing renown. When they quit making the trip to Bath County the mansion was discarded; by the late 1950s, the once-grand house was an outbuilding for hay storage. Cattle and horses tramped through its halls and high-ceilinged rooms.

The Forest Service bought the place in 1965 and nominated it to the National Register for Historic Places in 1972. But eighteen more years passed before the house finally found salvation in the Stidhams, who returned it to its original splendor, down to period furniture and drapes and oak floors polished to a high gloss. Ian and I drag our footlockers of food, clothes, and camping gear into the Library Room, which is the size of a small apartment, marveling at the completeness of the restoration, trying to imagine the sound of horses' hooves on the floors. Then, our stuff piled high in the room, we step onto the porch with a Primus stove, our cookware, and two freeze-dried meals to whip up dinner. The temperature has dropped into the high forties by the time we boil enough water to cook the two packets. Early September, and already winter's coming fast in these mountains; up on Jacob Hevener's much higher farm, it's no doubt even colder.

I measure out hot water for our dinners, stir in the powdery dinner mixes, and cover the pots. It's only when I lift the lid off mine after the prescribed ten minutes that I make an awful discovery: my chicken chili is a factory screw-up, missing its beans. Dinner is a thin soup of tiny chicken bits and spiced water. I'm too beat to fire up the stove again, so I force the soup down while Ian goes to town on a hearty pasta dish. Then we sit on the mansion's front steps for a while, the grounds black around us, marveling at stars that seem close enough to touch.

When I drift off to sleep, I recall something I saw on my hike, a reminder of where I'm headed, and how vast an effort is needed to protect it: a sign tacked up at a tree farm near the Blue Hole that read, "Forest Planted for the Chesa-peake Bay."

DAY THREE

About which the less is said,
the better

🐝 Over a lavish breakfast at Warwickton, Ian and I work out the morning's logistics. A system of trails follows the river from U.S. Route 220 to the mansion, so that Ian need only drop me off where we ended yesterday's hike, drive back here, and wait. I should show up by lunchtime. But after two days in the car, he's eager to do some walking himself, so we ask Pam Stidham if she'd consider driving us over to our hike's beginning either now—in which case we can leave the Volvo here—or at midday, to pick up the wagon left at the trailhead. Pam says she isn't busy at the moment, so we crowd into her pickup.

We pull off of 220 and jounce onto a narrow side road, cross a bridge over the Jackson, and pass what appear to be the ruins of a mill on the riverbank. Pam steers the pickup through a chain of tree-shaded curves that hug the stream, past clusters of small cabins and trailers lording over junk-strewn yards. A dog bolts from the roadside to give chase, abandoning the hunt as we roll past a spindly riverbank tree laden with a hornet's nest the size of a basketball. "Here we are," Pam announces. She stops the truck at a locked Forest Service gate. We sling on our knapsacks, step around the gate and wave goodbye.

The day's travels start auspiciously. Ian and I walk a broad dirt fire road that follows the river to Little Mountain Gorge, the first of several turbulent passes that the Jackson will carve through the mountains on its downhill run. Here the road disappears at an old ford across the river. We hop rocks at the foot of a three-foot-high, bank-to-bank waterfall, haloed in the sunlight shimmering on the river's surface.

The trail doesn't follow the road across the water. It bends off, climbing narrow and steep up the gorge's side, and we huff uphill through thick broadleaf forest until the path flattens. From here it clings to canyonside as the river below chatters over boulders and streams through rocky chutes, and we walk for miles in silence, the woods around us dark in shadow and sighing with the breeze.

Late in the morning the leafy canopy disappears, the gorge's steep sides veer apart, and we find ourselves in a sunlit, oval bowl of tall grass, honey-colored butterflies fluttering around us. The Jackson, we know, turns west through this Hidden Valley to pass in front of the mansion. Even so, we get lost briefly in the grass, which grows so tall we can't see where we're going. By the time we finish the seven miles to Warwickton it's high noon, and we're sweating buckets.

Later we'll blame our overheated condition for what happens next. As we cross the low bridge in front of the mansion, headed for lunch, we agree that the water downstream looks navigable. Not by canoe, perhaps—we can see that gravel bars are exposed here and there, along with the odd rock—but certainly, we figure, we can drop our truck inner tube into the Jackson and start traveling the river, rather than its flanks.

Pam has her doubts when we announce our plan in Warwickton's kitchen. "The water's about as low as it's ever been," she says. "You're going to be scraping bottom."

"We just had a look at it," I assure her. "We'll be OK."

"Well, if you can navigate it when it's this low, you're doing better than I can," she says. "This time of year, there's just no water in it."

I pull out my map. "It *is* low," I agree, "but I figure we'll try the stretch from here to Route 39—what is that, a mile? Two miles? If it's too low, we'll just switch to hiking at 39."

Ian and I consider driving to a gas station to inflate the tube, but I get impatient, and start filling it on the front porch with the bicycle pump stashed in the Volvo. The sun's directly overhead in a cloudless sky. It's furnace-hot. Brandy, the Stidhams' pony-sized Great Dane, sprawls, panting, a few feet away as I piston the pump handle up and down. Within a couple of minutes I'm seeing spots and panting myself. Ian takes over for a minute, pumping until he's queasy, then hands it back to me. Amazingly, we finish the job without getting sick. Then, with Pam wishing us luck, we strike across the mansion's front yard for the river.

At the water's edge I make some last-second adjustments to my gear, of which I'm taking an absurd amount: a waterproof fanny pack containing my notebook, a map, a jacket; canoe paddle, so that I can propel the inner tube downstream and push my way over rapids; life jacket, in case the water's so cold that I black out. Then I dump the tube into the water and fall backwards into its hole. Sure enough, the water's cold. My first full-body contact with the Jackson is shocking. I manage to stop gasping long enough to bid Ian farewell, and set off on what I figure will be an hour-long float to the highway bridge. Ian waves goodbye.

Five minutes later, I've floated perhaps fifteen feet downriver. Ian's standing on the shore, still waving occasionally. The current seems nonexistent, even though the Jackson has just tumbled through one gorge and not far downstream will drop eighty feet in another. I try using the paddle, but succeed only in spinning the inner tube in place. Disgusted, I climb out of the tube, sling it over my shoulder and start walking the slime-coated rocks on the riverbed. Ian again waves goodbye.

Down the Jackson I splash, kicking up a cloud of mud in the water behind me, desperately seeking traction on the glass-slick river bottom. Soon the water is waist-high, so I jump in the tube. Again, I go nowhere. I go back to walking, using the paddle as a staff, never quite achieving a comfortable balance on the uneven riverbed.

The afternoon sun crosses the sky. The scenery on the banks, farmland of yellows and greens, does not change; even on the river's bends I can pick out a tree up ahead and keep it in sight for twenty minutes. I'm trapped, I realize, by a terrible paradox. Deep stretches of the Jackson are utterly without movement; in fact, in one gust of headwind, I actually float upstream. The parts of the river with some velocity, on the other hand, are too shallow to clear. Ninety minutes into the voyage I round a bend and my heart leaps: a bridge! Up ahead, a concrete span crosses the stream, and I splash, slipping and lurching, toward it. Route 39, I think. Thank God, I've reached Route 39.

Only I notice that there's no traffic on it: in the minute it takes me to get fifteen yards closer, not a car crosses. Nor, I now see, does it sport the guardrails that typically gird Virginia bridges. As I get closer still, I see that it's only a single lane wide. It isn't Route 39, I realize. God help me, it isn't 39. I slump against one of the bridge's concrete piers and unfold the rolled top of my waterproof fanny pack, jam my hand inside in search of my map, and come up with a heavy lump of sodden paper. My notebook's trashed, as well. Great. Just great. I carefully unfold the map, peeling its mashed, softened layers apart until an edge starts to rip, then pulling elsewhere until its depiction of the river lies translucent and spongy before me. Sure enough, there's a bridge marked, faint but unmistakable—a farm road crossing. I follow the map's portrayal of the Jackson below here, and see, to my horror, that I'm only halfway between Warwickton and Route 39. Maybe a little less.

What the map doesn't show is that this narrow bridge stands within a few dozen yards of an important relic of American history. Buried beneath the gently rising farmland just west of the river are the remains of Fort Dinwiddie, for a few bloody years a key bastion in the nation's frontier defenses.

Few Americans would recognize its name. Few know much of the violence that sparked its construction. But in the mid-eighteenth century, a series of wars erupted in these narrow mountain valleys that pitted settlers against the Indians—particularly nasty tangles that made the later stuff on the Great Plains look like high tea. These wars sparked the massacre of entire frontier settlements. They were fought by some of the most fascinating figures in American history. And they saw some of the largest-ever battles between whites and Indians, an awful lot of which the Indians won.

Where I stand, beneath this concrete bridge, George Washington may have once brought his horse to drink. Raiding parties of the great Shawnee chief Cornstalk passed not far from here. Mad Ann Bailey, a grief-deranged widow who lived alone in a mountain cabin, dressed as a man, and blasted a gaping hole in the local Indian population, traveled this stretch of the Jackson in search of game and a good fight. I clamber up the riverbed to get a firsthand look at the past.

No Indians lived here when white Virginians first arrived on the Jackson— none had lived here for hundreds of years, in fact—but several tribes shared hunting rights in the river's valley and other valleys around it. Suddenly, in the 1730s and '40s, they encountered frontiersmen on these hunting trips—and, unbelievably, these whites claimed to own the land the tribes had used for centuries. Settlers weren't impressed by the Indians, either—particularly their everybody-shares-all view of the land and its bounty. "The white man despised the Indian as a heathen and was contemptuous of his rights," wrote Robert R. Howison, a mid-nineteenth-century historian. "He regarded him as a thief and wished he would keep out of the way."

Violence was only a matter of time. In 1753, the time came. Virginia's royal governor, Robert Dinwiddie, had received reports that the French were settling the upper Ohio lands claimed by England as part of the Virginia colony. In October the governor dispatched an emissary to make it plain to the French commander in the region that he was trespassing, and that if he didn't vacate the premises willingly he'd be forced to do so at the tip of a bayonet. Dinwiddie's messenger was a twenty-one-year-old major in the colonial militia, Indian-smart and backwoods-savvy far beyond his years. George Washington left Williamsburg on Halloween and, traveling north by horseback through the descending winter, reached a French outpost in present-day western Pennsylvania in early December. There he delivered his message. The

French chose to ignore it, and what became known as the French and Indian War was on.

The "Indian" part of its name grew out of French realism: outnumbered, they knew that if they were to have a prayer in a fight with the English they'd have to force their enemy to fight on two fronts. The French decided to concentrate their military muscle in French Canada, and fight the English from the north; their Indian allies would keep the English busy to the west by raising hell along the frontier. And so, from 1754 to 1758, a few hundred Indians held the Appalachian settlements in thrall. The Shawnee and the Delaware raided the rude mountain villages along the Greenbrier, just west of here. They sent murderous squadrons of warriors into the Jackson River valley and the Cowpasture. They didn't need much prodding to wage war: the tribes had seen English-speaking pioneers pushing into their territory. They'd spied survey parties along the Ohio. And they knew that if they failed to nip the English expansion westward, they'd be the worse for it.

They were an imposing lot—"tall, manly, well-shaped men of a Copper colour with black hair, quick piercing eyes, and good features," one eighteenth-century observer wrote, with "rings of silver in their nose and bobs to them which hang over their upper lip" and "plates of silver round their arms and in the hair, which is all cut off except a long lock on the top of the head." They plucked their eyebrows and eyelashes.

And they put up a heck of a fight. Early in 1755 the English, recognizing they had a full-blown war on their hands, imported one of their military stars to quell the Indian menace. Maj. Gen. Edward Braddock led a force of crack British regulars and colonial militia against the French and Indians on the Ohio, and promptly marched into an ambush in southwest Pennsylvania. The attackers fought as the Indians usually did, using trees and ravines as cover. Braddock, apparently believing that pretty columns of red-jacketed soldiers trumped well-aimed bullets fired from safety, forbade his army from following suit. Well-regimented suicide ensued; Braddock's army was cut to pieces.

"The Virginia troops showed a good deal of bravery, and were nearly all killed," Washington later said, blaming the defeat on the Redcoat regulars, who "exposed all others that were inclined to do their duty, to almost certain death" and "ran as sheep pursued by dogs. . . . It is conjectured, (I believe with much truth,) that two-thirds of our killed and wounded received their shot from our own cowardly regulars, who gathered themselves into a body, contrary to orders, ten or twelve deep—would then level, fire, and shoot down the men before them." Some of those there claimed that the carnage didn't end until one of the general's own men, a big, wild militiaman named Thomas Fausett, shot him to put an end to his orders.

When news of Braddock's defeat reached settlers in the mountains, a panic swept the frontier. Families abandoned their homesteads along the Greenbrier, the Jackson, even the Shenandoah to flee east, beyond the Blue Ridge. In a single day's fighting, an entire generation's work spent clearing and taming the frontier was laid waste. Those who stuck it out were terrorized by raiding parties that fell on villages as well as isolated cabins, killing and scalping the men within, braining the children against trees and rocks, and kidnapping the women they spared from death. Dinwiddie responded with a plan for a chain of forts the length of the frontier, from the Potomac south to the Mayo River, in southwest Virginia. Washington fiddled with the plan, adjusting the number of forts and their locations, and supervised their construction. Among the most important of the strongholds was the one right here.

At the top of the river's west bank I find a shelf of pastureland that rises to a terrace twenty-five or thirty feet high. Up there, invisible now, is what remains of Fort Dinwiddie, built near a spring that drains into the Jackson.

In May 1971, Virginia's state archaeologist, Howard A. MacCord Sr., supervised a dig with a backhoe here. Tradition had guided him to the place: the surrounding property was known as Fort Dinwiddie Farm, and a tumbledown nineteenth-century house nearby, long abandoned, was called the Fort Dinwiddie Mansion. No one knew for sure, though, where the fort had stood: no records pinpointed its location; no visible ruins remained. Like other forts along the Jackson—Christy's, which stood upriver, not far from Bolar Run; Mann's Fort, downriver some fifteen miles; and Fort Young, still farther downstream, in present-day Covington—Fort Dinwiddie had faded beyond the reach of memory. This despite the fact that it was among the most permanent of the frontier defenses, garrisoned by up to a hundred militiamen for thirty-five years.

MacCord's party crisscrossed the property with trenches for two days without finding a trace of the fort. He was beginning to think the tradition was just talk when the backhoe unearthed chunks of brick and several large stones: the mortarless rock foundation of a frontiersman's home, seventeen feet square. Then, several yards away, his group found traces of a perimeter trench—a remnant, perhaps, of the wooden palisade that once ringed the fort. Believing he'd located his quarry, MacCord ordered the dig stopped, figuring that proper excavation would come later. So far it hasn't. Dinwiddie still lies buried, awaiting the study it deserves.

I climb back down the riverbank to the inner tube and resume my listless drift downstream. A large farm passes slowly on the east bank, complete with the first dock I've seen on the Jackson, a tiny wooden pier jutting over a deep swimming hole. Not far away, an island splits the river into narrow, inches-deep channels swarming with mosquitoes and gnats. I trudge slowly, sloppily, through the shallows, lugging the inner tube in the crook of an arm or flinging it ahead to scare off snakes that in my imagination lurk by the thousands.

The minutes creep by. I round bend after river bend without seeing the hallowed bridge. My fanny pack, its contents soaked, weighs a good ten pounds. Big tough outdoorsman, I think. Look at yourself: Two hundred fifty years ago, you'd have been mincemeat out here. I eye the river's high banks, try to imagine the sight of a war party of Mingoes or Delawares suddenly appearing in the high grass—or, God forbid, Shawnees.

It was the Shawnees who struck the greatest fear into the frontiersman's heart. Headquartered in villages along Ohio's Scioto River, they joined the war on the English with relish. "Of all the Indians, the Shawanese were the most bloody and terrible," militia Capt. John Stuart wrote,

> holding all other men, as well Indians as whites, in contempt as warriors, in comparison with themselves.
>
> This opinion made them more wrestless and fierce than any other savages; and they boasted that they had killed ten times as many white people as any other Indians did. They were a well-formed, active, and ingenious people—were assuming and imperious in the presence of others not of their own nation, and sometimes very cruel.

The forts were cold comfort in the face of such an enemy, because a good many were little more than blockhouses—two-story log structures, second stories overhanging the first, with notches cut into their walls so militiamen could fire their rifles without exposing themselves. Others—such as Dinwiddie, presumably—were ringed by palisades, and a few were a combination of the two, with blockhouses at each corner. Even the stoutest forts were only limited successes, because the men within their palisades were often more scared of their surroundings than the civilians they were supposed to protect. Washington was disgusted by a 1756 inspection tour, reporting to Dinwiddie that he found the garrisons "very weak for want of men; but more so by indolence and irregularity. None I saw in a posture of defence, and few that might not be surprised with the greatest ease." Their troops afforded "no assistance to the unhappy settlers, who are drove from their plantations," he concluded.

My own trouble on the frontier is vexing enough without the Indians. I begin cursing the river's pretty rapids, dreading its soothing pools. After one gravel bar announces itself with a sharp rock—an announcement that, given my position in the inner tube, comes as a surprise—I start to worry about how vulnerable I am. Do snapping turtles live in the Jackson? I study the bottom as I sit motionless over one spot of turquoise deep. I don't see any, but the worry prompts me to fold myself cross-legged in the tube. In doing so I discover that if I sandwich the paddle's blade between my feet and do a sort of backstroke with my arms, I can get the tube moving at about half a knot. Until I grind on the bottom again.

Finally, three and a half hours into my float, the inner tube brushes against a shore-side bramble bush and promptly bursts. I clamber out into knee-high water, use the flattening tube as a cushion to claw my way over a chest-high thicket of nettles, reach a farming road and start hiking. Only a minute or two later I hear traffic, then see a whizzing truck through the trees, then—with such a rush of relief that I actually shout—round a bend to find Route 39 a handful of yards ahead. I stagger to the asphalt's edge and spot the Volvo parked across the road, and Ian running toward me.

"Earl!" he cries, throwing his arms around me. I step back and see that he's almost in tears.

"Are you OK?" I ask.

"I was so worried," he blurts. "I thought you were dead."

"You thought I was *dead?*"

"Or that you'd broken a leg, or something," he says, recovering enough to turn bright pink. "I couldn't figure out what could be taking you so long. I thought something must have gone wrong."

"Well, you were right about that," I say. "Believe me."

My first inclination is to head back to Warwickton, where we plan to spend a second night, and—after taking my lumps from Pam—soak in a bath for an hour. But another urge supersedes that: to scope out the river below here, and determine now whether I'll hike or float in the morning. I don't want to experience another afternoon like this one.

So after guzzling down a couple of Gatorades and describing my abortive voyage to Ian, I suggest we drive south to Richardson Gorge, where the Jackson has carved a high-sided canyon through the mountains. The gorge is deep in late-afternoon shadow. The road through it is little more than a single lane wide, and grips the vertical rock far above the river. From the Volvo's passenger seat, I find myself staring almost straight down at the Jackson. It's quickly clear that running it in the canoe is impossible: the streambed is more rock than water, a long, thin series of boulder-lined waterfalls only inches deep. "There's no way," I tell Ian. "Look at the thing."

"It looks worse here than it did back in Hidden Valley," Ian agrees. "And look where that got us."

"We're back to hiking."

DAY FOUR

On which we reach navigable water, traverse Lake Moomaw, and reflect on the high cost of recreation

The sound a mountain stream makes as it swirls through rapids approaches speech, at times. Water falling over limestone ledges, splashing against rocks, churning over gravel, makes a hiss studded with consonants. Its rhythm speeds and slows, its tone lilts with doubt, anger, glee. Sometimes it seems to possess distinct, recognizable voices. Close your eyes on the riverbank, and you find yourself in the company of a little girl asking questions, two hollering teenage boys, an arguing couple.

I'm eavesdropping on the Jackson shortly after daybreak as I hike the one-lane road that follows its bank through Richardson Gorge, straining to make out the river's words. They seem to dance just a breath beyond deciphering. Below, the stream threads cold and clear through dark stone, spills into black pools filigreed with noisy fizz, hurtles over shelves and down narrow flumes. An hour into the morning's walk, I realize what it's saying.

It's saying goodbye. For at the gorge's southern end I find two things that will change the Jackson's character for the rest of its length. Across the river, Back Creek Mountain—the steep ridge that since Vanderpool has formed the Jackson valley's western wall—abruptly dives to an end, and at its toe the river's first big tributary, the mountain's namesake, spews into the mainstream. With the merger, the Jackson is transformed: Back Creek doubles its strength, swells it from shallow mountain stream to bona fide river. And just a few yards farther down, the gorge's sides fall away, and the Jackson begins widening into a gargantuan sheet of water, Lake Moomaw. It has been shackled, its upland wildness tamed, by a dam twelve miles downstream.

We started the day early. An hour before first light, Ian and I tiptoed through Warwickton's big central hallway and out into a foggy chill that hovered over the fields of Hidden Valley. We drove south through Warm Springs, the Bath County seat.

Down a meandering side road we rolled, into a village of forty-two matching cottages, each painstakingly maintained and snugly arranged along three parallel streets. Bacova—an abbreviation for "Bath County, Virginia"—was founded in the 1920s as a company logging town by an outfit called the Tidewater Oil Company, and for a few years housed workers at what was reputedly the East Coast's biggest lumberyard. The firm went belly-up during the Depression, however, and tiny Bacova sank into idleness. Enter Malcolm Hirsh, a New Jersey industrialist. In 1957 he bought the entire town, resold its houses, and eight years later created a new company for Bacova's inhabitants. The Bacova Guild at first cranked out fiberglass stuff emblazoned with nature scenes, particularly mailboxes, but eventually branched into welcome mats, accent rugs, and bath decor.

West of the village we swung onto narrow Route 603, the Richardson Gorge Road, to begin the day's hike. The road hugs the left bank, twisting into the gorge high above the Jackson, diving down near the water's edge at a cluster of cabins owned by a hunting and fishing club. The encampment is guarded by signs warning off trespassers, a display of territoriality that seems out of place in this out-of-the-way canyon. Swathed in predawn gloom, cooled by the rushing river, the roadway snakes beneath hardwood and pine balanced on the gorge's steep walls. I stride briskly, eyes panning the canopy overhead, the water gushing between the boulders below, and in what seems like no time at all I've covered four miles and can see the mouth of Back Creek splitting the river's far bank.

No sign exists of an ancient homestead at the confluence, but it's said that an Irish family, the Hamiltons, settled here in the late eighteenth century, that one Osborn Hamilton bought land from the Indians. The story goes that the natives put Hamilton up while he built his house, and that he got on so well with them that for years afterward they returned each fall to hunt with him.

Hamilton's experience was not typical, however. By the time he supposedly settled on the riverside, the French and Indian War had been succeeded by another deadly conflict. The Pontiac War—a concerted push by allied tribes to stomp out white settlement west of the Alleghenies—had seen dozens of frontier families slaughtered. The Shawnees had swept through the Greenbrier settlements just west of here, practically erasing them, then had turned their attention to the Jackson and the Cowpasture. Their leader was a chief whose commanding presence and prowess in battle made him seem almost superhuman to the Europeans on the frontier. His name was Cornstalk. "His looks," wrote Col. Benjamin Wilson, who heard him speak years later, "were truly grand and majestic, yet graceful and attractive. I have heard the finest orators in Virginia, Patrick Henry and Richard Henry Lee, but never have I heard one whose powers of delivery surpassed those of Cornstalk."

John Stuart, of the Greenbrier settlements, wrote that in 1763 some sixty of Cornstalk's warriors descended on a settlement along Muddy Creek in the

Greenbrier country, and "introduced themselves into the people's houses under the mask of friendship . . . when, on a sudden, they killed the men and made prisoners of the women and children." From there they made for another settlement, where they found several families gathered in the home of pioneer Archibald Clendenin. "There were between fifty and one hundred persons, men, women and children," Stuart recalled.

> There the Indians were entertained, as at Muddy creek, in the most hospitable manner. Clendenin having just arrived from a hunt, with three fat elks, they were plentifully feasted.
>
> In the mean time an old woman, with a sore leg, was showing her distress to an Indian, and inquiring if he could administer to her relief; he said he thought he could—and drawing his tomahawk, instantly killed her and all the men almost, that were in the house.

So much for folk remedies. One settler, a fair distance from the house when the Indian administered his cure, heard screams and fled to the Jackson, where settlers refused to believe that an attack was under way until Cornstalk's warriors showed up nearby. The Jackson valley promptly emptied, the frontier families fleeing farther east, over the mountains to a big settlement along Kerr's Creek, in what's now Rockbridge County.

The valley had already seen Indian trouble. In October 1759, while the French and English still fought for control of the New World, a relatively small force of Indians had killed a slew of white families along the creek and taken several prisoners. The 1763 raid was far nastier. The fleeing settlers massed at a blockhouse at Big Spring, a broad, tree-rimmed pond a few miles northwest of present-day Lexington. "They were in a field, saddling their horses to ride to a meeting at Timber Ridge," Stuart wrote, "when the Indians cut them off from the blockhouse and commenced a massacre." One woman whose mother had been killed by Shawnees in 1759 reported that the Indians "had the ground all spied out," that they "came in like racehorses," and that in two hours they killed or captured sixty-three. Other witnesses reported that sixty to eighty people were killed, and twenty-five to thirty carried away, others that fewer than twenty died. Whatever the case, the fight was a lopsided one: no witness mentioned the Indians suffering a single loss.

The captives suffered "severe depredations," as writers of the day put it. Women were roughed up and enslaved, their babies beaten to death. The surviving prisoners were eventually released, according to the provisions of the 1764 treaty ending the war, but the Kerr's Creek massacre remained high in the frontier mind for years afterward—and its architect a figure of mystery, terror, and grudging respect.

Just as well. The frontiersmen hadn't heard the last of Cornstalk.

Below Back Creek the road swings across the Jackson on the narrow, concrete McClintic Bridge. I spot the Volvo on its far side, Ian beside it. He waves, yells hello, and his voice booms in the early-morning quiet, amplified by the silence of my hour-long walk. I wave back, pause to eye the river below the bridge. The Jackson arcs gently left as it heads south, wriggles through what looks to be a small rapids, then begins to broaden into the sheet of water that will become a huge multipurpose reservoir. Forty miles from the river's head, we've finally reached the point where we can put the canoe in the water.

"Well, here we are," Ian says, all smiles, walking to meet me at the bridge's middle. "I checked out places to put the boat in the water. We can do it right over there." He points just upstream, to a small parking area tucked into the curve that ends at the bridge.

"I can't tell you how ready I am to get in that canoe," I tell him. We head back to Warwickton. Our fellow guests—a young, exceedingly fit-looking couple from Richmond—join us in a huge breakfast of pancakes and scrambled eggs. An hour later we're packing the car, tedious work under an already-scorching sun. By the time we've finished I'm drenched in sweat, and the car seems even more stuffed than before. Ian helps me load the canoe onto the Volvo's rooftop rack, we say our good-byes, and we head back to the McClintic Bridge. As we approach the put-in, heat is rising from the road, creating mirages of puddles on its surface, making the air throb and distort a few inches above. I slather on sunscreen, which seems scant protection from the heat and light that await me. "After you drop me off," I tell Ian, "see if you can chase down some zinc oxide. I've got to get some extra coverage for my nose, or it's going to look like a burnt sausage by the time I cross the lake." I pull on a ball cap.

"OK," Ian nods.

"And a bandana," I add. I figure I can jam it under my cap, so that it hangs down and keeps the sun off my neck, à la the getup worn by the French Foreign Legion.

"OK, man."

We study our maps of the lake and arrange to meet a couple miles down, at a primitive campsite, then ready the canoe. It's a small boat, little more than fourteen feet long, built for a single paddler. Much of its interior is consumed by flotation bags, big yellow air bladders laced into the bow and stern—insurance policies, designed to keep the canoe from filling completely with water. I jam my rain jacket, sunscreen, notebook, and pens into a dry bag—a vinyl duffel—and toss it into the bow, just behind the flotation bag there, then bungee a cooler filled with ice, Gatorade, and water bottles into the boat behind my seat. Then, with Ian snapping pictures, I push off and head downstream.

So begins my first day under paddle. I glide through a narrow, marsh-fringed S-curve just below the bridge, over the riffles I'd spied from above, and into widening flatwater. A half hour later the river has become Lake Moomaw. Its water is deep, sparkling cobalt, and from the floor of the broadening valley soar mountains studded with oak, hickory, and tulip trees. The lake bends as I paddle southward, the canoe moving at what seems high speed, and with each curve a new squadron of fellow boaters swings into view, fishermen in tackle-packed speedboats and families on pontoon party boats and fat, tattooed bikers on Jet Skis. Most wave as they roar pass. It is a lovely place.

It has come at a price, however. Below me—deep below me—lies the course the Jackson took in its first dozen, spectacular miles after receiving the muscle of Back Creek. Before the lake's creation, this was one of the finest stretches of whitewater in the East, a fast-moving, noisy chain of rapids filled with trout and unspoiled by the surrounding country's sparse settlement. A dozen miles below the bridge, the rapids reached a crescendo in the Kincaid Gorge. The remote canyon combined exciting sport and high, exposed rock, and teemed with deer and wild turkey. And the outdoorsmen who braved bad roads and rough water to reach it had the place to themselves: Kincaid Gorge was largely undiscovered, never crowded. Unfortunately, its seclusion may have worked against it, for when plans for the gorge's destruction were hatched, few Virginians knew to object.

The lake I now paddle had its beginning in the late 1920s, when the Virginia Public Service Company hired a local timber broker, Thomas M. Gathright, to buy up the steeply sloped woodland straddling the Jackson here. The firm was a forerunner of the state's biggest electric utility, Virginia Power, and its consultants saw the gorge as a fitting home for a hydroelectric dam. The Depression intervened, however, prompting the utility to drop the project. Gathright turned the land he'd amassed into a wildlife preserve. Seasons passed. The gorge grew ever richer with life.

With the end of World War II came new plans for a dam across the narrow mountain cleft, this time as part of a massive Army Corps of Engineers scheme to better control water flow in the James River basin. Electricity didn't figure in these plans. The Corps aimed, more than anything, to limit flooding on the James by pinching off its chief headstream, and to smooth the cycle that each spring saw the river swell with rainwater and snowmelt, and each summer bake to a trickle.

Floods were an obvious worry to those living on the riverbanks, but low water, too, posed problems. The Jackson and James passed through dozens of towns, cities, and factories, all of which dumped their effluent into the waterway; the rivers also skirted hundreds of farms, which spewed fertilizer- and pesticide-laden runoff with each rain. When the rivers were full this mess was diluted and flushed, but during dry spells the James became thick with pollution, and downstream settlements drank from this tainted flow. Army engineers proposed storing the spring's surplus rainfall behind a dam on the Jackson, and releasing it as the river's level dropped later in the year.

Congress authorized the dam in 1946, then declined to cough up the cash the Corps needed to get started. The proposal hung in this limbo for nearly two decades, during which the Army busied itself restudying the project twice. The first time, it decided that plugging the gorge was perhaps not such a good idea after all—that the dam's "economic justification was marginal." When it took a second look, in 1964, it reversed its reversal; the dam, it decreed, was needed after all. Within a few years, Congress relented. The money was on its way.

At this point a fight erupted, picked by advocates for keeping the gorge as it was. One of them was the Environmental Protection Agency. The dam would "replace a unique and highly valuable resource, protected by public ownership, by a resource which is not in short supply and is distinctly less valuable on environmental grounds," the EPA said. "Virtually all of the uniquely valuable features would be destroyed by the reservoir." The battle for the Jackson was on. It would last for years.

The sun, high in the cloudless sky, is relentless. I can feel my skin drying, feel my neck burning. Sweat pours into my eyes. My mouth tastes of salt and iron. I slug down bottle after bottle of Gatorade, and still feel thirsty. After an hour, perhaps a bit more, a large marina looms on the west shore. Ian is standing on a pier that juts into the reservoir. He waves. I contemplate pulling alongside, then decide to beach the boat: the heat has put me in a darkening mood. I need to walk. I need shade. For two days I've been dying to get into the canoe, and now I can't wait to get out.

The bank is a mucky bog. I ride the canoe's nose into the mousse, swing a leg over the gunwale, and sink halfway to my knee in warm, black mud. Swearing emphatically, I flop back aboard, yanking my trapped leg out of the goo with a loud slurp. I walk to the bow, spy a chunk of scrap wood halfway between canoe and solid ground, and use it as a stepping stone to *terra firma*.

Ian's up at the car, unloading drinks, sunblock, and a bandana, the last item a square of fabric printed with a camouflage hunting scene. I stalk across the parking lot, sweating, my left leg caked in gassy-smelling slime, and take the bandana from him. "Nice," I growl.

"All they had," he replies.

"Great. I'm gonna look like something out of *Deliverance*."

Ian shrugs. "Actually, they did have one that looked like a rebel flag," he says. "I could go back and get that one, if you like." We exchange scowls. "Hot out there?"

"An oven," I tell him. "You get some sunblock?"

"I did," he nods. "No zinc oxide, though. They didn't have it at three stores I went to, and I think the three I hit are all there is."

We are, indeed, in an out-of-the-way piece of country. Call it bad planning, call it a quirk of the terrain, but one can't drive around Lake Moomaw. After lonely Route 603 crosses the McClintic Bridge at the reservoir's northern tip, it hugs the western shore for a few miles. Busier, more developed highways parallel the lake's east and south shores, but don't link with 603.

"I can't believe I've only come this far," I mutter. "Christ, I'm making no time at all. I've been out here for more than an hour, and I've barely started across the lake."

Ian frowns, confused. "I thought you were doing pretty well," he says.

"How do you figure that?" I nod toward the water. "It hasn't really even broadened, yet."

He wordlessly opens his map on the car's hood, and I see that my memory of the lake's shape is faulty: Moomaw stretches twelve and one-half miles, but its entire northern half is narrow, an esophagus that empties into a wide, round stomach six miles south of McClintic. A second fat gizzard lies below the first, marking the spot where the Jackson took a wide turn before spinning into Kincaid Gorge. "Chill out," he says quietly. "You're halfway across. You're making *great* time."

"Damn," I whisper. "I *am*, aren't I?"

"At the rate you're going," Ian says, "I'm going to have a hard time beating you to the boat ramp. You want some lunch?"

I shake my head. "I'll have a Clif Bar out there." I unfold the camouflage bandana, drape it over my sweating scalp, and pull my ball cap over it. "Lookin' good," Ian lies.

"Get me another bandana, when you get a chance."

"I think that one suits you."

"Get me another."

"It's not your average model. That's a *man*dana."

"Dude," I tell him, "be on the lookout for another."

A short time later I'm in the stomach, a lobe of water a mile and a half across, two small wooded islands hanging in its middle. I'm hugging the eastern shore, seeking shade under the conifers on the bank, maneuvering around discarded tires that clog the shallows. The best shade, I see, lies far across the broad water, south of the islands on the stomach's curving lower shore. It seems a fine place for lunch, so I head diagonally across the reservoir's widest point, dodging a squadron of long-haired, whooping Jet-Skiers who smile, real friendly-like, as they carve troughs all around me. Once in the shade I get off my knees and stretch, pull a Gatorade from the cooler, tear open a Clif Bar, sit chewing as a territorial bee circles the boat. I watch a speedboat across the water, so far off that the thuds it makes as it scuds through a wake are out of synch with its movements. A beautiful place, I think. A recreational paradise.

By the time the EPA raised its objections to the Moomaw project, work was already under way on the dam, and a lot of the locals were pushing hard for its completion. A highland reservoir was bound to draw tourists, and tourism dollars, by the boatload. Nowhere was this support as strong as in Covington, about nineteen miles downriver from the dam. The people there had more than income at stake: Covington was flooded on a regular basis by the Jackson and its tributaries. By snaring mountain rain and snowmelt upstream, the reservoir would keep big bulges of water from cascading into town. Plus, smack in Covington's middle was the Westvaco bleached-board plant, among the biggest paper mills of its kind in the world. A steady flow in the Jackson would carry its effluent downstream, making life easier for the plant and drinking safer for the locals.

The project's critics were unimpressed. They argued, first, that so-called multipurpose dams—those that provide recreation and flow augmentation, as well as flood control—simply don't work. If you're gunning for good boating and swimming and such, you need a reservoir filled with water. Raising river levels downstream during dry spells requires a good tub of water behind the dam, as well. But flood control—protecting a place like Covington— means keeping a lot of a hilltop reservoir empty, so that there's room for all the water that otherwise would be washing down into streets and homes. In short, the critics charged, multipurpose dams make promises on which they can't deliver.

Environmentalists found faults with the specifics of the project, as well. Even an empty reservoir wouldn't stave off some flooding in Covington, because right downtown a big tributary, Dunlap Creek, empties into the Jackson, and its flow would be unaffected by the dam. And while bolstering the Jackson's flow would improve water quality, its greatest effect would be felt along the stretch of river ten to fifteen miles below Covington, and its biggest beneficiary would be Westvaco. The dam was little more than a subsidy to private industry, the critics said. Instead of forcing the plant to clean up its act and reduce its pollution, the government was proposing to dilute the company's mess and push it downstream. The EPA went so far as to suggest that Westvaco be forced to reimburse the government for the "allocated costs of water quality and flood control benefits which accrue to them." That didn't happen. Nor did a lawsuit by a consortium of private-sector environmental groups derail the project.

At the southern end of the lake's second bulge I reach a fork in the waters. Off to my left, the reservoir curves eastward into Kincaid Gorge. Steep mountainside rises from both sides of the channel; beyond the bend rises the Gathright Dam, 257 feet high and 1,310 feet across at its top. Ahead the lake follows the valley of Fortney Branch, a creek that once dumped into the Jackson. At its head is a boat ramp, where Ian waits in the car.

An hour later we pull up to the dam. We park, wander across the road to the place where the grassy shoulder dwindles to nothing and the ribbon of baking asphalt ventures alone across the gorge. I stop near the dam's middle, peer over the guardrail down an unnervingly steep slope of carefully groomed gravel that dives between the buttresses of rock around us, into the gorge's shadows and down to the Jackson, narrow again after its sabbatical. I can make out rapids—motionless flecks of white from up here, soundless behind the distant roar of the dam's outflow, twenty-five stories below. That dim hiss is, in fact, the only noise: the place is empty of tourists, of traffic, of birdsong. It's as if the surrounding woods and water have been shocked mute by the dam's intrusion. Either that, I find myself thinking, or they've fallen silent in anticipation of some awful spectacle, the way cows instinctively seek high ground before a flood, or zoo animals get nervous before earthquakes.

The silence adds to the implicit menace that all dams seem to radiate, that fills you with the odd impulse, while standing at their centers, to eye the solid ground way off to your left or right and calculate how long it would take to sprint the distance. If I felt the dam shift beneath my feet, could I make it to the Volvo before the whole thing blew out? Could I stay one step ahead of the slumping gravel, the splitting asphalt and concrete? No way. I'm past fail-safe out here, a good hundred yards into a zone of blind faith in Army engineers. I stare down at the gravel, notice that it's held in place by chicken wire.

Chicken wire. An ideal material for penning fowl, no question, but a pretty poor confidence-builder here. That chicken wire holds the gravel in place, and the gravel blankets a thick mountain of rock, and that covers layers of chipped rock, sand and gravel. Finally, deep in the dam's heart, is a dense wedge of clay, what dam-builders call an "impervious core." The label seems engineering hubris, akin to calling the *Titanic* unsinkable. That many earthen dams bear the same terminology doesn't lessen its brazenness; American history is rife with catastrophe born of challenges to nature. One was the great Johnstown Flood, which killed more than two thousand Pennsylvanians in 1889 and followed a dam failure above town.

I start strolling back toward the gorge's side, toward the car, gravel skittering and scraping underfoot, fighting the urge to trot. Ian's staring down the upstream face, so I nonchalantly cross the road, gaze out over sapphire-blue water winking in the late-afternoon sunshine. The lake here, as elsewhere, is spectacular. "Wow," I say.

"Yeah," Ian nods. "Beautiful."

"That's a lot of water."

"It is." He shrugs to the south, up the road on which we've parked the Volvo. "I read on some sign that if you hear three horn blasts, this thing's about to go." I thank him for the heads-up, remind myself of something I read in a gung-ho engineering text: that these days, the risks inherent in earthen dams are about equal to those of concrete, that engineers have perfected, as much as they can, the math necessary to keep them intact and working over decades. That more than thirty-six thousand large dams—those more than fifty feet tall—store water around the world, and it's rare indeed that they fail. Just the same, I'm antsy to ease closer to the gorge's side. The water seems an impossible burden. The chicken wire seems so measly a last line of defense. And I'm nagged by something else I read in that textbook. Since 1900, a hundred-odd large dams have busted around the world. Roughly a quarter of them did so because they or their foundations were defective.

That might be a comforting statistic, except that I know that while the workmanship at Gathright is doubtless superb, the rock to which it's wedged isn't the best. More reading I've done, this time in old newspaper stories: a vast curtain of concrete hangs on the gorge's north side, giving the dam a hard surface against which to rest. Behind it is weathered, crumbly limestone honeycombed with caverns. The Corps knew from the start that Coles Mountain was full of holes; the wall was planned all along to keep water from using them to end-run the dam. But in June 1974, months after the environmentalists' last lawsuit failed, word got out that the caves were far worse than originally figured: some of them, just discovered, were huge, upwards of one hundred feet long and stuffed with creamy-looking formations. The mountainside was as much air as rock.

A contractor building the wall warned that the discovery would boost the dam's price by millions of dollars. *Engineering News Record,* a trade magazine, pronounced the gorge a dam builder's nightmare, with "rock like Swiss cheese," and condemned the project's site as "about as weak as its economic justifications." On the Sunday before Richard Nixon resigned the presidency, the *Washington Post* devoted as much of its front page to the situation as it did to the president's impending impeachment. Its headline asked: "Gathright Dam: Boon or Boondoggle?" The story strongly suggested that the answer was the latter.

But the Corps stayed true to its course. It had prevailed over the environmentalists; it wasn't going to be beaten by the environment. It spent the millions. It had the caverns filled with concrete. It finished the dam.

We pitch our tents in a well-maintained campground just uphill from the dam, cook macaroni and cheese mixed with canned tuna over the stoves, slap mosquitoes.

"Aw, man," Ian says through a mouthful of dinner. "This stuff is *great.*"

"Mac and Gack," I nod.

"Mac and what?"

"Gack. G-A-C-K. Mac and Gack."

"Mac and Gack," Ian whispers to himself. He stuffs a huge yellow gob into his mouth. "Mac and Gack," he says again. Then, in a singsong voice: "When I have a hunger attack, all I need is my Mac and Gack."

"Please," I say. "Not while I'm eating."

He launches into a louder, lustier second verse. "When I have a hunger aaaattaaaack, all I need to eat is my Mac and Gaaaack!"

"Ian. Really."

The sun sinks, and the light turns golden. Ian slides under the Volvo's front end to tinker with the transmission. While he struggles, grunting, with a torque wrench, I wash the dishes and wander through the campground. We're fifty miles into the trip, I reflect, and the fledgling James has already undergone profound change. While Gathright drew headlines, Virginia Power—which had bowed out of a Kincaid Gorge project long before—was quietly working on two Bath County reservoirs of its own. One is in the mountains 1,262 feet above Back Creek, a few miles north of its confluence with the Jackson at McClintic Bridge; the other is on the creek itself. When the demand for electricity is low, water is pumped uphill, from the lower reservoir to the upper. When demand peaks, the water is allowed to rush back down to the lower in huge tunnels, past turbine generators that produce a surge of power. It takes more energy to pump the water up than the utility gains in sending it back down, but because electricity's cost varies with demand, the Bath County Pumped Storage Facility is an economic success. Its presence, however, means that by the time the Jackson reaches Bath County's southern border, little of it has been left unmolested.

At about ten o'clock we turn in, agreeing to wake at six. Ten minutes later I'm lying on my back, staring up at bright green nylon, when Ian's voice reaches me, muffled by his tent's walls. "Earl?"

"Yeah."

"So what do we do if we hear the three horn blasts?"

I recall our conversation on the dam. "Well," I tell him, "I'd say we sleep in until six-thirty."

He chuckles, says, "OK."

Little do I know that he's misunderstood my joke. He resets the alarm.

DAY FIVE

Of whitewater
and wolf spiders, and the Jackson's
first brush with industry

🦡 Waking half an hour later than expected, I cram my sleeping bag into its stuff sack, deflate my sleeping pad, gather my gear, and crawl outside into the predawn gloom, eager to begin my first day canoeing on actual river. Ian buffaloes from his tent at the same time, and together we fire up the stove, boil water for coffee and instant oatmeal, and discuss our plan for the day.

Roughly nineteen miles separate Gathright Dam from the U.S. Route 60 bridge in downtown Covington. I figure that if I make decent time, I'll be in town by mid-afternoon. We study the map, see that several bridges cross the Jackson along the stretch, each with a canoe landing nearby. Ian will meet me at a couple of them, then wait in Covington.

By just before eight we're driving toward the put-in, a fishing area at the dam's downstream foot. We turn down a steep, switchbacking lane and coast into a narrow parking lot beside the water. I gaze into the river and feel my stomach tighten. Right beside the parking lot, a chain of boulders spans the streambed. Water sweeps black and fast among the rocks, splashes noisily below. Downstream, more boulders await. "Oh no," I mutter.

Ian pulls the car into a parking space and kills the engine. "What's the matter?" I nod toward the trip's first set of rapids. "Things move quickly here."

He beholds the rocks and current silently, then gets out. Swallowing my apprehensions, I untie the canoe at the Volvo's rear and help him loosen the straps lashing it to the rack, and we carry the boat to the river's edge. From here the water's roar is louder, the boulders more imposing, and I see that in passing through its first obstruction the Jackson abruptly falls a good two feet, maybe more. I bite my lip, grab my paddle, bungee the cooler into the boat's rear, toss my drybag in. "Ready?" Ian asks, snapping pictures.

"No," I grimace, "but waiting won't help." I climb in the boat as Ian holds it by the gunwales, wave him away, and shove a paddle blade into the water.

The boat veers from the shore. The current snags me, and the canoe spins sideways. I backpaddle, get it straight, keep paddling backwards to maintain my place. Ian jumps in the Volvo and rolls downstream, getting in position to photograph me going over the falls. He parks again, walks with his camera to the river's boulder-strewn edge. "How's it look from down there?" I yell. "What part looks the clearest?"

He eyeballs the rocks for several seconds. He tilts his head, eyes them some more. It's clear that no path through the rapids looks particularly good. "I don't know," he finally says. "Maybe the one kinda to your left. Right in the middle of the river." OK, I think, this is it. I plough with my right blade, swing the canoe left, try to snap the bow back around to thread the boat into the looming gap.

But something goes terribly wrong. The current sucks the stern around, and I hit the boulders broadside; I feel the canoe shift under me, and then I'm tilting, and tilting farther, and suddenly I've dumped the boat and I'm floating in water so unbelievably cold that it takes me a moment to shriek.

The canoe is pinned against the rocks. I let the current pull me to the stern and give it a tug, and it dislodges. Using the boat as a crutch, I lurch over the slick, rocky bottom toward shore. Ian, meanwhile, has apparently concluded that I am about to drown: Hollering unintelligibly, he throws down his camera, bolts down the riverbank and comes splashing in the water toward me.

"It's OK," I yell. "Everything's fine." I shove the boat's bow toward him, and together we lug it up the rock-strewn bank, water spilling from its cockpit as we go. On the lower side of the falls we dump out the remaining water and shove the canoe back into the Jackson. "I think we're in trouble," I gasp, winded.

"You hurt?"

I shake my head. "I'm fine. But imagine what the day's going to be like if this happens every time I come to a rapids."

Ian looks anguished. "Maybe you better not go by yourself."

The thought has occurred to me. Our plan for the trip is dependent, however, on having the car close by; without it, we simply can't carry all the crap we'll need to get home and to file newspaper stories along the way. There's no changing the plan, because even as we crouch on the riverside rocks, people in Hampton Roads are opening their newspapers over Sunday breakfast, and reading the first installment of a series about our trip down river. Tomorrow they'll read about my hike across Highland County, and the next day, my abortive journey by inner tube. We've created a beast that must be fed. It's too late to back out of the adventure now. And even if I wanted to take Ian along in the canoe, I couldn't. He's big. The boat is small. No way will we both fit.

"We have no choice," I tell him. "Just do your best to stay close to the river. If I seem to be taking too long to get someplace, head back upstream until you find me."

He pauses before speaking again. "Do you have any idea what you're doing?"

"Not much."

"I don't like this."

"Me, neither. But what are we going to do?"

After fishing my drybag out of the drink, I push off again and paddle with little confidence past a small island and around a sweeping bend to the right, mountains soaring high on both sides. I practice turning right, turning left, slowing myself to a stop. Then, within ten minutes of setting out, I encounter another test. The river crashes through a new tangle of rock and over another two-foot ledge.

I backpaddle for a minute, trying to find a gentle way past the obstacle, and eventually decide on a route that takes me hard against the left bank, through a sharp turn to the right and down a rushing but smooth channel of water to the river below. My apprenticeship continues to be harsh: the bow of the canoe snags on a rock as I make the hard right turn, and I wind up tangled in the branches of a willow bent overhead. Suddenly, spiders are raining from the tree into the canoe—and I mean hairy, fist-sized monsters, big enough to saddle up. I scream a string of profanities, smack several flat on the canoe's floor, crush others bare-handed against my life vest, fling my spider-covered drybag back into the river and cleave a couple others sprinting for cover with the blade of my paddle. Amid all this excitement the canoe dislodges itself from the rock, and I swoop down the falls into calmer water, where I jump over the side in an attempt to drown whatever spiders have crawled down my back or up the legs of my shorts. I fish the drybag out of the river, climb back in, and paddle on.

I'm now consumed with doubt about making it to Covington, let alone the James's mouth. I recall reading that this stretch of the Jackson is rated a Class I or Class II by river runners, a designation signaling little challenge. In whitewater parlance, a Class I rapids is a cakewalk, a mere riffle, requiring no skill whatsoever. A child could canoe it. A dog could. Class II is a bit tougher—you might want to pick your route through the rapids. You'll move a lot faster, and have to steer to avoid rocks. You may dump the canoe, though it's usually because you've done something stupid. With Class III, you encounter standing waves and pretty high speed and more difficult approaches. Picking the wrong route will roll you. You'll get a bit wet in an open canoe, and you could get bruised, as well. Class IV is fast and difficult, with major skill and even greater nerve required to get through the rapids, and the prospect of injury, boat damage, and stranding should you fail to make it. Class V is over-the-top scary, nothing but speed and foam and divine wrath. Mess up, and you could break something. You could die, even. There's a Class VI, too, but it's hardly worth mentioning. Think *suicidal.*

I stare back at the two-foot ledge as the river takes me southward. That's Class I, Class II at the most? An ominous bass chord rumbles on the day's soundtrack. Bigger water waits downstream. Class III at Balcony Falls. Class IV at Richmond. I can picture myself wedged between boulders at the state capital, the current yanking at my helpless body, limestone holding me in place by the temples. I can picture myself dumping the canoe at Balcony Falls' upper end and finding it busted in two at the bottom. I can picture myself busted in two. Jesus God, I think. What the hell have I gotten myself into?

An hour later, a few smaller rapids behind me, I'm feeling a bit more sure of myself, but just a bit. Holding my breath, I wobbily negotiate the small ledges and rock gardens that appear around each bend. I clumsily ward off boulders with my paddle. I can hear pebbles slicing the canoe's bottom. But I don't dump, and soon I've relaxed enough that I start paying attention to my surroundings.

High cliffs yawn overhead as the river switchbacks downhill. Through the riverside trees I can see their sandstone faces sculpted into curving hollows and humps by the abrasive force of running water eons ago—so far in the past that the water responsible has reached the sea, turned to vapor under the sun's rays, rained on some far-off continent, seeped through soil and rock to the water table below, bubbled up in a foreign spring, flowed in another river to another sea, found itself again in a cloud, rained somewhere else, and so on, hundreds and thousands of times. Or so I imagine; perhaps, I think, a few of the water molecules flowing around the canoe today were part of the Jackson when these cliffs were just short mounds being chewed away by an infant river. Perhaps some have made this trip many, many times.

Sycamores, tulip trees, ash, and maples crowd the banks. An occasional cabin slides by, tucked deep in the forest's shadows. This stretch of the river is infamous for the people living in some of these cabins. For decades the landowners here claimed they owned the riverbed, as well as the land on its flanks, and that fly-fishermen wading into the shallow water were trespassing. Longstanding practice holds that American rivers are public, everyone's to use, but the Alleghany County landowners produced deeds that backed them up, and eventually the courts took their side. These days, it's OK to canoe the upper Jackson—it is, after all, a navigable waterway, at least to a decent canoeist—but make personal contact with the river bottom, and you're courting a summons.

Another half hour passes, and I don't see a landowner, hostile or otherwise. I thump over more small rapids, gracelessly flail at the shallows, further gouge the canoe's plastic. And slowly, cautiously, I begin to enjoy having the Jackson to myself. As I round one bend, I catch a doe and fawn drinking in knee-high water off the right bank. I drift silently, coming within twenty yards of them before they glimpse the canoe and high-step downstream, then up the riverside.

A few minutes later a beaver cuts across my path, a broad V rippling behind him, and disappears in the long grass that fringes the stream. In three days I've seen two beavers, counting the dead one on Route 220, which is remarkable—the toothy creature has had a tough time of it in Virginia. Prized for its pelt, viewed as a nuisance by corn farmers and lumbermen, the rodent was hunted with prejudice throughout the eighteenth and nineteenth centuries. By the 1850s it survived in the Mid-Atlantic only in a few remote corners, and didn't last long there: the last Surry County beaver died in 1895; the last in Nelson County in 1902. Someone killed the last Powhatan County beaver in 1907. And in 1911, the last Virginia beaver—the very last one seen—was killed in Dinwiddie County, down south of the James. *Castor canadensis canadensis* was extinct in the Old Dominion.

The beaver I've just seen isn't a Virginia beaver at all, but the descendant of transplants. In 1932 and 1937 the state, along with several private benefactors, bought beavers from Pennsylvania, New York, New Hampshire, and Michigan, and released them in a few of the animals' former haunts. Along the James and its tributaries, the creatures have reestablished themselves. You could argue they're better off today than they were 150 years ago.

A few miles below the dam I round a sharp right turn and spot a stream splashing into the Jackson's left bank: Falling Spring Creek. Three miles up this small brook waits one of western Virginia's great natural attractions, a waterfall that carries the stream's rushing waters over a precipice visible from U.S. 220. "The only remarkable Cascade in this country," Thomas Jefferson wrote of Falling Spring Falls in his *Notes on the State of Virginia*. "About three quarters of a mile from its source, it falls over a rock 200 feet into the valley below. The sheet of water is broken in its breadth by the rock in two or three places, but not at all in its height. Between the sheet and rock, at the bottom, you may walk across dry." The falls seems quite a bit shy of two hundred feet to me, but true, you can descend a path from the road and, reaching the cascade's bottom, venture into a damp, noisy corridor between rock and water.

I'm interested by more than the natural beauty of the place. A few yards from the cascade, a roadside boulder announces that nearby stood the cabin of one Ann "Mad Ann" Bailey, one of the most intriguing characters on the Virginia frontier.

Bailey was an Englishwoman, born Ann Dennis in Liverpool in 1742, who came to Virginia as an indentured servant. At twenty-three, while living in Staunton, Ann married, and in 1767 gave birth to a son, William, here on the Jackson at the mouth of Falling Spring Creek. Today a small village called Falling Spring occupies the oval of bottomland off to my left, invisible beyond the riverside trees. But in the late eighteenth century the place was home to little more than a rough stockade—Mann's Fort, also known as Fort Breckenridge, another in the chain of defenses that Washington had built to guard against French and Indian attack in the 1750s. The fort saw little direct action, though fifteen men were reportedly killed by Cornstalk's warriors in an ambush just to the south.

The details of Ann's life around Falling Spring are sketchy, but it is known that in 1774 her husband was killed in battle with Cornstalk's forces. Crazy with grief, she vowed to even the score. Leaving young William with a family here, she took up wearing buckskin britches and a man's jacket, and proceeded to cut a bloody swath through the rapidly thinning Indian population. She soon acquired a reputation for backcountry know-how unmatched by most men of her day. Aboard a black pony named "Pool," short for "Liverpool," she supposedly carried letters from Fort Young, in modern-day Covington, to Point Pleasant, a strategic wedge of forested land at the junction of the Kanawha and Ohio Rivers, way out in Shawnee country. She's also said to have appeared at Fort Young one night with a fresh scalp.

She "rode like a man, with a rifle over her shoulder, and a tomahawk and a butcher's-knife in her belt," a nineteenth-century historian recalled. "At night she slept in the woods. Her custom was to let her horse go free, and then walk some distance back on his trail, to escape being discovered by the Indians. After the Indian wars she spent some time in hunting. She pursued and shot deer and bears with the skill of a backwoodsman." Her most famous stunt reportedly came in 1791 at Fort Lee, a stockade in present-day Charleston, West Virginia. The garrison there was under Indian siege and low on gunpowder. Ann bolted out of the fort, rode through the attacking masses to Fort Union—now Lewiston, West Virginia—and rode back with a supply of powder aboard a second horse, saving the outpost.

Short, mannish, foul-mouthed, handy in a fistfight, prone to drunkenness, she nonetheless snagged a second husband, was widowed again, and eventually retired to her son's farm in Ohio. There she built and moved into a rough cabin. She died either there or, depending on whom you believe, in a shanty along the Ohio, just below Point Pleasant, in November 1825.

During her remarkable eighty-three years, her "shooting, riding and profanity out-masculined the fiercest masculine proficiency of her day," as one Depression-era writer put it. That she isn't known as well as Calamity Jane or

Annie Oakley is an oversight we'd do well to correct. Mad Ann Bailey was one of the most formidable figures to ever live in these mountains.

The fight that killed Ann's first husband is as unknown to most Americans as Ann herself, despite its role as a turning point in the struggle between white settlers and Indians on the Virginia frontier. For ten years after Pontiac's war, the Shawnees and whites lived an uneasy *détente,* during which the Indians were further shoved off their traditional hunting grounds by white encroachment into the Ohio Valley. Indian resentment mounted. White settlements grew jittery. A showdown seemed inevitable. Families on the Cowpasture, Jackson, and Greenbrier kept their rifles close at hand.

In April 1774, as Britain's high-handed treatment of the colonies edged Americans ever closer to revolution, a squad of frontiersmen opened fire on several canoes of unarmed women and children on the Ohio, slaying the family of a friendly Mingo chief, Logan. Bent on revenge, Logan and a confederacy of tribes, already itching for a fight, swooped down on the cabins and villages of the western Appalachians. Some whites in turn embarked on preemptive attacks every bit as savage as the worst the Indians could muster; others fled by the hundreds back east across the mountains. That May, Virginia's House of Burgesses implored the colony's royal governor—John Murray, the Earl of Dunmore—to fix the situation. Dunmore initially took the defensive, but Indian attacks only increased. Stronger action was needed, and the governor eventually decided on a military thrust deep into the heart of the Shawnee nation.

It became fashionable after the Revolution to accuse Dunmore of having incited the hostilities to divert Virginia's attention from the growing schism with the mother country. This conspiracy theory, perhaps the earliest embraced by a nation fond of them, won favor mostly thanks to timing: the Boston Tea Party took place that spring, and the Virginia legislature—meeting far downriver in Williamsburg—adopted a resolution sympathetic to the Massachusetts port, prompting Dunmore to shut the group down. That, in turn, spurred the legislators to get together at Williamsburg's Raleigh Tavern, where they called on each of the colonies to send representatives to a general congress in Philadelphia later in the year. The seeds were sown for the coming war for independence.

This is known for sure: Dunmore answered the Indian threat by ordering Gen. Andrew Lewis, who lived a few days down the James from here, to raise an army. Lewis, an experienced colonial militiaman, had earned a towering reputation as a leader, a fighter, and a military strategist—all of that on a frontier where even the weakest settler was tougher than the toughest modern-day outdoorsman. Dunmore would muster his own fifteen-hundred-man army and meet Lewis at Point Pleasant, on the western edge of what's now West Virginia.

That summer Lewis amassed a militia of well-armed and experienced Indian fighters. He arranged them in two regiments, one of 450 men from Virginia's southern frontier and led by Col. William Fleming, and the other a 600-man force from the north, led by the general's own younger brother, Col. Charles Lewis. The army that started marching for Point Pleasant that September had much in common with its enemy: its volunteers were feral, attuned to the woods, kin to each other, armed with flintlocks and tomahawks and scalping knives, and they were led by a great warrior. Waiting for them was an army of Shawnees, Mingoes, Delawares, Wyandots, and Ottawas, eight hundred to a thousand strong. And Cornstalk.

In early October Lewis's army reached Point Pleasant to find that Dunmore hadn't shown. In his place came a messenger with word that the governor was marching straight to the Indian settlements in present-day Ohio, and asking Lewis to do the same. What Lewis didn't know was that he'd been watched for days. Cornstalk knew exactly where he was and how many men he had, and knew that Dunmore was too far away to lend a hand if Lewis got into trouble. The Shawnee chief hatched a plan to attack Lewis's army, wipe it out, then take on Dunmore's.

So shortly after Lewis's arrival at Point Pleasant, Cornstalk led his army through the woods to the west bank of the Ohio, about three miles above the white encampment. With nightfall, the entire Indian force crossed the river on rafts and moved south, toward the sleeping Virginians. A half hour before sunrise, two of Lewis's men out hunting deer stumbled on Cornstalk's army about a mile from camp. One was killed, but the other raced back to sound the alarm, shouting that he'd "seen about five acres of land covered with Indians as thick as they could stand one beside the other." Almost simultaneously, another two soldiers raced into camp to report they'd just seen Indians, too. Imagine the terror Lewis's soldiers must have felt, roused from sleep, fumbling for their muskets, blood busy with adrenaline, the woods around their camp shrouded in the predawn dark.

Andrew Lewis sent his little brother with 150 men to scope out the surrounding forest, and Capt. William Fleming with 150 more. A half mile from camp the Indians attacked, zeroing in first on the column led by Charles Lewis. The young colonel almost immediately caught a bullet in the chest.

Fleming now came under attack, and was hit three times—twice in the left arm, once in the lungs. Andrew Lewis ordered two hundred more men into action. They arrived as the battle was going against the militia—so much so that the men in camp started building a timber breastwork, just in case the fight turned into a last stand. But the new outfit slowly forced the Indians back.

Dug in just yards apart along a front a mile and a half long, the two sides fired on one another, tried to outflank each other, strained to see through the battle's smoke. Between shots the Indians cursed the Virginians as white sons of bitches—many an Indian could cuss eloquently in English—and yelled taunts. One, apparently, was an allusion to the fifes played in British army advances: "Why don't you whistle now?"

Among the whites who lived to talk about the fight, Cornstalk was a favorite subject. Throughout the battle, they'd remember, he ran from tree to tree along his lines, exhorting his men to "Be strong! Be strong!" When one brave didn't show the kind of spunk his boss expected, Cornstalk downsized him with a tomahawk chop to the skull.

Eventually the Virginians sneaked around the Indian line, and Cornstalk pulled out, retreating across the Ohio after night fell. He left behind a frightful scene: scores of white militiamen lay dead or wounded, the estimates of their number ranging from 160 to 228. Capt. John Stuart, who wrote the most celebrated memoir of the battle, said 75 whites were killed and 140 wounded—or roughly one in five. Col. William Christian, who reached Point Pleasant a few hours after the shooting stopped, wrote that he had "been through all the camps, and believe that many more men will die. . . . They are really in a deplorable situation—bad doctors, few medicines . . ." Cornstalk's casualties were never figured with certainty. A day later the militia "found twenty-one of the enemy slain on the ground," Stuart reported. "Twelve more were afterwards found, all concealed in one place; and the Indians confessed that they had thrown a number into the river in time of the battle; so that it was possible that the slain on both sides, were about equal."

Regardless, the militia had scored a victory by driving the Indians over the Ohio. Now Lewis set out to finish the job and to avenge his brother's death. As soon as he made provision for the wounded, he took chase after Cornstalk with his remaining army—looking, as they said back then, to "chastise" the enemy. Meanwhile, Cornstalk called a meeting of his confederacy's chiefs on how best to handle the situation. As he saw it, they had to make peace or to kill all their women and children and fight to the last man. The chiefs didn't mull the options long before voting for peace.

It came in the nick of time. Lewis, closing in on the Shawnee towns, was intercepted by a messenger who told him to back off, a treaty was at hand. The general ignored those instructions and the army pressed on until it was in sight of an Indian village on Ohio's Kilkenny Creek, where Dunmore himself appeared and ordered Lewis to turn back. Grumbling, the Virginians returned to Point Pleasant. A short time later the treaty was fact.

For many years after the smoke cleared, the battle was the subject of song and poem. When it's remembered at all these days, it's usually as a formative experience, for many of the fight's survivors went on to later glory. Seven officers at Point Pleasant became generals in the Revolutionary army. Six captains commanded American regiments. Four officers led the June 1776 attack on Gwynn's Island in the Chesapeake Bay, where Dunmore was sent packing back to England. The battle left a lasting impression on the Indians as well. Among the warriors killed at Point Pleasant was Puckeshinwa, father of a six-year-old boy named Tecumseh. The son would later become one of the greatest Indian leaders in the East, the organizer of an abortive, last-ditch confederacy against the white population's westward expansion.

To the Virginians living along the Greenbrier, Jackson, and Cowpasture, the battle's legacy was immediate and welcome: After Point Pleasant, the Shawnee never again threatened the eastern Appalachians.

Paddling south through Alleghany County, I scatter a flock of Canada geese, its members dashing flat-footed and honking across the water and into the air, headed downstream. A few minutes later I round a bend and surprise them again, and a half-mile farther, shoo them a third time.

I pass over limestone ledges bearded in moss that dances with the current, can see river bottom six feet below the canoe in photographic detail. Palisades of dark rock tower overhead. Trout glide by in shadows along the banks. Small rapids break the Jackson's surface, gurgling, every fifteen minutes. I don't see another canoe all day. The trouble at Gathright fades. I only occasionally imagine a spider crawling on my legs.

Then I notice a smell—just a hint, carried on an occasional southerly gust. Akin to boiling sauerkraut, but smokier, slightly sulfurous. A while later I notice that a white haze obscures the upper reaches of the riverside bluffs. It is a foreshadowing of the pristine Jackson's first meeting with heavy industry. About eighteen miles below the dam I swing around a bend and find my way blocked by a curtain of plastic tubing that dangles from a wire suspended high over the water. A sign on the left bank blares that I am about to enter a hazardous industrial area filled with chemical pipes and dams. It implores me to exit the water immediately.

Ian is waiting nearby, at a boat ramp built next to a water treatment plant. He looks a little too pleased. "Yeah!" he hollers. "You made it!" I laugh as the canoe glides to the foot of the ramp. "A shock, isn't it?" I beach the boat, step over the side into calf-deep water, splash up the sloping concrete. "Wow," I say, nodding toward the curtain. "Weird."

Ian nods, says he's spoken with the Westvaco mill in Covington, which put up the signs and runs a portage service to haul canoeists around their spread just downstream. The plant's public relations officer, a woman named Ricki Carruth, is dispatching a truck for us. "Well, I guess we ought to wait, then," I say. "Not be rude."

"How'd it go?"

"It was . . ." How best to put it? "Shaky. I didn't dump again, but only because I was lucky. I came real close."

"Does it feel like you're getting the hang of it?"

"Slowly," I tell him. This shortchanges the fear I'm really feeling: three or four days downstream, the river carves its way through the Blue Ridge at Balcony Falls. The rapids there will be a lot bigger than the piddly little bumps on this stretch of the Jackson. Between here and there I'll have to become expert at handling the boat, which strikes me as highly unlikely.

We haul the canoe out of the river and wait. Ten minutes click by, and the truck doesn't show. Impatient, we lash the canoe to the Volvo's rack, to which Ian has tied the boots and socks he soaked back at Gathright. I'm admiring the Okie ambiance this creates when a pickup comes bouncing up; its driver climbs out and introduces himself as a Westvaco employee dispatched by Ms. Carruth. Do we need any help portaging?

No, thanks, we tell him. We've got it covered. We make small talk, during which I mention that we have to be going so that I can write my story, and Ian and I can file the series' next installment. Where you going to do that? he asks. I admit that I don't know—perhaps we'll try the Covington paper, the *Virginian-Review,* I say. We jump in the car and drive into town.

It is an unpleasant little place. Alleghany County's seat is dominated by Westvaco's bleached-board plant, which occupies the town's gut with a cancer of stink, smokestacks, and high-rise machinery. Clanking and hissing and mountains of wood chips rise from the Jackson's flood plain. A concrete pool filled with chocolate-colored goo squats on its bank. "Good God almighty," I mutter as we roll along a ridge overlooking acres and acres of environmental bruise. Even had I not spent the day paddling a beautiful mountain stream, Covington's ugliness would be jolting. And its smell—its smell is sharp, all-pervading. "How can anyone live here?"

Complain about Covington's stink, and invariably a townie will tell you that if you think it's bad now, you should have tried breathing here years ago. There's truth to that: in January 1939, a photographer for the Depression-era Farm Security Administration fired off a picture of Covington in which the mountains crowding the town were all but invisible behind a thick, smoky shroud of bad air. Thirty years later, Shelby Coffey III, destined to become editor of the *Los Angeles Times,* wrote of a "thick bluish haze" over downtown Covington that turned Main Street into "a blurred image like a faded, aging photograph of the little town your grandfather talked about spending his hard but fair childhood in." Stick around, Coffey wrote, and "there comes a sense of claustrophobia. You can't get away from the smell, the haze, the feeling that your lungs are swallowing in some vaporous disaster. As if you stepped into a room where a hundred chain smokers had just held a two-hour meeting."

It is, by all accounts, a much healthier town today, my horror notwithstanding. Westvaco has spent hundreds of millions of dollars to clean up its act. Still, to an outsider, the plant's ever-present odor takes some getting used to, and when Covington is in the grip of a temperature inversion, so that Westvaco's exhaust is trapped by the mountains that encircle the city, the place reeks.

The factory's effect on the river is just as startling. Clear, cold mountain water is sucked into its intakes, put to use making the stiff paper in food and cigarette packaging, and pumped back out in a substantially modified form. The water goes through a lot of cleaning before rejoining the river; even so, the Jackson turns a deep, opaque sepia, not unlike weak coffee. It smells of detergent. It's warmer, meaning that it can't hold as much dissolved oxygen, on which fish depend. It bears little resemblance to the river I sampled in my spill at Gathright. It looks spoiled. Beaten.

Ian and I pull into the *Virginian-Review* to find the newspaper offices locked tight. We're coasting back out of the lot when our friend from Westvaco pulls up in his pickup and invites us back to the plant. Ms. Carruth, he reports, will be happy to give us a place to work. So we follow him through the business district to Westvaco, park the car, and haul our equipment into an air-conditioned guard shack, where we wait for a while until Ms. Carruth appears to escort us into the company's offices. We cross a pedestrian bridge over the river, glimpse it rolling below, and snake through a labyrinth of corridors to her snug office.

Carruth is a friendly, upbeat woman, eager to present the company's case. We talked on the phone before Ian and I began the trip, and she knows that I stumbled on Shelby Coffey's old story, and that I'm underwhelmed by Covington myself. She notes that the operation is huge—it includes this bleached-board plant, another facility that produces activated charcoal, a corporate research center, and a few miles downriver, a paper-coating plant, employing all told about two thousand people—and argues that given its size, it's impressively clean. "We're big," she says, "but because of this mill's position on the Jackson River, and in a valley, we have pioneered some very innovative environmental measures that have been emulated around the world."

"This is a very low-odor mill," she says. "I've been around a lot of paper mills, including this one fifteen, twenty years ago. And when I returned to the Alleghany Highlands about a year ago I thought it was marked, how much less noticeable the odor was."

I nod, relieved to be visiting Covington today, rather than fifteen or twenty years back. Carruth produces other evidence of the company's clean-up efforts: over the past ten years, according to Westvaco and to state regulators, the plant has reduced its pollutants by two-thirds, no longer dumps dioxin into the river, and has managed to improve the color of the downstream flow.

All of which impresses me, but not as much as a figure I find in one of Westvaco's company reports: With all those improvements, the Covington operation still spews more than 4.5 million pounds of pollution per year. Carruth responds that sixty percent of the mill's emissions are methanol—wood alcohol—which is released into the air, rather than into the Jackson. A good-sized forest produces a similar amount, she says, just in the course of looking good and providing shade.

Maybe so. But given the choice between a forest and a paper plant, I decide I'll go with the woods. They don't stink.

Wanting to put Covington behind us, Ian and I drive the canoe to a muddy, rutted wasteland beneath the U.S. Route 60 bridge late in the evening, aiming to get a little paddling in before the sun goes down. We bounce the car through potholes and around trash and chunks of concrete. Doing our best to ignore the soapy aroma that seems to waft from the stained water, we quickly unlash the canoe and walk it to the bank. But now we encounter a snag. Our maps don't show any downstream access to the river; we can't tell where Ian might be able to get the car close to the bank so that we can load up the boat and head to a campsite we've booked a few miles north of town.

What seems like deliverance comes in the form of two teenagers loitering under the bridge on mountain bikes. I ask one of them, a portly lad with an evil-looking scar on his nose, where we might be able to pull the canoe out of the water downstream.

"You could go to Clifton Forge," he offers.

This I know to be poor advice: Clifton Forge, a down-on-its-luck railroad town and the second-biggest settlement in Alleghany County, is a good fifteen river miles away. "Tonight," I say. "We need to get to a place downriver tonight, and we only have a little while—what, an hour?—before sunset."

The kid shrugs. "Clifton," he says. "You won't have no trouble getting to Clifton. This river's fast, man. It's rough, real rough. It moves along real quick. You'll get to Clifton, easy."

"Not Clifton," I tell him. "Forget Clifton. Is there anything else close by? Like, three miles from here?"

He changes the subject. "You want to get to Richmond, don't you?"

"Yes," I mutter, exasperated. "But not tonight."

"I'm telling you, man, Clifton," he insists. He looks at his buddy, a scrawny kid with a crew cut and teeth like an old fence. His buddy nods. "This river's rough," he says again. "It goes under this one railroad bridge, past the legs of it, and—" His face contorts into an expression intended to convey serious whitewater. At least, that's what I think it's meant to convey.

Ian comes over with the maps, and for a few minutes the kids study them. Over behind this one shopping center, they say, you can bushwhack to the bank. That might work. But they can't find the place on the map, and lose us in their explanation of how to get there.

Eventually the kid with the scar leaves us, wandering over to the river to take a dip. In a moment he's waist-deep in the Jackson, no more than five hundred yards downstream from where the Westvaco plant dumps its effluent into the river. Ian and I watch him for a minute, then decide to load the canoe back on the car and call it a day.

DAY SIX

On which the expedition
battles its way past all manner of
obstacles to reach the James

❧ Early morning, and we're again on the urban desert under the Route 60 bridge. Just above here a wide creek, Dunlap, dumps into the Jackson's gurgling brown stream. Downriver, their combined flow surges southward through Covington. Right in front of us, it splashes noisily over a small ledge, perhaps eighteen inches high. "I've been thinking," I announce.

Ian is nervously eyeing the ledge. "What?"

"I'm no good at this," I say.

He makes no attempt to contradict me. "And I'm thinking that Balcony Falls could be a real problem," I continue. "So sometime this morning I need you to get to a phone and see if you can round up a guide to help me get through it."

Ian nods slowly. "OK," he says. "That's good to hear." He helps me carry the canoe to the water's edge, then stands tensely on the bank as I shove off, back the canoe into the channel's center, and line myself to go over the drop. "Set it up for Thursday or Friday," I yell to him.

"Be careful," he hollers. I wave, paddle hard, and swoop over the ledge.

Ian applauds. I whoop. For a moment, it almost feels as if I know what I'm doing.

That doesn't last. The kid under the bridge was right: The Jackson does, indeed, move toward Clifton Forge at a fast clip, its width split by rocks and churned by rapids, and soon I'm struggling. I paddle without mishap through downtown Covington, but the river swings wide to the west just below, turns sharply south, then cuts east, and each new bend brings a rapids nastier than the one before. Every hole I pick through each of the stony falls proves to be the wrong one. I run aground, scrape hard against sharp, submerged rock slabs, get wedged against boulders. I slide over small ledges sideways, the canoe rocking wildly. I do a lot of screaming.

All of this comes as a shock, because around me are the sounds of people, civilization—car engines and the whoosh of traffic and horns and clattering trains. Bridges loom overhead, booming with the muffled drumrolls of truck tires. The water's untamed rush seems weirdly out of place. Then, after negotiating a chain of sharp-cornered oxbows, the river sweeps beneath the railroad bridge the kid had warned me about, swings to the east—and gets rougher. I gallop down a long straightaway, Interstate 64 high to my left, boulder fields jutting from the water all around me. Gray rock hulks on the streambed, breaking the river into narrow flumes, sending it over drops two, sometimes three feet high.

Diving over one falls, I miscalculate the water's force and wind up slamming into a car-sized boulder so hard that I'm thrown off my knees and against the rock. Somehow I manage to stay balanced enough to keep from flipping the boat. In another chute I get hung up on a submerged snag, spin 180 degrees and, shrieking at the top of my lungs, plummet backwards over a two-foot drop into a froth of whitewater, looking over my shoulder as if backing out a drive. I again avoid getting wet. It seems a miracle.

Before Westvaco turned Covington into a real city, the hills flanking the Jackson here were occupied by widely scattered backwoodsmen. Among them was Peter Wright, who was out hunting one winter's day when a sudden snowstorm trapped him in a rock shelter east of town. He had to eat his moccasins to keep from starving.

By that standard, I have it pretty easy. Still, it's a long morning of noisy water, violent collisions with stationary obstacles, and rapids that spit me downstream faster than I can run. With each new terrace or rock garden I try to apply lessons learned upstream. Sometimes a discovered technique actually seems to work more than once; more often, I'm worse for my wisdom. But by lunchtime I've reached, through all this experimentation, one hard and fast conclusion: fortune favors the bold. I almost always fare better when I attack a rapids, rather than tiptoe in. Timidity was my undoing at Gathright, it seems to me; negotiating rough water depends on picking a route through the rocks, committing to it, and going at it full-tilt.

That certainty carries me through rapids that come three or four to a mile until, shortly after noon, I paddle into what's clearly an artificial stretch of river, perhaps half a mile long and arrow-straight. A glance at the map confirms that I'm paddling a shortcut carved across an old oxbow. It's a boring traverse—minus curves by which to measure my progress, I seem to crawl downstream—but the man-made channel offers one break: for a brief while, I needn't worry about whitewater.

It returns soon enough, as I loop around another bend, then another, but the day's toughest rapids are behind me. Around another curve I find Ian standing on the riverbank, and with amazement watch him walk across the Jackson's surface. "Watch out," he yells. "There's, like, a dam here." As I paddle closer I see that he's actually standing on a concrete ford, a third of it green-slimed and invisible under a few inches of water, the rest of its length crossing the river just above the surface. I bring the canoe slowly to the point where the ford slips underwater, and Ian grabs its nose. I clamber up beside him. "Where are we?"

"Dabney S. Lancaster Community College," he says. "Car's just uphill." We leave the boat on the ford and hike a narrow drive up the bank. The Volvo's parked beside a brick maintenance building, and we sit on its stoop, eating PBJs and studying our maps. Big, red-bodied wasps buzz lazily around us, seeking mud nests in the eaves.

"Thank God we didn't listen to that kid last night," I say. "Can you imagine how late it would have been when I got here?"

"*If* you got here."

"Ten-four to that."

"Speaking of dying on the river," Ian says, "I tried calling the James River Canoe Livery, in Lexington. The guy I needed to talk to wasn't around. I'm supposed to call back." I nod, and notice for the first time that Ian's arms and legs are scraped bloody. He explains that after making the call at a K-Mart in Covington, he charged through a riverfront thicket of wild raspberry, redbud, poison oak, and spider webs to hand off a fresh supply of Gatorade, only to reach the water just as I rounded a bend way downstream. Cussing, he hacked his way back out to the car, drove a couple miles downriver, and clawed through another stand of bushes, sure he'd be snake-bit, to the Jackson's muddy edge. He waited for more than an hour before deciding I was either dead on the rapids upstream or that I'd passed the spot before his arrival, so he bushwhacked to the car, shredding the few square centimeters of flesh that hadn't been lacerated earlier, drove upstream, again shoved his way through riverside bushes to the Jackson, again saw I wasn't there, and, spurting blood by this point, headed back through the brush to the Volvo.

"Too bad we didn't pack a machete," I say.

"Seriously, I'm thinking about hitting a store," he says between bites, "and buying a Weed Eater."

A half hour later I paddle into the outskirts of Clifton Forge, and encounter the most vexing obstacle of the day, this one entirely man-made. As I near a railroad bridge over the Jackson, reputed to be the widest such bridge in the world, I find the river blocked by a gravel causeway, its flow channeled into several large corrugated pipes. A sign in fluorescent orange instructs me to portage to the left, but once out of the canoe I find that the sign is false advertising: there's no easy way to put the boat back in on the causeway's far side, nor even to reach it; my path is blacked by jagged rocks bigger than beach balls.

Across the river and uphill a ways, a couple of construction workers are talking beside a big piece of earthmoving equipment. I haul the boat ashore as far as I can, then clamber over the boulders toward them. They don't see me coming. When I yell a hello and they turn to face me, I can see that they're not accustomed to the sight of a sunburned paddler in shorts and a bright red life jacket on their construction site. When I explain that I need a hand moving my boat, however, one is quick to volunteer. We cross the Jackson to the north bank, grab the canoe by its ends, and haul it, lurching, over the rocks, the beefy construction hand toting the load easily, me gasping and grunting behind him.

The causeway's downstream side lies in the shade of the railroad bridge, and a few yards away the river flows smooth and cool away from us. But in between are the pipes carrying the river under the gravel. Water is barreling from them in thick, roaring jets. My helper drops his end of the canoe. "There you go," he says.

"What am I supposed to do now?" I ask him.

He shrugs. "Put it back in the water and start rowing, I guess."

"Where am I supposed to do that?"

Another shrug. "Right here." He points to the water exploding from one of the pipes. As confident as I'm starting to feel in small rapids, I'm not ready for this. "No," I say. "No way. We can't put in there. The canoe'll be in Lynchburg before I can swing my leg into it."

He shrugs again. "I don't know what you want me to do."

I study the causeway's edge and see that in one place the corrugated metal cofferdam with which it's buttressed extends a few yards downstream, away from the surge. If we can carry the boat over there, I tell him, I believe I'll be able to push off without flipping. He studies the route we'll have to take. It isn't attractive—a high-wire act, really, on the cofferdam's top edge. We'll have to shuffle a dozen feet out over the water, balancing while carrying the canoe. "I don't know," he tells me.

I feel a twinge of panic. Ian is already motoring to a rendezvous a couple miles downstream. I can't carry the loaded boat out there by myself. If the construction worker backs out, I'm stranded. "Look," I say, "I really appreciate the help you've given me—but I need just a little more. Just get me out to the end of that cofferdam, and I'll be on my way and out of your hair." My helper is still eyeing the narrow ledge. Finally, he sighs. "All right," he grunts. "Whatever."

We edge our way onto the cofferdam, tiptoe out over the water. At one point I slip and fall off, planting one leg knee-deep in rocky water, but manage to climb back up, still clutching my end of the canoe. A few tentative steps farther, and we've reached a relatively calm pool of water at the cofferdam's tip. I thank the guy as he helps me lower the boat onto the river, shake his hand, and push off under the railroad bridge.

In days past, Clifton Forge was the dominant burg in Alleghany County, home first to an ironworks that gave the place its name, then to a railroad yard that employed thousands. Covington, though older, was pretty much dormant, awaiting Westvaco's arrival at the turn of the twentieth century. An 1872 magazine article called it "the City of Great Expectations . . . though it has attained only the importance of a village." Now, on the brink of the twenty-first century, the towns' places have been switched. Covington is the county seat, the locus of political and financial power hereabouts, and Clifton Forge—though still possessing a compact, busy-feeling downtown and traffic-snarled streets— is on the wane. The forge is ancient history. Railroad jobs have dwindled.

The city lies entirely on the Jackson's north bank, and I paddle to a melody of gurgling river, clanking and banging train cars, honking horns, the jake brakes and squeals of logging trucks off to my left. Then the river turns abruptly south, and with the bend comes an asset that Clifton Forge enjoys for perpetuity, something that Covington will never have. Ahead lies a narrow canyon punched through the 3,200-foot Rich Patch Mountains. Vertical cliffs rise high on both sides. Across the face on the left soars a gargantuan arch of white stratified rock, its apogee four hundred feet high and centered in the towering wall, its curve gentle but unmistakable. The Rainbow Gap.

The same 1872 article in *Scribner's Monthly* called Rainbow Gap "one of the grandest of gorges," a place "where the Great Architect has revealed the processes by which the mountains were made in baring to the view a mighty arch of a half mile chord and a thousand feet to the key-stone." And, in fact, the river has bared a heck of a geology lesson in carving through this uplift, one in which you can readily see how once-horizontal strata of rock have been bent and warped by forces deep within the earth. I push downstream at the gorge's toes, neck craned to take in the rainbow high above me, almost missing an ancient stone forge on the right bank.

Then, suddenly, the high ground falls away, and I'm surrounded by shelves of low farmland. A few minutes after that, I'm grateful for the day's whitewater apprenticeship, for off to my left a new stream spills into the Jackson, wide and cold and clear. The river ahead is a much bigger waterway, wider and deeper and with far greater power than the stream I've traveled from its highland headwaters.

I have reached the confluence of the Jackson and Cowpasture Rivers.

The Head of the James.

DAY SEVEN

On which we paddle
through a furnace, and among
boomtowns gone bust

❧ It's hot by midmorning, so hot that I pass two hundred cows or so belly-deep in the water beside me. Some are spooked as my canoe approaches. They bound gracelessly up the banks, the bells around their necks clanking, glancing back with wild eyes as I glide past. Most, though, seem too eager for relief from the broiling sun to care much.

I'm on the James now, having left its parent, the Jackson, at a lonely confluence a couple miles downstream of the Rainbow Gap, just outside of a narrow roadside settlement named for the gorge—Iron Gate. Most descriptions of the confluence dwell on its contrasts—the meeting of the pristine Cowpasture, tumbled from the highlands on a looping course roughly parallel to the Jackson, and the Covington-stained waters of the Jackson itself. Read older accounts of the place, and you're left with the impression that the infant James is split in half, clean on its left side, fouled on its right, and that it runs this way for miles. In person the difference doesn't shock. The Jackson, though dyed, has shaken off most of its detergent stink, its suds, and even some of its brown

EARLY MORNING:
GETTING READY TO SHOVE OFF
INTO THE WIDENING JAMES.

hue by the time it reaches the junction. The two combine seamlessly beside the Head of the James Farm, run for generations by the Gibson family.

Ian and I met there briefly yesterday, walked up a farm path past a pair of caged Saint Bernards the size of Holsteins, and met Charlie Gibson, the patriarch of the spread, as he pulled his pickup truck into the carport outside his brick rancher. He sat with us in the carport for twenty minutes, all of us drinking sodas, Charlie talking about life with the James's changing moods. Rain's been in short supply the past two summers, he told us, and the river's low now, as low as he could remember seeing it. But in times past, it has jumped its banks and stormed across the 150 yards of flatland between the streambed and his house, has doubled in size, tripled, quadrupled. At times it's gotten so high, it seemed it might carry the whole farm off.

Now sweat soaks my T-shirt. My life jacket, far too warm to wear, is tossed in the bottom of the boat behind me. And as I paddle in the James's sluggish flow past gargantuan bluffs and the drooping, dry-leafed maples that rim its great bends in Botetourt County, I recall Charlie's description of the river in flood. It seems unreal amid the desiccation of drought. The James is a more muscular stream than the Jackson, eighty feet across and four feet deep, but the heat seems to have sapped it of its vigor. I slug down quart after quart of water, dip my hat in the river every few minutes to enjoy cool rivulets down my neck and back. Still, I'm cooking as I float among the pocked limestone cliffs, past cattle farms and weedy railroad embankments. The going is slow.

Ahead, however, waits the promise of relief. Eagle Rock looks to be a fair-sized place, judging from my maps, with a grid of roads and clusters of buildings and bridges over the river, the sorts of attributes that might bring with them an air-conditioned room. Maybe a restaurant. At the least, a Coke machine. Late in the morning I round a sharp bend to the left, pass a flotilla of fishermen hovering in canoes at the mouth of a fat, fast stream, and spy Ian waiting on the left bank. I beach on a shelf of grassless bank rutted by four-wheelers, dark in the shade of a grove of oaks, maples, and ash. The Volvo is parked a few yards from the water's edge.

"Hiya," I say, stepping ashore, rubbing my knees. Five days of kneeling in the boat have left them skinned and sore, and the unelastic muscles in my legs cramped. Standing after hours under way is a slow, unsteady exercise. Grimacing, I straighten up. "How's Eagle Rock?"

"Slow," he says.

"See a restaurant?"

"No." We unload the canoe, carry my gear to the car, then hoist the boat onto the roof and begin tying it down. OK, I think to myself, maybe there's no restaurant. But surely there's a place to rest a while, get out of the heat, use a phone—I have a story on my laptop computer, written in camp last night, that I have to transmit to the paper. "Well," I say, "let's have a look." We head up a deeply gouged dirt drive through chest-high grass to town.

What greets us is, alas, something less than an oasis. Eagle Rock at midday has the barren ambiance of a spaghetti western: the downtown commercial strip, which faces the river and the CSX Railroad's tracks, is sun-bleached, deserted. In the middle of the block, yellowing newspapers cover the windows of an abandoned feed store. At one end of the block, a flaking Greek revival facade announces a bank, apparently without customers—the Volvo is alone on the street. Downtown Eagle Rock is empty. We drive a block uphill, away from the James, passing plain but well-kept houses on small yards. We see no one outside, no signs of life. "It's like the place has emptied out," Ian says.

"It is," I agree. "It's creepy." We turn onto a street that parallels the business district. A firehouse looms. "They're bound to have a phone, at least," Ian says. He steers into the lot, and we climb from the car, walk to a side door. It is witheringly hot. The concrete and asphalt around us radiate wickedly. I rap on the firehouse door. We wait. Nothing. I pound on it again, then check the building's front, to make sure I didn't somehow miss another entrance. Ian knocks. Seconds tick by. "Unbelievable," I mumble. "Where the hell is everybody?"

"Good thing there isn't a fire," Ian observes.

We turn away from the building. Just across the street stands the sleepy-looking Eagle Rock Funeral Home. A car's parked out front, all its windows down. The mortuary's front door is ajar. "Want to try it?" Ian asks. It seems the only place in town. "Might as well," I answer, and we saunter across the pavement and step through the doorway into a darkened foyer. A bright office is way in the back, at the far end of an unlit hallway, and in it sits a beefy fellow. "Come on in!" he hollers.

Bill Simmons is seventy-five, and he's been running the funeral home for fifty years. He invites us to use the phone, has us sit and pass some time in air conditioning that blasts noisily into the room.

He is sitting behind the busiest desk I've ever seen. While explaining what we're doing, Ian and I become mesmerized by how much stuff he has within reach—videotapes, three-way lightbulbs, two TV remote controls, a thermometer, miniature screwdrivers, two phones, scissors, an adding machine, hand lotion—and how little room it leaves for actual work.

The walls are crowded, too, and as Ian transmits his photos over the phone I wander the office and the foyer, looking at pictures. In the hallway I find one that depicts a busy little city crowded on a hillside. Houses, lots of them, march up the hill, along with churches, a fine-looking school. An industrial operation is under way at the foot of the settlement, and the main drag is crowded with shops and lined with parked cars. I notice that the street looks down on railroad tracks and a river.

It seems impossible, but sure enough, it's Eagle Rock—I can make out the bank we saw earlier, and a church Ian and I had admired uphill, now abandoned, but in the photo trim and bright. Simmons and another visitor who's strolled into the office and eased onto a sofa, an Eagle Rock longtimer named Emmett Dudding, explain that this used to be a busy, exciting place. "When I was born my daddy was a farmer, and he didn't want to do that as a career," Simmons tells us. "So there was an opening at the Ford agency here, and my daddy sold Fords here from 1925 to 1928."

It takes me a moment to process what I've heard. "Wait a minute," I blurt. "There was a Ford dealership *here?*" Dudding smiles, nods sagely. Simmons keeps going: "Then he switched to Chevrolet, and he sold Chevrolets here until my brother and I bought the business from my daddy, and we ran it until 1960."

"There was a *Chevrolet* dealership here, too?" I ask.

Dudding again nods. Until a few years after World War II, they tell us, Eagle Rock boasted a thriving industrial base—extracting limestone from the surrounding mountains and "cooking" it into lime. Simmons himself worked for two lime companies in town, and recalls making thirty cents an hour on the job. Twelve bucks a week. The town also was the shopping hub for the farms and rural crossroads dotting this part of the county. "When I grew up here you could buy everything you needed—clothing, groceries, hardware," Simmons says. "We had a doctor, a drugstore."

"Didn't need to leave Eagle Rock to shop," Dudding agrees. "Used to be you couldn't get around. Everybody was on horse and buggy. Going to Roanoke was a two-day trip."

"So what happened?" I ask them.

Dudding sighs, leans back in the sofa, gives the floor to Simmons. Limestone grew too expensive to mine and process here, he says, and modern highways put Roanoke's shopping malls an easy drive away. Within a few years, Eagle Rock lost both its workers and its customers. These days, Simmons concludes, "the businesses are pretty slim."

We're digesting this understatement as we head back toward the river on still-empty streets, passing part of the old lime operation on the way. The kilns, idle for decades, are filled with algae-carpeted water. They're among many vestiges of booms gone bust along this stretch of the James. As I paddle into the afternoon, I pass the ruins of bridges swept away by floods and never rebuilt, the foundations of riverside businesses vanished, entire towns faded to historical footnote.

Among the most remarkable relics comes before Ian and I even reach the water. The rutted track to the river shares its turnoff with a small, well-tended rectangle of garden-fringed lawn called Last Lock Park. We explore it on foot, and just a few yards from the roadside find a long depression in the grass, the remains of a great dream that captured the imagination of Founding Fathers and generations of entrepreneurs, travelers, laborers, and farmers. We're looking at part of a mammoth undertaking in public works, a canal stretched across Virginia's middle that linked the mountains to Richmond, and a deepwater port to the sea.

The James River and Kanawha Canal never made it to Eagle Rock, but the canal company's craftsmen hand-cut and laid stone locks and aqueducts in anticipation that the ditch itself would follow. Alas, the completed canal only got as far as Buchanan, 197 canal miles upstream of Richmond and a day and a half downriver for us.

Just the same, the undertaking was some kind of audacious. The canal was intended to snake up the James and Jackson, tunnel through the Alleghenies, and connect with the headwaters of the Kanawha River, in what's now West Virginia. There everyone and everything would be loaded onto canal boats traveling down the Kanawha to the Ohio River at Point Pleasant. The ruined old lock Ian and I examine in Eagle Rock is part of a long-ago scheme to link the Atlantic and Mississippi.

A couple of big names were among the early visionaries. George Washington mulled the idea of connecting the eastern and western rivers in 1784, and Thomas Jefferson published an early call for the project. Describing the James in his *Notes on the State of Virginia*, the future third president added that "the expence would not be great, when compared with its object, to open a tolerable navigation up Jackson's River and Carpenter's Creek, to within 25 miles of Howard's Creek of Green briar, both of which have then water enough to float vessels into the Great Kanhaway." In 1785 the James River Canal Company organized, with Washington as its honorary president, and built a canal stretching seven miles upriver from downtown Richmond. Over the years it was lengthened, widened, and connected to the James downstream, below the seven-mile-long falls that blocked, and still prevent, boats in the freshwater from reaching the tidewater.

It wasn't until nearly fifty years later, after hard times, a state takeover, and reorganization, that the James River and Kanawha Company began the westward push. Ahead lay a task of daunting scale: building a wide, well-tended waterway that for most of its length followed the James's northern, or left, bank; creating a towpath alongside it; and fashioning aqueducts to carry the canal's water over the many streams and sizeable rivers that interrupted the river's shore. Locks were needed to stair-step the canal up central Virginia's steadily rising terrain, and dams to keep it filled with water. The banks crumbled. Floods were frequent, destructive, and dangerous.

Even so, in December 1840 the canal boat *General Harrison* became the first freight boat to cruise the 146 miles from Richmond to the tobacco warehouses of Lynchburg. The new canal reduced travel time between the cities from ten days to thirty hours. Packet boats made the journey three times a week. The following spring the company began work on the project's second phase. It was a tough 51 miles to Buchanan, uphill into the Blue Ridge foothills and through the range's spine in the pass at Balcony Falls, and the job was made tougher by cash shortages. It wasn't until November 21, 1851, that the packet boat *John Early* arrived at the canal's new western terminus. The 197 miles of completed canal had cost $8.26 million—more than the Erie Canal, which was nearly twice as long.

Ian and I return to the riverbank, dump the canoe in the water, arrange to meet a few hours downstream at another town faded with the loss of its industry—Salt Petre Cave, once devoted to extracting the ingredients of gunpowder from riverbank hills. I paddle through the heat, looking for signs of canal work, seeing few. One thing I do notice: along this stretch of river, my maps give names to all the rapids. I wonder whether those names are leftovers of the surveying teams and work crews that planned the canal upstream of Buchanan.

While that work was under way, traffic on the completed stretch exploded. Soon after the waterway linked Richmond and Buchanan, 195 freight boats plied it regularly. Passenger boats made the trip, which had taken the better part of two weeks early in the century, in just 47 hours, and daily service carried travelers between the capital and Lynchburg six days a week. Horses on the towpath pulled the narrow packet boats along at four miles per hour, while the travelers inside or riding on the roof enjoyed "luxurious accommodations and polite Society," as one newspaper ad put it, their relaxation interrupted only by shouts of "Low bridge! Everybody down!"

By 1860, the canal's relatively speedy pace was being eclipsed by the new darling of westward expansion, the railroad. The Civil War hastened the canal's passing, but it was already plain that it would happen; for most of its length, it's nowadays a silted-in dry ditch, overgrown with weeds and trees and alive with all manner of varmint. Its towpath is still an important part of Mid-Atlantic commerce, however: after the canal's decline, the Richmond and Alleghany Railroad bought up the canal, laying its tracks on the smooth, level path beside it. The Chesapeake & Ohio later bought out that railroad, and today the C&O's descendant, the CSX Railroad, still rides there.

Late in the day I spot an opening in the picket line of ash and old man's beard along the left bank, see the CSX tracks at the top of a steep embankment hard against the shore. I beach the boat, climb the embankment's soft gravel face to the tracks, and look down, sweating, on the handful of old houses that form Salt Petre Cave. A single barking dog is the only sign of higher life. Ian pulls up in the Volvo while I'm on the tracks, and follows me back to the boat. Hauling it up and over the old towpath proves brutal: the heat is relentless, the rise steep, the footing loose. We swear extravagantly.

We're strapping the canoe to the roof rack when a freight train rumbles by, creating its own wind, rustling the trees, filling the air with a deep throb. Remarkable, I think as I watch it clatter and squeal by, that moving freight through the mountains still depends on a project conceived more than two hundred years ago.

Late at night, after we phone in another story and pictures, we drive through the dark to a new campsite. We've camped for the past two nights north of Clifton Forge, and found we like not having to break camp every morning. Now we've picked a site way downstream, near Natural Bridge Station, figuring that by setting up there we can remain encamped for three nights straight. It's black as pitch when we reach the Campground at Natural Bridge, a sprawling RV resort on the hilly south bank, its highest ground occupied by a barnlike two-story building of showers, bathrooms, and a big rec room filled with pinball machines and video games. The grounds are silent, the rec room empty, the combination office and camp store, over near the entrance, dark. It seems we'll be the only campers here tonight.

But as we weave the curving lanes, trying to pick out a campsite, a little Dodge Neon pulls into the campground and follows us. When we select a treeless hilltop site and start unloading the car, the Neon pulls into the site next door, and a young woman in the front passenger seat lowers her window. "Is it open?" she asks. Her English is halting, heavily accented. I stroll over to her car, and see that another young woman is behind the wheel, three others squeezed into the snug back seat. "I don't know," I say, "but we're staying."

"Would it be OK if we camped here, next to you?" she asks.

I have the sense that I've seen this scene in a movie. Or dreamed it. "Sure," I tell her. "That'd be fine." So while Ian and I pitch the tents, open a couple of beers and fire up the stoves on a picnic table, the five women—visitors from the Czech Republic, they tell us—putter around across a few yards of dark. A small dome tent rises from the grass in their car's headlight beams. They take turns changing into pajamas behind the Neon, the others keeping an eye on us.

Ian seems edgy, excited. I can't tell whether it's the Czechs or the fact that we're having Mac and Gack for dinner. He begins yodeling while he stirs the macaroni. "When I have a hunger attack, I always—"

"You know," I interrupt, "it makes me so sad when you do that."

He completes the verse anyway. "By the way," he says, "I finally got ahold of the guide this afternoon."

I'm almost ready to forgive his singing. "I talked to him," Ian says, "and he seemed to think you wouldn't need him."

"Oh yeah?"

He pulls out a pad, holds it near the two candle lanterns we have burning on the picnic table, reads from notes he took during the phone call. "Said if you've made it this far, you'll have no trouble—that the worst of it is a high Class II."

Hmmm. "I've *barely* made it this far," I remind him. "It's been pure luck that I haven't dumped the canoe a dozen times. Hell, more than that." We drink our beers, thinking. A high Class II? It's the first time I've heard Balcony Falls described as a high Class II. I could probably fake my way through a high Class II. I've been through that, or worse, upriver.

Or have I? Truth is, I'm a bit fuzzy on where a Class II ends and a Class III begins. I'm not sure about the distinctions between any of the classes, really. If I were without my maps, or my photocopied descriptions of the river's whitewater stretches, I'd have no clue as to what I've been through. Besides, I think, it's not like gauging the rapids accurately has had much bearing on my ability to survive them. I've nearly been undone by supposedly low-rated rapids, particularly the ones back between Covington and Clifton Forge.

"I'm a bad canoeist," I announce. "The guy saying I don't need a guide is an expert canoeist who doesn't understand just how bad I am." Ian opens our cooler, digs around for another beer in silence. "I just don't want to take the chance," I tell him. "I'm not worried about getting hurt. But if something goes wrong, and I'm stranded—well, it'd be no good to be out there by myself. It just seems smarter to have someone else along. And what really worries me is: What if I lose the boat? What if something happens and I dump, and I'm OK but the boat floats off or gets busted up, or something?

"We'd be screwed," I conclude. "I think we ought to go with a guide."

Ian exhales loudly. "OK," he says. He smiles, visibly relieved.

DAY EIGHT

Of oxbows, old stone, and the ghosts of a frontier past

The James River swings through a series of oxbow bends in Botetourt County, some so looping that after four miles of hard, hot paddling, I'm within a few hundred yards of where I was an hour ago.

It's 10:00 A.M., and already it's been a long morning. Awake at dawn, I walked uphill from camp to the showers, doused myself with scalding water, strolled back outside through the empty game room to a chorus of bleeps from idle video and pinball machines, and loped back to our campsite. From fifty yards away I could see that Ian was holding court. The Czechs were up and gathered around our picnic table, one of them serving as spokeswoman for the group. Once I joined them I caught on that they'd been vacationing in Florida, and had decided on a "quick" visit to Washington, D.C.

"It must not seem very quick in that little car," I said. The spokeswoman, petite and dark-haired, chuckled at that. "It is not bad."

"And that tent," I said. "You guys are all crowded into that one tent?"

She shrugged. "You Americans," she said, "you need so much space." I glanced over at our own relatively opulent spread. My tent alone had more floor space than they had shared.

They were eager to get back on the road. They broke camp and loaded up the Neon while we ate breakfast, and were ready to go at the same time we were. "Are you going to pay?" the spokeswoman asked—an odd question, I thought. "Yeah," Ian said. "We're going to stop by the office on our way out." She nodded, we said our good-byes, everyone climbed into the cars, and we cruised over to the campground's office-store. I jumped from the Volvo and jogged to the door. It was locked. I turned back to Ian just in time to see the Czechs wave and gun it down the drive. "Wow!" Ian yelled. "Did you see that? They just took off without paying!"

I nodded. "They wahooed the place."

"Man," Ian sighed. I couldn't tell whether he disapproved of their behavior or admired it. We backtracked upriver to Salt Petre Cave, Ian reenacting his campsite conversation with the women. "Did you notice the one with the blond streak in her hair?" he asked.

Tall. Slim. Almond-eyed. Late twenties, early thirties.

"Something happened there," Ian said. "There was something between us."

"Ten feet of air," I suggested.

"Really, we connected. I felt something, and she felt it, too."

"Did she tell you so?"

"No," Ian replied. "It was the way she was looking at me."

"She felt something," I mused. "Was it nausea?"

"I don't think so," he said, laughing. "She gave me these." He produced two postcards of Prague's downtown skyline. There was nothing written on the back of either.

"She didn't leave you her name? An address?"

"No," Ian said. "Well, you saw how it was. There wasn't much time."

"What a drag," I said. "Another two minutes, and you might have had some chance of meeting someday."

"It's true." Ian nodded, keeping his eyes on the road.

"Now you'll never see her again."

"I know," he said solemnly.

"And you'll have to pay for a hotel if you ever go to Prague."

"It's tragic," he said. "Really, it is."

At the put-in we slid and skidded down the railroad embankment with the canoe, and I pushed off, hoping to make good time to our planned lunch stop in Buchanan. But almost at once I was struck by a wicked headwind that cut my speed in half, and it has stayed with me for well over an hour, making the already slow oxbows torturously so.

Just a little ways upstream, above Eagle Rock, I paddled a straightaway miles long; here the James curves so severely that it nearly makes islands of the land snared within its loops. The short explanation is that a river does, as the old saying goes, follow a path of least resistance. It runs straight until it's deflected by an obstruction, and bounced against its valley's side—prompting it to flow back across to the valley's far side, then turn back across, and so on, until its course downhill has turned snaky.

What happens to these bends over time depends on the kind of rock through which the stream runs. If the rock is hard stuff, resistant to wear, the river will maintain a relatively narrow channel, with little dry valley floor around it. If, on the other hand, it's weaker rock, the river will gradually carve itself a broad, flat valley. A river snaking through such a valley chews at the banks on the outside of its bends, and redeposits this borrowed rock and soil on the insides. Played out over lifetimes, this bottomland give-and-take changes the shape of the river's curves, redirecting its flow around the valley floor. Thus, a river's channel wanders all over its bottomland. Its shape is always on the move, nomadic, over time sweeping back and forth across the width of the valley. Old maps and a lot of study convinced the Army Corps of Engineers that the Missouri River, parts of which have valley floors a mile wide, normally steals and redeposits thousands of bottomland acres a year—so much, in fact, that it would take the Missouri only seventy years to borrow and lend all the land on the valley floor around it. We often label these valley floors "floodplains," which might give the impression that they're created by floods. The fact is that most aren't; their rivers create them just in the course of flowing.

So why is it, you might now ask, that a river in a widening valley doesn't automatically get wider itself? Why doesn't it spread out? Stretch its legs? Because a river's streambed has been fashioned by nature to carry water and sediment downstream, and if it's not of the proper width and depth, it won't be able to pull this mission off. Too wide a channel will slow the river's flow until it can no longer carry its load of sediment; too narrow a path will spur the rushing waters to gnaw faster at the banks. So, in normal times, a river—this river—maintains a balance between the extremes.

Knowing all this doesn't make the oxbows any easier to paddle, unfortunately. Getting nowhere fast, I have time to wonder whether any spiders survive in the boat. I'm reasonably sure I didn't kill all of them during my tangle with the willow tree below Gathright. God knows how many are crouching under the flotation bags. I find myself eyeing the edges of the bow bag for a glimpse of hairy legs.

I also find time to study the bridges carrying the CSX railroad tracks across the necks of the bends, and I notice they have in common an odd detail: The lower two-thirds of the piers rising from the James's rocky bottom are built of massive, hand-cut blocks of stone. The upper reaches are made of smaller, newer-looking slabs. The answer to the riddle is that they weren't built as bridges, but as aqueducts, some of the improvements finished in anticipation of the JR&K's westward push from Buchanan. When the push failed to come, the work was stopped, here as at the last lock in Eagle Rock. Later, when the railroad came through, it topped off the bridges—built low because they were to support an artificial channel of water several feet deep—and laid tracks on the old canal route. The railroad put other canal construction to use around here, too. At the end of one bridge, CSX trains today disappear into a tunnel through one oxbow-ringed mountain that was dug for canal boats.

Eventually the river straightens a bit, and a highway bridge appears up ahead: Springwood, site of my morning rendezvous with Ian. As I near the bridge I glance to my right, into a deep, shaded cleft in the bank, and see a small, postcard-perfect waterfall dappled with sunlight. It's gone in a second as I drift downstream.

I find Ian waiting beside one of the bridge's massive concrete legs, and convince him to wade upriver with me to have a better look at the falls. We splash about a hundred yards through cool water, eyes peeled for snakes, then feel the river turn icy as we near the mouth of a small stream flashing shallow over gravel and into the James. Stepping into the narrow chink in the riverbank, we climb the bed of Spreading Spring Branch into the shade. The air temperature drops at least ten degrees. And before us is a bank-to-bank waterfall rushing in cold, clear sheets from a curved limestone lip. The water drops about five feet to a crystal pool.

"Aw, man," Ian moans. "Look at that."

Planted in the pool's bottom is an old water heater.

Three miles below the Springwood bridge, Looney's Creek gushes into the James from the right bank. These days the confluence is on the western edge of Buchanan, though I can't see much sign of a town on the river ahead. Two and a half centuries ago, it was on the edge of the frontier—and smack in the middle of trouble.

On one of their many raids on Virginia settlers during and after the French and Indian War, the Shawnees paid a visit to the scattered settlement of Looney's Ferry, using mountain trails and creekbeds to avoid a fort that stood on the James here, at the mouth of Looney's Creek. By the time an alarm was raised, Cornstalk's warriors had killed and scalped a passel of men and dragged off several women and children. One of the prisoners was a terrified, grieving young woman who was destined to became a hero.

Her name was Hannah Dennis, and she lived with her husband and small child on a homestead on Purgatory Creek, just north of present-day Buchanan. On a late July day, probably in 1761, the Shawnees swooped down upon the Dennises' spread, killed Hannah's husband and child before her eyes, and took her prisoner. The Indians then struck the neighbors: at Robert Renick's home, they seized Mrs. Renick along with her four sons and a daughter, then pushed on to Thomas Smith's homestead, where they shot and scalped Smith and the visiting Robert Renick, and captured Mrs. Smith and a servant.

The Indians split up, and Hannah Dennis was suddenly alone, separated from her friends and forced to march back to the Shawnee towns. The journey took her up the Jackson, over the Alleghenies, and across hundreds of miles of wilderness essentially unexplored by whites, until Looney's Ferry seemed an impossible distance behind her, an insurmountable series of obstacles—mountains, rivers, wild animals—away.

Dennis must have known that the odds were against her returning to white society. So she went native. She learned the Shawnee language. She dressed and painted herself as a Shawnee squaw. She performed the tedious, tiring grunt work expected of Indian women. More importantly, she learned Shawnee custom and religion, and over time managed to convince the Indians that she possessed the powers of magic and medicine. Escorted into the woods and fields around the Indian towns, she'd pick herbs that she mixed into healing elixirs and pastes. She made no effort to deny rumors that she could see the future. She pretended to speak with the dead. She chatted with animals.

Time passed, and the Indians came to view her not only as one of their own, but as an officer of the tribe. Eventually they no longer sent an escort along on her forays into the woods for herbs, and on one such trip, when she'd strayed far from the village, Hannah Dennis ran. She tore through the woods and crossed fields, forded streams, and climbed rock faces. She crisscrossed the Scioto River three times, bent on erasing her trail.

When hours had passed without her return from the woods, the Shawnees got wise and dispatched a team of warriors, familiar with the territory and accustomed to speedy travel, to track her down. They came within sight of her as she forded the Scioto a fourth time, took a few shots, missed. Nursing a cut foot, Dennis searched for an escape as the warriors crossed the river after her. With no time to spare, she crawled into the hollow shell of a fallen sycamore and waited.

And waited. The Indians gathered nearby, stumped by her disappearance, spooked by the notion that she might have used magic to escape. They stepped on the log in which she hid as they searched. That night they camped a short ways off, well within earshot of the hollow tree. The next morning, unnerved, the warriors elected to give up the chase and crossed back over the Scioto. Dennis moved on, traveling in the cover of darkness, crossing the Ohio on a piece of timber, living on roots, herbs, grapes, wild cherries, and river mussels, hiking across the mountains for twenty nights until she was found by three white pioneers and taken to their settlement on Muddy Creek, in the Greenbrier country. Fed and rested, she traveled by horse to Fort Young, in Covington, then downriver to Looney's Ferry.

Her story is a testament to pluck, of course, but it also survives because her experience was a rare one. For the half-century in which whites and Shawnees tangled on the Virginia frontier, the Indians gave better than they got, striking terror into a much more powerful foe, killing scads more English than they, themselves, lost. They rarely lost a fight against a like-sized army. They were rarely outmaneuvered. That Hannah Dennis managed to beat them was a remarkable feat.

As for Cornstalk—well, his story took an unexpected and ugly turn. Three years after the Battle of Point Pleasant, and sixteen after Hannah Dennis's kidnapping, Virginians occupied a rude stockade at the confluence of the Kanawha and Ohio called Fort Randolph. It was 1777, and the Revolution was on. American leaders feared the British would incite the Shawnees and other Ohio Valley tribes to attack. Tension in the stockade was high. A raid could come at any time, and if the fort fell, the Virginia frontier would be vulnerable all the way east to the settlements beyond the Jackson and Cowpasture.

At this point, in early November, Cornstalk appeared outside the walls. No army followed him on this trip to Point Pleasant; he was backed up only by another chief, Red Hawk, and a third Indian. Why exactly they made the visit is open to conjecture. Whatever their intention, Cornstalk wasted no time in making clear that trouble was on the way. He was opposed to joining the British in the war, he announced, but all of his people were for it, and he imagined that he'd have to run with the stream. The fort's commander, Capt. Matthew Arbuckle, was a skilled frontiersman and Indian fighter who'd done battle with Cornstalk on this very ground. On hearing that the chief might soon take up arms against him, he ordered his visitors detained.

Even as this was happening, American volunteers were gathering at Fort Randolph for a visit to the Shawnee towns to cement the tribe's neutrality in the War for Independence. The fort got even more crowded on November 9, 1777, when Cornstalk's son, Elmipsico, popped up across the Kanawha and yelled a hello. The chief "immediately recognized the voice of his son, got up, went out, and answered him," Capt. John Stuart later recalled. "The young fellow crossed over, and they embraced each other in the most tender and affectionate manner."

Elmipsico spent the night. The next day, the fort's leaders held a meeting at which Cornstalk again predicted that his people would fight with the British, then launched into a strange monologue: "When I was a young man and went to war," Stuart quoted him as saying, "I thought that might be the last time, and I would return no more. Now I am here amongst you; you may kill me if you please; I can die but once; and it is all one to me, now or another time."

Not long after the meeting broke up, two young frontiersmen were off across the Kanawha hunting for deer. Returning to camp, they passed some Indians spying on the fort from the cover of weeds, and drew fire. One of the men, named Gilmore, fell dead on the riverbank. Capt. Arbuckle was standing across the Kanawha with John Stuart when the shooting started. They were wondering who could be responsible when the surviving hunter bolted down the far bank and screamed that Gilmore was dead. His fellow volunteers jumped into a canoe, crossed the river, rescued the survivor, and brought Gilmore's scalped and bloody corpse back to the point. No sooner had the canoe nosed ashore than the cry went up: *Kill the Indians in the fort.* Guns in hand, a mob headed up the bank toward Fort Randolph. Arbuckle and Stuart stepped in its path and urged the men to cool off. In answer, Stuart reported, the men cocked their guns and ordered the commander to step aside.

As the mob approached the prisoners' quarters, Elmipsico began to panic. Cornstalk tried to calm him, telling him "the Great Man above had sent him there to be killed and die with him," Stuart wrote later. "As the men advanced to the door, the Corn-stalk rose up and met them; they fired upon him, and seven or eight bullets went through him.

"So fell the great Corn-stalk warrior,—whose name was bestowed upon him by the consent of the nation, as their great strength and support. His son was shot dead, as he sat upon a stool. The Red-hawk made an attempt to go up the chimney, but was shot down. The other Indian was shamefully mangled, and I grieved to see him so long in the agonies of death."

American leaders denounced the murders as deplorable, despicable, cowardly. When one of the men reportedly involved in the killings was brought to trial, however, he was acquitted by a jury of his Rockbridge County neighbors.

The sun is broiling when I meet Ian under Buchanan's Main Street Bridge, where we find a local examining the river shallows beside a boat ramp. I realize he's looking at a foot-long, motionless bass that's trapped in a pebble-rimmed pool. "I caught it this morning," he tells us, "and then I decided to put it back in the water, so I can catch it again when it's bigger." Ignorant of fishing clichés, I consider pointing out to the guy that Buchanan, while small—its only fast-food joint shares a roof with a gas station—probably has a significant population of anglers among its 1,200 souls, and that he might not have the chance. But his tone, and the fact that he's returned to the ramp hours later, tell me that he has a personal relationship with this fish. I hold my tongue. "I don't understand why it's not moving," he says. I stare down at the fish with him. He's right: its speckled form is utterly becalmed.

"Could it be dead?" I ask, still standing ankle-deep in water at the boat ramp's foot. "The water feels awfully warm." I lean down, gently touching the creature's back. It weakly waves a pectoral fin. "No, it's not dead," he judges. "Maybe it needs deeper water." He looks at me. "Would you mind picking it up, moving it over into the river?"

This is a development I could not have predicted at the start of the day. "I don't know how to do it," I tell him. "How do you pick up a fish like this?"

"Well, usually," he says, "you do it by the mouth."

I reply that I'm worried I'll hurt it, and after regarding me with a blend of mild disgust and pity he shuffles up the ramp and across a gravel parking lot to his car, returning a minute later in dark green waders. Then he bends down, cradles the bass in both arms, and carries it, splashing, a few feet out into the James, where he gently lowers the fish into the current. It hovers for a moment, then darts off. The man sighs with relief, waves goodbye, and trudges up the ramp. "Well, that was weird," I note.

Ian nods. "Sure was." We head up the ramp toward the car, where lunch waits—the usual peanut butter and grape jelly on wheat bread, water and Gatorade. The heat is oppressive, the sun scorching, the gravel parking lot around us brilliant with reflected light. Wasps loiter under the wayback's open hatch. "So what's the latest with our guide?" I ask through a mouthful of Jif.

"I talked to the livery people, and they said that if you want to go through the falls on Thursday, the owner will take you. If you want to go Friday, they'll have someone else do it."

"Somebody good?"

"Somebody named Hope."

"A woman?"

"No," Ian says, "it's a guy. Owner said he's real experienced."

"Well, we're halfway through Wednesday," I say. "I can make some miles this afternoon, but I don't see any way in a million years we're going to make it to the head of the falls by tomorrow night."

"It wouldn't be tomorrow night, either," Ian says. "The guy said it usually takes something like four hours to get through the falls. So you'd have to meet him at, like, three o'clock."

"No way," I decide. "Looks like it's Hope."

Buchanan is a picturesque little place, with homes on both sides of the river linked by its Main Street, and a classic small-town American business strip lining the road just south of the James. There are churches, and a bank, and a town hall, and down by the water an old, burned-out hotel awaiting restoration. Most of the businesses that grew up with the place are gone, replaced by the sort of tourist-oriented enterprises that characterize burgs just off the interstate: a longtime drugstore and tobacconist has become an antique shop, the duckpin bowling alley in its basement closed. Dry-goods stores and five-and-dimes have shut down, and bookstores and yuppie sandwich shops have sprouted in their place.

What has kept Buchanan's downtown alive—has kept it from fading to dust and memories, like Eagle Rock's—is the same thing that attracted the original businesses to the town, and its early settlers, too: Buchanan sits at the intersection of two centuries-old transportation corridors. One, of course, is the James, Virginia's primary east-west thoroughfare in the days before highways and railroads punched through the Blue Ridge. The other is a road that runs along the floor of the Great Valley of Virginia, the trough of fertile pastureland between the Alleghenies and the Blue Ridge.

The road has existed for untold hundreds of years. It may have had its start as a game trail, a migratory path used by elk, deer, and buffalo on their seasonal moves from one grazing area to another. By the time the English settled downriver, at Jamestown, it was the Warrior Path, a trail used by Indian hunting parties. The path was wide, deeply worn and hard-packed, and stretched from the Potomac southward along the Shenandoah River, into the James River's basin, and beyond, toward the Tennessee line. In the first half of the eighteenth century, white settlers took up residence in the Valley of Virginia not by traveling up the James or over the Blue Ridge's gaps—journeys, both of them, that were all but impossible with any sort of payload—but by traveling down this old Indian trace from Pennsylvania. The path quickly evolved into a wagon road, often called the Pennsylvania Road to reflect the source of its traffic, and by the 1740s it crossed the James on Looney's Ferry. Before too long a settlement arose around the ferry, and commerce with it, for here goods bound for market in the Tidewater could be hauled to the river by wagon, loaded aboard boats, and shipped downstream.

Eventually the ferry, which had replaced a ford probably first used by animal herds, was itself supplanted by a covered bridge. The rough path down from the Potomac became the Valley Turnpike, one of three hundred such toll roads built in Virginia in the first half of the nineteenth century. With only slight modification, the turnpike became U.S. Route 11 in the early twentieth century. By the late 1960s, that highway had, in turn, been trumped by Interstate 81, which braids with Route 11 from New York state to Knoxville. The upshot is that the interstate, which passes just west of Buchanan today, is the descendant of paths used by men and beast for as long as both have traveled in the Valley. And for two and a half centuries, anyone or anything traveling that path to the James encountered the settlement that eventually became Buchanan.

In Hannah Dennis's day, such outposts held tremendous importance, for settlements west of the Blue Ridge were few—it took as long for European civilization to push from Jamestown to here as it did to gallop westward from here to the Pacific. These days, the Valley's dangers are pretty tame. But settlements along the interstate, and especially their fast-food franchises and gas station bathrooms, are as important as ever.

Buchanan has something else going for it. Ian and I meet Harry Gleason, who first ventured to the town as a student of landscape architecture and urban planning, saw promise in the place, and returned after graduation as a full-time employee and booster. Since then, the longhaired, gregarious planner has worked tirelessly to promote Buchanan as a town apart. We meet him at Buchanan's town hall, a former fire station crowded with desks and stacked paper, and listen as he recounts local history (Buchanan dates to 1811; Pattonsburg, the portion of town on the north side of the James, to 1788), waxes about the beauty of the surrounding mountains, pays homage to the river, and talks about the future. Buchanan is as auspiciously located today as it was two centuries ago, he says. The town's potential—as an employment center, a tourism destination, an historical treasure—is virtually limitless. It's as can-do an advocacy as I've ever heard. By the time we leave him, Ian and I are believers.

He mentions one other thing shortly before we head out. Just downriver from the Main Street bridge, Gleason says, is a rock formation that attracted a good bit of attention from nineteenth-century tourists. A few minutes after I shove off from the boat ramp, after paddling down a gently curving stretch of calm water, I see a quarry looming on my right—and, on my left, the formation.

Its surroundings are unassuming. A cliff rises from beside the river, a railroad track at its foot. Weeds and scrub thrive at its feet. No roads approach it. But in the rock is a partial circle of striated rock, shocking in the smooth perfection of its arc. It center is carved most deeply from the cliff, and with each stratum of surrounding curve, it stair-steps closer to the bluff's face. It looks like the entrance to an ancient cathedral. Directly across the river is a sewage treatment plant and a small dump, through which today's curious must walk to enjoy this natural wonder.

Over the next few hours I paddle around several large oxbows, steep mountainsides hard against one side of the river, then the other. Cows abound in the water; in one cliff-bound bend, I share the James with a dozen or more just as two trains rumble and clatter past, one on each bank. The bluff on the outside of the riverbend forms an amphitheater, amplifying the roar of the freight trains and terrifying the cows, who begin lowing as a chorus. For a few minutes the remote bend is almost deafening.

Just downstream, at Alpine—marked as a town on my map, but a lonely, houseless farm road in reality—I meet Ian and load up the boat. We drive back to the campground, which seems strangely empty without the Czech women. Ian, apparently pining for the woman with the streaked hair, is visibly needy. It seems a good night for comfort food. I fire up a batch of Mac and Gack.

"Ian," I warn him, "don't."

DAY NINE

On which the expedition
braces for big excitement and the
prospect of crippling injury

🐝 Awake before daybreak, I crawl from the tent and shuffle up the hill to the campground's showers, aim closed eyes into the spray, and head back to find that Ian is up and has water boiling on the stove. Over coffee we review the day ahead. For me it's a short one, a nine-mile paddle from the roadside at Alpine to Glasgow, at the head of the James River Gorge. Ian will call the canoe livery people back and finish lining up a guide for the run down Balcony Falls. We'll meet just once along the way, at Natural Bridge Station.

I'm on the water at 9:00 A.M., paddling slowly along a shallow, limestone-studded stretch of river, pastureland on my left beyond a picket of wilted trees and the CSX's trackbed, round-shouldered peaks rising on my right. Crimson damselflies hover and dart over the canoe's bow as I study the thickly wooded slopes. These are not the towering cliffs that lined the river's curves just yesterday; the mountains here, while bigger, approach the water's edge gently, without the craggy severity of the miles upriver. I know that'll change: up ahead I can see the high, kink-backed spine of the Blue Ridge, the Great Valley's eastern wall, hazy in the distance, and I feel a twinge of excited dread. God, I think, I hope Ian nails down that guide.

Then, halfway through a wide bend to the right, I notice a shady cleft in the north bank, and from it a narrow creek spilling into the river. The stream seems big enough to canoe for a short distance, but then passes beneath a narrow bridge and dwindles as it climbs. Beside the bridge is a cluster of homes, a church—the hamlet of Gilmore Mills. And the stream beneath it, I learn from a glance at my map, is Cedar Creek, a waterway that has occupied a place of renown since the mid-eighteenth century. You'd not know it to look at it here, but a few miles upstream the creek has carved a deep gorge, spanned high above by the famed Natural Bridge, billed by its owners as one of the world's "Seven Natural Wonders." It hangs 215 feet over the creekbed, measures 90 feet long and 40-odd feet thick at its middle—statistics which, like the umpteen words spilled in its description, fail to capture the force with which it smacks you when you're standing beneath it. Photos don't do it justice; the scale of the rock formation so far exceeds expectation that even visitors jaded by its image on postcards, place mats, and in practically every Virginia guidebook ever published can't help but feel awe in its presence.

It so moved George Washington that he carved his initials high in the rock beneath the span, a piece of eighteenth-century vandalism that remains visible today. Thomas Jefferson wrote that it was "impossible for the emotions, arising from the sublime, to be felt beyond what they are here," and believed those words enough that in 1774 he bought the bridge and the acreage around it. John Edwards Caldwell, a New Yorker touring Virginia in the summer of 1808, wrote a friend that he was so affected by the sight that he "could not in plain rational language convey to you my ideas of what I had seen." And David Hunter Strother, who using the nom de plume "Porte Crayon" produced a popular run of nineteenth-century travelogues, wrote that he'd encountered "few objects in nature which so completely fill the soul as this Bridge in its unique and simple grandeur."

Ascending Cedar Creek to the bridge might have been possible in years past, but now, my map suggests, a dam crosses the stream between its mouth and the formation. The only practical approach is by road, where the bridge is announced by an explosion of souvenir shops, petting zoos, and motels in what seems the middle of nowhere. A cavern and a wax museum hawk their attractions. One tourist draw advertises "Studio Tours"—whatever that means—with a giant roadside rhinoceros sprouting butterfly wings.

Eyeing the bridge itself requires a visit to the center of this mercantile clot, a big mock-colonial place that houses a ticket booth and a sprawling gift shop. A stroll through the store, choked with the bells, spoons, ashtrays, and bad art that America's natural wonders seem to breed, does little to whet your desire to behold the bridge. But the payoff for braving the store, plunking down eight bucks, and descending the quarter-mile trail to Cedar Creek, is huge. The bridge is not only shockingly big, but seems almost too perfect, too well sculpted, to be real: the way its belly meets the gorge's curving sides to form an oval of light between water and rock, the angle at which it vaults the chasm, its melding of massiveness and odd delicacy—all of that seems more the product of an architect's eye, of careful attention to size and scale, than it does an accident of erosion.

"In consideration of the perfection of its adaptation to its surroundings," Crayon rightly testified, "the simplicity of its design, the sublimity of its proportions, the spectator experiences a fullness of satisfaction which familiarity only serves to increase; and while that sentiment of awe inseparable from the first impression may be weakened or disappear, wonder and admiration grow with time." Look at the bridge and you understand why Jefferson, an ingenious architect and the most artistic of the nation's Founding Fathers, had to own it.

In Jefferson's day, and for decades after, you could enjoy the Natural Bridge from its top, as well as from the creekbed. The adventure, it seems, was terrifying. "Though the sides of this bridge are provided in some parts with a parapet of fixed rocks, yet few men have resolution to walk to them and look over into the abyss," the future president wrote in his *Notes on the State of Virginia.* "You involuntarily fall on your hands and feet, creep to the parapet and peep over it. Looking down from this height about a minute, gave me a violent head ach." That reaction was shared by a good many other visitors. In his *Virginia Illustrated,* published in 1871, the intrepid Porte Crayon recounts a trip to the place with three lady friends:

> Porte started up, and intimated to the ladies that if they would walk with him a short distance, they might have a distant glimpse of the bridge without delay. Starting from the tavern door they followed the public road by a gentle ascent for sixty or eighty paces, when they came to a gate. Here Crayon entered, and taking Minnie by the arm, he pushed aside the branches of an arbor vitae, and led her forward several paces, until they reached a rocky barrier.
> "Look down, Cousin."

She shrieked, and would have fallen but for the support of her companion, who hastily withdrew her from the spot, and seated her, all pale and trembling under the shade of an evergreen.

"What's the matter? What is it?" inquired the others, with alarmed eagerness.

"Oh, Porte, how could you do it! The Bridge! the Bridge! we're on the Bridge! It was terrible!"

On hearing this Fannie and Dora looked wildly about, as if seeking some place of refuge, and finally fled through the gate by which they had entered, and only halted when they had gained the middle of the highway.

"Come back, you silly creatures!"

"No, no! Not for worlds! We would not go on it again."

"Don't you know that you are on it now?"

Dora would have taken to her heels again, but Fannie stopped her. "Don't mind Porte's quizzing," said she. "Don't you see we are in the public road and not on any bridge?"

Porte succeeded in capturing the runaways, and holding them securely before he gave the information, explained to them that they stood over the center of the arch, and yet so entirely hidden was the chasm which it spanned, by the natural parapets of rocks and trees, that he had himself seen persons pass over without being aware of it.

People still travel the bridge without knowing it: U.S. Route 11 uses it to cross Cedar Creek, and the gorge below remains hidden. Only "the natural parapets of rocks and trees" have little to do with it. These days, carefully placed billboards and fencing block the view, along with access to the span's edge.

I paddle on, rounding a wide curve to the left, then a sharp one to the right, and spot Ian up ahead, standing on the bank beneath a concrete highway bridge. "I called Hope," he says as I glide toward the bank.

"Excellent," I say. "Everything lined up?"

"Pretty much. He wants to know whether to bring a canoe just for himself, or whether you want to go through the falls with him in a two-seat canoe." He hauls the canoe's bow onto the bank, and I step out, stretch my back. There's a certain purity to paddling the rapids in my own boat, I think. But to do it in a two-seater would be worry-free. Fun, even. "I'll go with him," I say.

Natural Bridge Station is named for a building that hasn't existed in years. The railroad spawned the settlement, at a time when rail was the quickest and easiest way to reach not only the Natural Bridge but also Lexington, the Rockbridge County seat and a busy college town even in the nineteenth century. A Dumpster is parked next to the weedy flat where the station and platform once stood, where passengers boarded the Norfolk and Western. From there you can watch modern-day Norfolk Southern trains round the bend on the river's far shore, swing onto a bridge of black trapezoids, and clatter toward you through its girder sheath.

The Chesapeake and Ohio stopped here, too, on the riverside tracks at the bluff's foot. Long ago, an elevator lifted its passengers up the cliff to the speck of a town that sprang up around the station. The tiny business district was dominated by a three-story edifice of rusticated cement block, built in 1910. Its lowest floor, facing the station and the wide main street, was the Chiles-Barger Company, a general store; the upper two comprised the Alhambra Hotel, which one reached by scaling a steep side alley and entering around back. Next door to the general store stood a combination restaurant–post office, and beside that, an auto shop. A store was next, apartments on its second floor, and a short ways downhill from this dwarf downtown was a barn for the stagecoaches that carried the railroad's debarking passengers to the county's various attractions.

Eventually the passenger trains stopped coming, and Natural Bridge Station swiveled on its axis, moving its financial and social center out to Route 130, the new vein of incoming cash. The old business district withered to nothing. Or almost nothing. Today the Chiles-Barger store is blacked out behind plywood, the company name over its doors barely legible. A sign on the building's side wall has been devoured by rust, but after studying the cinnamon-colored flakes I realize that they vary in texture, that they still form letters once painted bright and crisp: I can make out "The Alhambra," and the word "Tourist," and beneath that, "Steam Heat." At the bottom, the word "Entrance" is accompanied by an arrow pointing up the alley.

Behind the building, a low white fence surrounds the hotel's yard. A fossilized neon sign, again advertising steam heat, hangs from a staple-shaped frame among the trees. I walk back to the main road and wander past the old post office, the long-closed auto shop, and the apartments. Across the road, I pause at the north end of the railroad bridge, peer down the bluff, can see no sign of an elevator. Then I stroll to the old station site and look downhill, away from the river, where a bare lawn marks the site of the old stagecoach barn, and try to imagine the metal-on-metal squeal of the train's brakes, the hiss of the steam engine, the chatter of excited conversation as high-collared ladies and squared-away VMI cadets stepped off the train and sashayed to waiting carriages.

Not long ago, really. Rockbridge County surely has a good many old-timers who remember the Alhambra's glory days, and who can scarcely believe they've lived long enough to see it so desolate. Lives were spent nurturing this little settlement, building it up, I think to myself. Adults devoted their imaginations and energies to it, and their children dodged horses in this once-bustling street. Now the adults are dead, their labors memorialized by this fast-decaying shrine, and the children who return here receive a none-too-subtle reminder of their own impermanence. Soon rust will eat clean through the sign on the hotel's side wall, and wind and rain will scour the last ghostly vestige of the general store's name from the facade, and the number of people who can recall it being otherwise will dwindle to none.

Like drops in the river, we move on.

Day's end is just four or so river miles downstream, beyond a handful of shallow bends. I'm eager to get there and head back to camp, so after slugging down some water I push back into the James. Both sides of the river are relatively flat, though I can see that won't last long: the flood plain narrows dramatically up ahead. The Blue Ridge's long spine arcs gray-blue above the trees, a seemingly impenetrable wall. This much river cannot pass gently through that kind of barrier, I think. But even as the thought fades, I realize that my guts no longer churn at the prospect. I'll be sharing a boat with a pro. No worries.

Just downstream from the Route 759 bridge, narrow Elk Creek enters the James to my right, and with it comes another reminder of the rugged going ahead: my topo map shows that the creek bends through a fertile bottomland, the Arnold Valley, and intersects with a smaller stream, Belfast Creek, the bed of which climbs a thousand feet up the side of a wooded ridge to something called the Devil's Marbleyard. Two small brooks, the Little and Big Hellgate creeks, come off Gunter Ridge, as well.

It's a safe bet that early settlers didn't name places for hell or the devil because they found them pleasant. To underline the point, there's an Indian legend about the Marbleyard involving divine rage and natural disaster. The story goes that after a missionary couple converted the local Indians to Christianity, a terrible drought and famine hit the Arnold Valley that the tribe blamed on the newcomers. The missionaries were dragged up the side of 2,700-foot Gunter Ridge and burned atop a sacrificial pyre. Within minutes the sky blackened, a ferocious wind swept up the mountainside, the forest burst into flame, and rain fell that blistered the skin. Every member of the errant tribe was wiped out, and the site of their great sin, the story goes, was left empty of life, a heavenly memorial and warning. Climb the Belfast Trail today, and two-thirds of the way to the ridgetop you reach an acre-big, treeless jumble of light gray boulders that stands out on the otherwise thicketed mountainside like a gleaming scar.

A little ways past Elk Creek I paddle past our campsite, where the tents remain pitched on the knoll. The place looks otherwise empty. Before long the high ground south of the river sidles up beside it, and as the sky rapidly clouds and the river turns gray I spot a railroad coaling tower jutting from the trees to my left. Ian and I are to meet somewhere near it, so I hug the river's north bank, alert for his call. As I pass the tower I see an island in the stream ahead, most of the river passing on its right side; Ian is standing on a mud bank beside the shallow, sluggish left channel. I paddle toward him and, as I slip between the island and shore, find my progress blocked by shoals of sand and mud. I climb over the canoe's side, eyes peeled for snakes—the water swirling blood-warm around my ankles seems perfect soup for them. I yell to Ian to be on the lookout for telltale wriggles, then quickly splash across the forty yards that separate us.

After hauling the boat onto the bank we grunt up an overgrown path to the railroad tracks. The putty-colored coaling tower rises beside them a few dozen yards away. Dead ahead is an old wood-frame depot, an island among several parallel tracks. CSX trucks and track repair gear and cricking grasshoppers abound, but just one house—there's little clue that we stand at a town's edge. Ian and I stroll to the station, peer in its windows, stare down the tracks. I notice the depot displays the Chesapeake and Ohio's name for the stop: "Balcony Falls." The slightest twinge. "What do you say we drive downstream, and see if we can get a look at the rapids?" I say.

"Sure," Ian agrees. "By the way, I drove over and paid for the campsite. We're all set. And I checked back with Hope. He's bringing the canoe." As he says it, I feel a surge of almost giddy relief. I'm set, I think. I'll make it through Balcony Falls.

"We meet him outside the grocery in Glasgow at ten tomorrow morning."

"Know where the grocery store is?"

"He said we'd have no trouble finding it." We load up the car and bounce uphill into Glasgow. Mountainsides rise sudden and steep at the town's edge, looming high on three sides, and at their feet weave narrow country lanes fringed with dogwood and old man's beard and the pink-flowering Judas tree. The air smells of pine. On a misty autumn evening, it all might pass for the Highlands.

But as Ian and I pull up to Route 130, the town's main drag, the sun's still high in the sky, the September air is gummy and hot, and Brooks and Dunn blasts from the open window of a passing pickup truck.

Virginia's Glasgow is a mountain town. A lone peak, conical Sallings Mountain, guards the settlement's western flank; to the east the view is dominated, and travel blocked, by a long, high hogback—Three Sisters Knobs—that rises abruptly from the alluvial shelf on which Glasgow's crescent-shaped grid of small houses and churches is perched. It is a river town, too, of course. The

Maury River, the last of the James' big mountain source streams, joins the bigger river in a rocky confluence at Glasgow's southeastern corner, so that the place is hemmed by water on two sides. But more than anything else, Glasgow is a resilient place, a survivor of lousy luck and booms gone bust, a place where floods are benchmarks for bad times and watersheds by which births, deaths, and weddings are remembered.

Hints came early that life here might be complicated. In 1740 the bottomland at the confluence received its first white settler, a Pennsylvania German named John Peter Salling. Two years after building a homestead in what's now central Glasgow, Salling had a visitor, a fellow frontiersman named John Howard, who had just won a commission from the colony's governor to travel west to the Mississippi on a mission of discovery. He promised Salling a piece of the payoff—scads of land—if he signed on. The pitch caught Salling in "a very unlucky hour," as he put it. He signed on.

What followed was one of the most remarkable adventures in frontier history. In March 1742, Salling, Howard, and three other men headed west from the homestead to the Natural Bridge, then southwest to the New River, where they killed five buffalo and stretched their skins over a wooden boat frame. In this rude coracle the five and their cargo descended the New until its cascades got nasty, hiked a ways, then descended West Virginia's Coal and Great Kanawha rivers to the Ohio. In early June they reached the Mississippi.

Nearly a month later, Salling and company were about 120 miles above Natchez when they were captured by Frenchmen and Indians, who dragged them before the French governor in New Orleans. He promptly jailed the trespassers as spies, and informed his bosses that he planned to ship them off to the mines of New Mexico. But bureaucracy got in the way. The governor, LeMoyne de Bienville, was a lame duck, and decided to let his successor take responsibility for transporting the prisoners. The new governor was slow in showing up: more than two years passed, Salling and the others behind bars all the while, and the man from Glasgow began to get a little restless. In October 1744, fed up beyond fear, he busted out of prison with a Creole robber named Baudran.

Crossing Lake Pontchartrain in a hide boat, they "tied the Shoulder Blades of . . . Bulls to small sticks, which served us for paddles," Salling reported— then traversed Mississippi's Bay St. Louis and Biloxi Bay, hiked to the Chattahoochee River, and made their way by water and land to present-day Augusta, Georgia, and Charleston, South Carolina. Salling's journey didn't end there. The small schooner on which he sailed for Virginia was intercepted at sea by a French privateer, the crew of which held him prisoner and robbed him of his provisions. Back in Charleston, Salling elected to head north by land. The trip took a month, but on May 17, 1745—three years, two months, and a day after leaving—John Peter Salling came home.

If that was the first evidence that life here would be eventful, clue number two came late in 1742, a few months after Salling left on his trip. A band of thirty-three Iroquois happened by present-day Glasgow. A local, Capt. John McDowell, entertained them for a day, after which they struck off into the wilderness. Soon word came along that they were camped beside a tributary of the Maury, raising all kinds of hell, so McDowell gathered a militia of thirty-four men and set out to move them along. The captain and ten of his men died in the resulting forty-five-minute battle.

The clues kept coming. Midway through the nineteenth century came the James River and Kanawha Canal, and the first practical cargo link between the Valley and Richmond. Before long another canal connected the James with Lexington, up the Maury. Packet boat traffic was heavy. Alas, a town had little time to spring up at the confluence before Yankee troops ruined the James River canal.

Railroad tracks were laid through the Blue Ridge, though, and before long a dozen trains a day were passing through present-day Glasgow. And trains, like modern interstates, promised money. In 1890 a company of land speculators led by Gen. Fitzhugh Lee—soon to win fame as the chargé d'affaires in Cuba when the battleship *Maine* exploded—bought up a lot of local land, divided it into lots, and announced a great city in the making. It was a preposterous claim: Glasgow was, in effect, a paper city created in anticipation of a boom fueled by the creation of the paper city. But these were weird times in the Valley. Nearby Buena Vista was sprouting on similar wishful thinking, and Glasgow, with its railroads and rivers and the prospect of iron mining in the surrounding hills, seemed at least as good a bet. Lee and company built a power plant and a fancy hotel, and attracted such far-flung investors as Britain's Duke and Duchess of Marlborough.

The bubble burst. No big factories moved in. The iron played out. The power plant never operated, and the hotel, never opened, was sold for salvage. Homes were picked up and moved to Clifton Forge. Though it incorporated in 1892, Glasgow faded so dramatically that in a Depression-era guidebook it was labeled "the remnant of a town."

But it is, like I said, a resilient place. In 1935 redemption arrived in the form of Lees Carpets, a Philadelphia outfit that opened a giant weaving mill on the banks of the Maury. Over time the plant added spinning mills, expanded to cover thirty-four acres, and put hundreds of locals to work.

Ian and I drive through town on Route 130, a road paralleling the James and linking Glasgow with Natural Bridge Station. The heart of the business district consists of a small, bright blue motel and restaurant, a couple of gas stations, the firehouse, the grocery store. Hope was right. It isn't hard to find.

Blue Ridge Road branches off to the left, and along it lies the town's historical center. Town Hall, the library, a school turned apartment house, and brightly flowered, block-sized Centennial Park are down here, as well as the side road to the carpet mill and the bulk of Glasgow's homes. Back on 130 we cross a steel bridge over the Maury, spot the factory beside it just upstream. It has kept spinning and weaving despite nature's efforts to wipe it and Glasgow off the landscape.

They've been strong ones. About once a generation the James and its tributaries, the Maury included, have jumped their banks to hammer the communities along their course. The James is particularly moody at Glasgow, perhaps because the narrow, boulder-studded gorge waits just downstream to pinch its flow. In 1771, 1842, 1847, and 1870 the rivers inundated the bottoms that would become the town; in March 1936 another flood put roads to Glasgow under ten feet of water.

But it's been three more recent floods that have truly tested the place. In August 1969, the remains of Hurricane Camille spawned an overnight deluge that flash-flooded central Virginia. The Maury's volume was about 170 times the normal. Fourteen feet of water swirled over Glasgow's streets. Just three years later, Hurricane Agnes pumped nine feet of water into town. Then, in November 1985, yet another disastrous storm dumped eight and a half inches of rain on Glasgow in two days. Again the rivers left their beds. By the time they returned, dozens of homes and businesses throughout the town were stripped of their contents and thigh-deep in mud.

Glasgow is, luckily, a resilient place.

On the bridge's far side the road hits U.S. Route 501, which carries traffic through the James River Gorge above Balcony Falls. We pause as a chain of empty logging trucks rumbles by, then follow its tail into the gap. The highway here follows the bed of the old stage road from Lynchburg to Natural Bridge. Because the canal and towpath left no room for a nineteenth-century road at the riverside—and the railroad leaves none now—501 snakes along a contour line far up the gorge's northern wall. A traveler "follows its tortuous course up the mountain's side," as one 1845 account said of the route, "until it gains an elevation of hundreds of feet above the river, which it appears to nearly overhang. Gigantic mountains hem him in on every side; while far, from the dark ravine below, comes up the roar of the rapids."

As advertised, within minutes we've risen five hundred feet above the James, and Ian pulls the Volvo into a shallow crescent of gravel on the highway's shoulder. Trucks swooshing past, we get out to take in the river below, but can glimpse only small stretches of the far-off water through the roadside redbud and pine. What we can see, however, is impressive: the James is frothing with whitewater, and the river's roar can, indeed, be heard over the rustle of the forest around us. It occurs to me that as ominous as the rapids seem from up here, they'll look a lot nastier up close.

We head back to town and turn down a narrow lane that parallels the Maury. It dead-ends in a small parking lot, from which we follow a footpath through waist-deep weeds that meanders farther down the stream to the rocky point where it meets the James. Of the confluences along our route, this is one of the biggies, known to pioneers as the first "fork of the James" west of the Blue Ridge. The Maury, called the North River at the time, was a key to the nineteenth-century canal system that moved freight and people beyond the range. The twenty-mile North River Navigation intersected with the James River and Kanawha Canal right here, within yards of where we stand. It's difficult to picture it today—the Maury churns through a boulder-cluttered rapids at its mouth, and riverbed and banks show no evidence of past taming—but for more than twenty years, beginning in 1860, packet boats from Richmond could turn off the main canal here for the quick stab into Lexington. The entire trip from the capital took about forty-four hours.

The North River Navigation might be a rather insignificant footnote to the canal era were it not for the quality and durability of its construction, for many of its locks and dams have survived the years since its demise and today rank among America's premier exhibits of nineteenth-century engineering. The best-known is the Ben Salem Lock between Lexington and Buena Vista, where you can park within a few yards of a spectacularly preserved structure of hand-cut limestone block. The river beside it probably looks quite a bit shallower and faster than it did just after the Civil War: the North River Navigation was not a canal this far upstream, but a chain of dams that harnessed the swift-flowing stream into flatwater lakes, with locks to stair-step boats up and down the height differences between the ponds.

In those days you'd find yourself facing such a dam at Ben Salem, and a nine-and-a-half-foot difference in the water level between its upstream and downstream sides. If you were bound for Lexington, you'd approach the lock when its upstream gates were shut and its lower, downstream gates open. Your canalboat would slide into the lock. The lower gates would shut behind you, and sluice gates in the dam's upstream end would open, filling the lock with water until its level equaled that of the dam's upstream side. Then the upper gates would part, and away you'd go.

Below Ben Salem the Maury is regularly punctuated with locks and the ruins of navigational dams; they crop up every minute or two along Route 633, a narrow two-laner that hugs the river for seven miles below Buena Vista and was, for part of its length, built on the North River Navigation's towpath. One such lock, at Miller's Dam, marks the upstream end of a four-and-a-half-mile canal that carried river traffic to just above the James. The canal itself is all but vanished.

Ian and I linger at the confluence as the sky further clouds and a wispy mist builds in the gorge downstream. The James is two hundred yards wide here, and through the haze we can make out the boulders it has battered for eons on its race through the Blue Ridge. They sit midstream and jumbled along the banks, so big they have names, strewn among cascades and rapids. It looks to be a bony piece of river. We can't see the stormiest stretch of falls: the gorge's curving walls block our view of those places where the water attacks the mountains with the greatest fury. The racing, foaming water we do see is just practice. "Aw, man," Ian says, staring downstream.

I chuckle. Now I'm looking forward to tomorrow. Sharing a canoe with Hope promises to be a little like riding shotgun with A. J. Foyt on the Capital Beltway: it might get exciting, sure enough, but the guy'll know what he's doing. I'll be fine. The worst that can happen? I might get wet.

We drive down 130, over the river and back to our campsite. It's not yet mid-afternoon, and we luxuriate in the time we have to do laundry, shower, unpack and repack the Volvo. I write my day's story in the campground's "adult lounge"—an apartment stocked with paperback books, just above the game room—and file it with the laptop plugged into a phone jack behind the register in the camp store. Ian talks longingly of the Czechs. We cook up a mountain of Mac and Gack. Ian recounts his conversation with the Czechs, the metaphysical link he felt with the one. We enjoy a leisurely couple of beers at the picnic table.

I try to steer our conversation away from the Czechs. I succeed, but just the same, we turn in early. I dream of rough water, of rocks and races, falls and foams. But it's more a workout than a nightmare.

DAY TEN

On which we risk soaking
and arrest in the foam of Balcony Falls,
then behold a river robbed

The James has meandered along a lazy northeasterly course since Buchanan, sidling up to the flanks of the mountains along the way, bending around them, nosing its way deeper into the foothills of the Blue Ridge, seeking a path downhill. But at Glasgow it abruptly bends to the southeast, leaving the city at the point of one of its many zigs. Swollen with the waters of the Maury, the river punches through the Blue Ridge's highest heights in a steep-sided gorge, its water falling some 11.5 feet per mile through the gap, twice the rate of the streambed between Buchanan and Glasgow.

The gorge is a spectacular, noisy place, the water frothing over a staircase of boulder-studded rapids, its roar amplified by the walls of sandstone and quartzite that leap skyward from the river's banks. This deep trench, for years the only practical corridor between the mountains upstream and the Piedmont below, has long vexed the people traveling the James. Not me, however. I know my limitations. I know that luck, more than skill, has saved me from turning turtle any number of times upstream. I know that the mightiest rapids ahead, Big Balcony Falls, will require plenty of skill. So Ian and I are loitering outside the Glasgow grocery when, at ten sharp, a shiny black Ford pickup pulls into the lot with a long red canoe roped to its roof.

Hope Zollman couldn't look more relaxed as he steps out of the cab. He's tall and thin, imbued with the rangy nonchalance that comes with absolute expertise. He tips his ball cap, bill bent into a parabolic curve, smiles through a short beard, and fires up a Salem. Ian introduces himself, shakes Hope's hand. "Are we glad to see you," he tells him. Hope nods. "You're paddling with me today?"

"Uh, no," Ian says, and points to me. "This is Earl."

We shake hands. "Well," he says, eyeing me, "you ready?"

"You bet," I say. And something about the guy—his calm, perhaps; or his unpretentious, beat-up old life vest; or his accent, which oozes campfire smoke and game trails and a lifelong friendship with the river—makes me mean it.

We'll need to put Hope's truck at the gorge's far end, so he and Ian devise a plan for the shuttling necessary to get it there. We drive both the truck and the Volvo down to the weedy point at the confluence that Ian and I visited yesterday. We unload the canoe and the equipment we'll need. I stay with the boat and gear while Ian follows Hope to a boat ramp four miles down 501, where we'll pull the canoe out of the water. Assuming, that is, that all goes well and we make it that far. Hope leaves his truck at the ramp, and as Ian drives him back, they stop at a driveway that Hope knows. Hope says he can't recommend it, because it's illegal, but Ian could wander down that drive and find himself alongside the river, if he wanted to. And if he were to walk downstream along the tracks, he'd have a front-row view of every big rapids in the gorge. He could get close-up pictures of us as we shoot Big Balcony, for instance.

Of course, it *is* trespassing, Hope says. The CSX is touchy about people walking its tracks, and it patrols that stretch. There might be a ticket in it, or worse. It might be dangerous, besides—some parts of the gorge leave little room to get out of a train's way.

While they're having this conversation, I jump among the rocks on the riverbank and explore the overgrown tract at the confluence. Some people in Glasgow have plans to make this place a park, a monument to the hero of a particularly dark day in the unhappy history of navigation at Balcony Falls.

On a cold Saturday morning in January 1854, the canal boat *Clinton* was headed upstream in the James River and Kanawha Canal when it encountered what was still called the North River. A heavy rain had fallen the night before, and the North was running several feet higher than normal. As a mule team strained to pull the boat across the smaller stream's mouth, the towline snapped, and the *Clinton* spun out of the North and into the James and back toward the gorge.

Aboard were about forty-five souls, most of them railroad hands bound for work upriver. As horrified onlookers watched from shore, the boat raced toward the gorge's rapids and another, more immediate, peril—the Mountain Dam, which stretched across the James at the gorge's head. Its spillway created a huge drop in the stream—all but certain destruction for a boat like the *Clinton*—and an impoundment so deep on its upstream side that the crew couldn't touch bottom with their poles to slow themselves down.

About one hundred yards above the dam seven men jumped off. Four made it to shore; three went over the dam and drowned. Not having any other options, the boat's captain used the tiller to straighten the *Clinton* out, and with nearly forty people hanging on for dear life the big vessel shot over the precipice.

Incredibly, it held together. But now loomed the falls, a series of named boulder fields and terraces. The *Clinton* faced an "awful crisis . . . to run through the White Rock, the Little Balcony, the Great Balcony falls and the Tobacco Hills," a witness, Capt. Edward Echols, observed, "places that formerly made the boldest hearts quake, and the strongest nerves give way under favorable circumstances." As Echols wrote to the *Lexington Herald,* "the scene became most thrilling and exciting to observe, the boat crowded with human beings hurried on, as it were, by the boiling waters with the speed of a race horse, down the river, as we all supposed, into the very jaws of destruction."

When the *Clinton* swept within a foot of the first boulder field, called White Rock, the skipper and four others jumped for it. The boat continued downstream, leaping the Little Balcony, bulling its way over Big Balcony, missing every danger until it hung up gently at the Tobacco Hills. The excitement wasn't over, however: five men were stranded on White Rock, and more than thirty on the boat, which remained midstream. Those on shore would have to brave the rapids themselves if they were to attempt a rescue.

"No time was to be lost, the river was still rising, and the wind by this time was blowing a perfect hurricane through the gap of the mountain," Echols reported, "making the adventure the next thing to madness.

"But the question was propounded, 'Boys, who will go?' When out stepped some half dozen or more brave hearts, among them an old boatman named Frank Padget. . . ."

That's how it began.

Ian and Hope pull back into the parking lot. We zip into our life vests and lug the canoe down the rocky bank to the James, bumping and scraping its plastic hull as we go. It seems the *Bismarck* next to my tiny boat—nearly three feet longer and six inches beamier amidships, where a truck inner tube is stuffed beneath the thwarts. Hope jams the cooler into the inner tube's hole, lashes it in place, hands me a plastic-bladed paddle. We climb in and shove off into the swirling current.

Ian waves as we chug away from the shore, then dashes for the car. Hope briefs me on my role in the boat: I'm to relax. Keep paddling. Enjoy the view. "So you've come all the way down the river?" he drawls from the back as we reach midstream.

"I have," I say. "Though I gotta admit, it's been more the river's doing than mine."

"Well, I'm sure you'll do just fine today," he says. "You know, when we finish, you're probably going to wonder why you even had me along."

I'm pretty sure he's wrong about that.

We swing east toward the first of the rapids, and I sense with a little thrill that between my paddling and Hope's steering we have total control of the canoe. It feels nothing like the long hours I've spent in my boat, wallowing sluggishly into and over the rocks: despite its size, the *Bismarck* snaps to our commands. Its nose swivels exactly where we want it. There's no unnecessary swearing and splashing.

Up ahead, a foot-tall drop in the river marks the ruins of the old dam the *Clinton* overshot. Years after the canal failed, it was rebuilt as the Balcony Falls Dam and modified with a powerhouse to generate electricity, and its impoundment pond became popular with Glasgow boaters. Then came Hurricane Camille. Many in Glasgow argued that the dam had contributed to the flooding in 1969 by impeding the high-running James and Maury, and four years later county officials asked the feds to order its removal. The first attempt to blow it up failed, but eventually the James flowed free into the gorge for the first time in well over a century.

We slalom effortlessly among slime-covered rocks, swoop over the dam's remains, wriggle through low water at Flat Rock Falls. Hope steers toward the south shore, where a flat-topped castle of rock the color of old bone rises from the water. We slip the canoe into a shallow beside it and step out. "This is what we call the White Rock," he says as we climb up the formation. It stretches twenty yards by fifty, a knot of mounds and shelves and boulders, its dimples and potholes glistening with warm water. "Normally you don't see nearly this much of it, but the water's about as low as I've ever seen it."

I try to imagine the river high up the rock's creamy sides, the *Clinton* surging past it, the five panic-stricken leapers diving over the side. It's sunny, though, about eighty-five degrees, the rock warm, almost hot, to the touch. I can't quite muster a picture of how it must have been to cling to its slick surface while showered with icy spray, the James up and bellowing all around, rescue only the faintest of prayers. Frank Padget surely had doubts when he jumped into a batteau and set off on his mission that day. But somehow, with the help of two gentlemen and two hand-picked assistants—both, like himself, black boatmen with years of experience on the James—he snuck the big, double-ended cargo boat into an eddy behind White Rock, where he plucked the stranded skipper and four passengers from their perch.

Hope and I climb back into the canoe and strike diagonally for another whitewater stretch, its centerpiece a two-foot drop that creates a wavering cowlick of water downstream. The approach is difficult: the canoe grounds against several submerged rocks, barely squeezes between others. There seems no straight-line route to Little Balcony Falls. "That's going to be our challenge today—trying to pick our way between the rocks," Hope shouts over the water from behind me. "When the river's up higher, you don't even see them."

Just a handful of feet from the drop's lip, Hope elects to change course, so that we attack it from a different angle. Were I to try this alone, all would be lost—I'd no doubt roll my canoe sideways over the brink, pitch myself into the rocky swirl—but to my amazement we poke our way across the top of the rapids, swing the boat back on itself and rocket into a chute. In an instant, we're flying down river. I let out a whoop.

Now, Big Balcony waits. Hope guides the canoe toward the top of the rapids, then veers right, so that we can see over the lip and into the confusion of spray and stone below. The James drops five feet here, over what appears to be a triple terrace. The result is a chain of standing waves of tremendous height and power. Even in low water, it's impressive. We ease the boat against a gargantuan slab of gray rock overlooking the falls, climb out, pull the canoe up after us. From the outcropping's crown we study the rapids. In places the water gushes smooth and clear over barely submerged boulders, creating sparkling veneers. Between them, the James spills white and violent. Our route will take us through the messy part.

A movement on the north shore catches my eye, and I look up to see Ian on the CSX tracks. He's in a hell-for-leather sprint, stride weirdly elongated to match the spacing of the railroad ties. It looks as if he's cross-country skiing. "There's your buddy," Hope drawls.

"Yeah," I say. "He's getting a workout."

"Moving along, all right." We watch him go for several seconds, until he jumps off the track and scrambles down the bank to a broad stone shelf on the far side of the falls. He waves. We wave back.

I go back to staring at the water. In 1854, Frank Padget blasted over these falls in the batteau, now carrying the five people retrieved from White Rock, only to find that the *Clinton* no longer waited just downstream at the Tobacco Hills: the canal boat had dislodged from its snag and flown farther down the gorge to another hang-up. Worse, one of its passengers had jumped over the side and now stood shivering on a midriver rock.

Padget couldn't get to the man. Instead he aimed for the *Clinton*, where he supervised the rescue of all aboard. Then he dropped off the canal boat's passengers, pulled the batteau upstream through the canal and headed back into the James above the falls.

"Well, what do you think?" Hope asks. "Think you could have done it in your boat?"

I answer before I think. "Sure," I say. Then I come to my senses. Who am I kidding? Riding solo in my boat I'd stand no chance here. As easy as the gorge has seemed today, I know better than to think that I could wrangle it alone. "Well, maybe not," I tell Hope. "Maybe not."

We return to the *Bismarck*. As we're settling into our seats, Hope gives me a last-minute briefing. "A lot of times you'll be going down the river with somebody and you'll get to here, and they'll take a look at the rapids and they'll stop paddling and just grab the gunwales. We call 'em 'gunwale grabbers.'" I nod. It seems a good name. "You don't want to be one of those," Hope says. "Don't let go of your paddle and grab the gunwales. If you do, we're gonna get wet for sure. Just keep paddling."

I promise I will, and we paddle back across the top of the drop. The falls are roaring. Foamy flecks of water catapult into the air just beyond the lip. "Here we go!" Hope yells. And as the current sucks us broadside toward the brink, we spin the canoe in a picture-perfect 120-degree turn and fall into the foam.

I'm still paddling, but the river is in charge. In the water's grasp we nose-dive into a tunnel of splashing thunder, sliding through the drop so quickly that I instinctively lean back. The bow slams down—*whump!*—and I'm enveloped in spray that catches the light like shards of a shattered mirror. Down the second terrace we leap—*whump!*—and the third, our speed building all the while. Then the canoe is riding atop a standing rooster tail of water, and another, and another, each progressively smaller.

And then it's over.

RIVER GUIDE HOPE ZOLLMAN,
RIGHT, AND I APPROACH BIG
BALCONY FALLS.

We steer the boat to the rocks at the river's edge, where Ian grabs the bow. Hope says he has something to show us, and we jump from the canoe and pull it ashore, then climb the bank to the railroad tracks. On their far side, between the trackbed and the gorge's north wall, is a trench some ten feet deep, overgrown with weeds and small trees. I realize that I'm looking at one of the best-preserved stretches of the James River and Kanawha Canal. Hope leads us down-river. A few yards along, a pair of stone walls line the canal: a lock. Not much farther, another lock, dry but wonderfully intact, missing only its wooden gates, rises from the brush. And near it, on the canal's far side, is a small monument.

It commemorates heartbreak. On that bleak winter's day in 1854, Frank Padget made his second run down the gorge in the batteau, this time with eight aboard, aiming to rescue the lone *Clinton* passenger left in the river. They quickly reached the rock on which the stranded man stood, and for a moment it must have seemed that Padget had accomplished the impossible. But the batteau hung up on a rock as the stranded man was pulled aboard. The vessel swung broadside to the current and was instantly crushed.

Five aboard leapt onto a rock, and were rescued the next morning after a cold, terrifying night. At least one more drifted to shore. But two, Frank Padget and the stranded boatman, drowned in the James. The monument is a copy of an obelisk Capt. Echols had erected on the spot shortly after the disaster. It and the original, which now stands in Glasgow's Centennial Park and is destined, someday, for display at the confluence, read: "In Memory of Frank Padget, A coloured slave, who during a freshet in James' River in January 1854, Ventured and lost his life, by drowning, in the noble effort to save some of his fellow creatures, who were in the midst of the flood, from death." It is a reminder of just how powerful and capricious this river, any river, can be.

We stroll back up the tracks, Hope providing helpful information as we go—"Uh, Earl, that's poison oak you're standing in"—and clamber down the embankment to the canoe. I pause before getting into the boat to gaze onto the James. The mountainside on the south bank rises straight from the rocky river, soaring through forest and exposed rock to a conical peak a quarter mile up. "It's pretty country, isn't it?" Hope almost whispers. I nod. The falls are roaring. Sunshine falls bright and golden on the boulders. A heron, wings flapping heavily, makes a splash of gray-blue against the trees. The riffles at our feet are sparkling. "It sure is," I say.

Hope tips his ball cap back. "I've been in Rockbridge County just about my whole life," he says. "Been other places—been paddling in Costa Rica and Belize, spent some time in Canada and out West. But I haven't found that any other place suits me as well as this." I'm not sure, at that moment, that I've felt any place suit *me* so well. Despite having just visited the Frank Padget monument, I suddenly feel a tremendous trust of the river and ease with my place on it. For just an instant I also feel an almost overwhelming urge to go get my boat and run Balcony Falls myself. But I quash it. Instead, Hope and I return to the canoe and paddle a series of smaller rapids—Willow Notch, Tobacco Hills, Velvet Rock—into a long reach of flat water.

The lakelike stretch takes us forty-five minutes to traverse. I've cleared a hurdle, I think as I paddle, one that I've feared since beginning my trip. I'm buoyant as Hope and I pull the canoe from the water at a boat ramp five miles downstream of Glasgow. But within minutes of bidding Hope goodbye, Ian and I make a frustrating discovery: there's no returning to the river for miles. Just downstream from its tumultuous surge through the Blue Ridge, the James is blocked by a massive hydroelectric dam that runs diagonally from bank to bank. The Cushaw Dam itself is no surprise; it appears plainly on my topo maps, and created the flat water that Hope and I have just crossed. What the maps don't show is that there's no portage around it, no access back to the James on its downstream side.

We arrive at this revelation while parked alongside U.S. 501 just below the dam. The highway crosses the river on a narrow, high bridge, and from its middle—which we reach via a precarious walk against traffic, a long drop to the river on one side, rushing trucks on the other—we notice that no road, no path, no nothing descends to the river's edge within our view.

We look down on the Cushaw's huge concrete spillway. Just below it, the river churns over boulder-strewn rapids, and it strikes me that if it weren't for this dam, and the impoundment pond that drowns the rapids upstream, the Balcony Falls whitewater would run unbroken from Glasgow to this point and beyond. The Cushaw is twenty-six feet high; the river would fall much of that distance on its own if the dam were not here to absorb the drop.

"Man," says Ian. "That is one ugly dam."

"Sure is," I reply. "I wonder how they decided that this is where it belonged."

"And who decided it," Ian says.

"Yeah," I nod, getting indignant. "Who does decide something like that?"

We stare at the water sliding down the spillway and the dam's red-brick powerhouse, Soviet in its functional charmlessness, leaning against the guardrail and away from the rumble and smoke of fast-passing semis. I notice a white rectangle painted on the back of a nearby road sign: a blaze. Motorists share the crossing with hikers on the Appalachian Trail, the 2,150-mile footpath that traverses the Eastern mountaintops from Mount Katahdin, in the North Maine Woods, to Springer Mountain in Georgia. The southbound trail drops onto 501 upstream of the dam, follows the highway to the bridge, crosses the river and immediately veers off the blacktop and climbs into the James Face Wilderness, a rugged, roadless chunk of the Jefferson National Forest. A hiker's brief encounter with the James doesn't come with the river looking its best. How sad, I think, that such a spectacular water gap ends like this—with an ugly slab of concrete that contributes nothing to the landscape.

Nor much to anything else. For all of its intrusiveness, the Cushaw is no great source of power. Built in 1928-29 and placed in service in 1930, it generates 20,000 megawatt-hours of power per year. That sounds like a lot, until you divide that number by the 12 megawatt-hours of power the typical home consumes over the same time. Cushaw could power a burg of fewer than 1,700 households. In fact, it produces less electricity in a year than the Bath County Pumped Water Facility on Back Creek can generate in a *day.*

And it's not as if the dam is a big component of the local economy: Cushaw keeps one caretaker employed part-time. Virginia Power could restore the gorge to its natural, glorious state, and nobody would miss the dam or its trickle of electricity.

The first turnoff that promises river access comes a mile below the bridge, on the river's north side. But the promise turns to vapor within a few feet of the highway: it's the entrance to the Snowden Dam, a zig-zagging concrete wall that shunts the James's flow into a narrow channel on the north bank. This raceway feeds a powerhouse with which the city of Bedford generates electricity.

Downstream from the Snowden, the river is straddled by the Blue Ridge Parkway's James River Center, a wayside on the beautiful, 469-mile ridgetop road through Virginia and North Carolina. At the north end of the parkway's bridge is a first-rate nature walk and a visitors' center with exhibits on the river's canal days. A footbridge slung beneath the parkway links the complex to a restored lock on the south bank, complete with wooden gates. Visitors to the James find the river here uncharacteristically placid, for its waters are sliding into another impoundment. Around a downstream bend, and just three miles below Snowden, a third dam blocks the river. The Big Island Dam dates to the 1840s, when it was built to irrigate the James River and Kanawha Canal; these days the eleven-foot-tall rock-and-concrete structure is put to use by a containerboard plant, a confusion of stacks and steam and stink on the south bank.

Bluffs rise along the floodplain just behind the mill, and matchbox houses crowd their tops. The view from their yards isn't a pretty one. A short distance downstream, the riverbank is pocked by a chain of squarish ponds tainted with the mill's effluent. Ian and I find a boat ramp between the mill and ponds, but little more than four miles downstream yet another blockage waits, Georgia Pacific's Coleman Falls Dam, and we can find no place near it to portage.

But wait. There's more. The hydroelectric Holcomb Rock Dam, five hundred feet long and fourteen high, crosses the James just a short ways below Coleman Falls, and there's no legal access to the river around it. We bounce the Volvo over a railroad track and into a Georgia Pacific parking lot several hundred yards below the dam, snoop around the small powerhouse there—a blue, prefab metal shell built atop brick and a much older foundation of stone—and drive a wriggling, one-lane road upstream to the dam, Ian honking the horn as we swing around blind curves. Just below the dam we make an astounding discovery: along the south bank is a beautifully preserved stretch of the canal, one of only two still filled with water. But putting the boat in there is out of the question— rather than offering the safe passage for which it was built, the canal now flows into the dam's powerhouse. I'm not in the mood to make close acquaintance with an Allis Chalmers vertical-shaft turbine. We drive on.

Downstream waits the massive Reusens Dam, another obstruction that had its beginnings in the mid-nineteenth century and was later converted to hydroelectric power. And three miles beyond Reusens, the Scotts Mill Dam is part of Lynchburg's water works. Cushaw, it turns out, is a prelude to the next twenty-seven miles. From the bottom of the gorge to downtown Lynchburg, seven dams pen the James's flow, making it less a river than a string of windswept pools.

This is how the Piedmont welcomes the James River after its tumble from the mountains.

DAY ELEVEN
Fleeing Lynchburg

Early morning finds us on the Lynchburg riverfront, seeking a place to put the canoe in the water. We've looked forward to our arrival in the city: here the last foothills of the Blue Ridge melt into the relatively flat uplands of the Piedmont, a broad stair step that in Richmond will give way to the coastal plain; the river's rapids calm to riffles, its bed broadens, its current slows. And the ghosts of two hundred years of busy river history wait. Lynchburg was a major station on the James River and Kanawha Canal, the largest on the Upper James, and even before work crews carved the waterway into its downtown waterfront, the place relied heavily on the river. Here, we figure, the population is well-attuned to the James' pulse, and stream and city will be seamlessly one.

It is not so. We find Lynchburg built with its back to the river. The James is virtually invisible on the downtown waterfront, obscured by a clutter of railroad tracks, factories, hollow-eyed warehouses. Its weedy south bank is littered with old tires, cast-off machine parts and blowing fast-food wrappers. Blue vinyl banners reading "Welcome to Lynchburg's Riverfront" are tied to a chain-link fence that parallels the bank and borders a large parking lot—a lake of asphalt built on filled-in canal.

"Check out those signs," I say to Ian.

"Aw, no way those are serious."

"I don't see how they can be."

"*What* riverfront?"

I find myself growing angry that a city spread along a glorious, bluff-lined reach of river could forsake it so. We find no acknowledgment that where the car now rests a canal once flowed, no clue that here stood one of the East's great nineteenth-century inland ports, nothing to remind visitors—or residents, for that matter—that before railroads and interstates, this was a thriving metropolis because it was built on the shore of a great waterway. Nor, in our wanderings over and between a braid of railroad tracks, can we find a place to lower the canoe down the bank. I resort to the maps, and eventually navigate the Volvo to a boat ramp in a parking lot beneath a high concrete bridge. The ramp is chained. A sign hanging from the barricade warns that it can only be used by emergency vehicles.

Ian brakes the car and we study the sign in silence for a moment. This is my map's only marked put-in. It hasn't occurred to me that it might be private. In fact, we seem to be trespassing even here: we're surrounded by pallet piles and stacks of foot-wide black pipes, at the edge of what's obviously a large industrial complex. A guard shack stands nearby. "We're an emergency vehicle," Ian suddenly declares. He looks at me and shrugs.

"Well," I say, "we're sure enough gonna have an emergency on our hands, if we can't put the boat in the water." So, without another word, we go for it. We unrope the bow and stern, pop the hatch, pull paddles, the cooler, and my life vest from the wayback. Ours are the spare, efficient movements of sailors at their battle stations, and in under a minute we've only to unstrap the canoe from the rack. Two minutes more and I'll be on the river, and the Volvo will be high-tailing out of the lot.

That's when Ian mutters, "Busted." I turn to find Sgt. Melissa A. Osborne, hard-hatted private security officer for the Griffin Pipe Products Company, marching toward us. "You can't launch that canoe there!" she shouts.

"Ignore her," I whisper to Ian. "Keep unloading stuff. Maybe we can sweet-talk her." We're pulling the rack straps through their buckles as Sgt. Osborne reaches the car. "You can't launch that canoe here," she says again.

I let the strap go and turn toward her. "Why not?"

"This ramp is owned by the Griffin Pipe Corporation," she answers. "It's private property."

"Well, I don't see the Griffin Pipe Corporation using it at the moment," I say. "We just want to put the canoe in, and we'll be out of here. It'll take no time at all."

"You can't do that," she rules. Well, I say, maybe you could give us the phone number of the president of the Griffin Pipe Corporation so that we can call the guy and get permission to launch our canoe from his ramp. She rattles off a number. I grab our cell phone. She informs me that it won't do much good: no one will be available to answer my request for forty-eight hours.

Look, I tell her, we're on a tight schedule. We've driven all over looking for a place to put the boat in. "At the foot of Ninth Street," she says. "There's a public boat ramp at the foot of Ninth Street." We're all unloaded, I whine. How can it hurt to let us use the ramp just this once?

Sgt. Osborne stares at me.

Sgt. Osborne isn't budging.

Sgt. Osborne won't be sweet-talked.

We pack up and drive on.

This isn't our first hint that our visit to Lynchburg might be a grim affair. Last night we pulled into town from the west on 501, cruising along an avenue of grand houses and the turreted grace of Randolph Macon Women's College, all built on a headland thrust high above the river. Tucked behind one section of mansions we found Riverside Park. We pulled in, thinking we could get to the water.

We could not. The park clung to a clifftop just downstream from an enormous railroad trestle. A few walking trails dropped off the precipice to weave along ledges a few feet below, but we could find none that descended to the bluff's foot, where we saw railroad tracks hugging the James's south bank. I'd expected a park cozied up to the shore, partly because of its name and partly because I'd read in some guidebook that the remains of a packet boat were on display here. The *John Marshall* made the Richmond to Lynchburg round-trip three times a week in the canal's heyday, and carried thousands of passengers into the interior. But it won particular fame for a 1863 run upriver, its cargo the body of Confederate Gen. Thomas "Stonewall" Jackson. Most of his body, anyway: his left arm, amputated after he was accidentally shot by his own troops at Chancellorsville, wasn't aboard—it was destined for a separate grave outside of Fredericksburg that's still a destination for oddity-seekers. The roughly seven-eighths of Jackson that was on the *Marshall* was bound for Lexington, where he'd worked as a professor at the Virginia Military Institute before the war, and where he was to be buried.

It's difficult to overstate the reverence Virginia holds for Stonewall Jackson, particularly that part of the population that to this day calls the Civil War the "War of Northern Aggression" or "The Lost Cause" or "The Late Unpleasantness." A lot of southerners figure him a leader of such genius and pure gall that, had he survived, the South might well have whipped the Yankees; his tragic death dealt the Confederacy a blow from which it never recovered. His face is instantly recognizable to most Virginians—more so than some of the state's eight presidents. The *Marshall* left Lynchburg that May, traveled the James River and Kanawha Canal to the North River Navigation, and made its way slowly through the locks upriver. And for this, it won a place of esteem accorded no other canal boat.

Was the *Marshall* really here, I wondered, so far above the James? We scanned the park, saw nothing that resembled a boat, came close to bagging the search. But near the park's highest spot, where the bluffs rose to their peak, stood a chain-link fence, topped with barbed wire, and within it there lay a long, ragged keel of black iron on concrete cradles. Its metal edges curled skyward like a dying leaf's. Rust had chewed away the hull's chines and clean through most of its bottom.

We left puzzled. The park kept the river at arm's length, and its historic centerpiece was decaying by the minute. We continued into the city hopeful that it was an anomaly. Our stay only darkened, however. Later in the evening we pulled into a local fast-food joint and found ourselves in the midst of a hellish take on "American Graffiti." Tattooed, evil-eyed youngsters cruised the parking lot, stared sullenly as we loaded up on food inside. The security guard standing near the door did little to bolster our comfort level: he was fat, wearing a mammoth handgun on his hip, and shockingly cross-eyed. "If there's trouble and that guy starts shooting," I whispered to Ian, "he'll have to fire twice to make sure he hits the bad guy."

"No kidding," Ian said, unable to keep from staring. "At least if a bad guy shoots us, it's intentional."

"I'm using you as a human shield," I told him. "Just so you know."

"Thanks, pal."

"Nothing personal. Gotta finish the trip."

That was last night. Now we drive, per Sgt. Osborne's instructions, to Ninth Street. At its foot we leave the car to find that the "ramp" is a steep concrete staircase. It dives down a gravel bank to the water's edge, which it meets beneath a railroad trestle. Litter rustles in the weeds straddling the path. A quick glance at the water itself tells us it's not the James: it's a skinny little stream, on the far side of which more pipe is stacked next to an abandoned cold-storage warehouse. Faded lettering on weathered wood announces it as the Lynchburg Diamond Ice Factory.

"What creek is this?" I ask Ian. I can make out few details on my maps: the photocopied topos show a bank overlaid with railroads. The riverfront's natural lines have been pretty much blotted out. Ian shrugs. He's never been to Lynchburg. "Hell, I have no idea where we are," I mutter. "I don't see how this can't be the James, but clearly, it's not."

"If it is," Ian says, "it's gotten real small, real quick."

Just then I glance across the parking lot and notice a creamy yellow quartz boulder squatting at its edge, close to five feet high and crisscrossed with veins. On its face is a plaque affixed by the Daughters of the American Revolution that reads, "Site of First House and Lynch's Ferry, 1757." That would be the house and ferry of John Lynch, first settler hereabouts, the farsighted fellow who opened a private ferry here at seventeen and was surrounded by a boomtown by the time he died. Lynchburg became the biggest tobacco market in the South, the inspection and shipping point for farmers throughout the Piedmont. Hundreds of hogshead-laden batteaux left for Richmond each year in the early nineteenth century, infusing the place with a prosperity outproportioned to its size. "Some of our stores are so extensive and elegant," an 1843 sketch boasted, "as not to suffer by a comparison with those of Philadelphia and New York."

None of this could have happened, of course, without the James. The river gave the settlement a highway link to the sea, an advantage that earlier towns in the region lacked. Take New London, just south of Lynchburg and today all but absorbed by it. Before the Revolution, this was among Virginia's principal towns, with "at least 70 or 80 houses," a courthouse and a government arsenal, clustered around the intersection of two major overland roads. It dwarfed Lynch's Ferry. When war came with Britain, local revolutionaries demanded that its residents take an oath of allegiance to the cause, and a passel of New London's merchants refused. The rebels didn't take this kindly, and pretty much encouraged the Tories out of town. New London's economy abruptly imploded, and with the physical advantages offered by Lynch's Ferry, just a few miles away, the place never recovered. The courthouse became a barn, the arsenal was moved to Harper's Ferry, and New London dried up and died. Had it suffered through the same economic collapse in Lynchburg's location, it might have bounced back. But it lacked the river. It missed that vital link.

I turn away from the boulder, take in the bleak urban desert around me, the warehouses lined forlorn at the foot of the hill that rises to downtown's modern heart. The river was good to the place for a long time, but eventually the city's economic lifeblood left the James, and the people running the place made the same decision folks in Natural Bridge Station did: they abandoned one source of sustenance for another, and refigured their town to reflect the shift.

"Well, what do you think?" I ask Ian. "Think we can get all our stuff down that staircase?" He eyes the drop. "It's not the best," he says. "There's got to be better."

"OK. Let's look a bit longer for another ramp, and if we don't find one, we can head back here."

Downstream the riverfront road, the remnant of an old turnpike, carries us past a breastwork of towering warehouses, their sooty red brick interrupted by massive windows. Most seem empty. Off to our left, in the James, the wooded lump of Percival's Island rises, linked to the city by a curving train trestle that's been converted to a pedestrian walk. The bank around it offers no path to the river, however. We push on.

After a thirty-minute search we find access to the James from the parking lot of yet another paper plant, the Rock Tenn Company's Lynchburg Mill. A rough concrete path, maybe a foot wide, dives to the edge of a narrow channel between the south bank and Percival's Island. Our launching spot is hard against a decrepit concrete dam and strewn with waterlogged pages from porn magazines. A twisted length of railing, scum-smeared and draped in rags and driftwood from some past freshet, curves above the dam's top like a foul arbor. "Jesus," I say. "Look at this place."

"Totally disgusting," Ian says, face screwed up.

We gingerly descend the path, plop the canoe in the water. It's tough to find a place free of sharp metal, but we eventually jimmy the boat between the riverbed debris in such a way that the plastic hull won't be sliced when I climb in. Before I shove off, though, I have to settle an urgent need. "It's imperative that I get to a bathroom," I announce.

Ian chuckles unsympathetically. "Aw, man. *Here?*"

Here, I tell him. It can't wait.

"I'm glad I'm not you," he tells me. I clamber up the concrete to the parking lot, scan the riverfront. My only option is the mill. A couple of hardhatted workers are loitering outside a door there, smoking cigarettes. I jog to them, ask if there's a bathroom around. A beefy guy in a beard nods. "Yeah, sure." He steps into the doorway, waits for me. I follow him in. "Head down there, and it's back on your right," he says, pointing. "Be careful."

So I set out into the plant. It's dimly lit, sweltering, swarming with fat pipes and crowded with huge, sinister-looking machinery. Loud hissing and thumping drowns out all other sound. Everything's sweatered in grime. The bathroom is a worn, tiny reprieve from the din. Then I'm headed back out through the steamy gantlet.

"Don't go in there," I tell Ian when I get back.

"Don't worry," he assures me.

"Where do you want to meet?" We review the maps, and see that although a small highway, Route 622, veers near the river's north bank in places, it doesn't appear to get close enough to offer Ian easy access except at a couple of hamlets, Riverville and Allens Creek—and those are so close to the day's destination that stopping at either makes no sense.

No, wait a minute; at the edge of one map sheet is another small town—maybe not much more than an old stop on the railroad, a place called Galt's Mill. It's ten miles downriver by the CSX railroad mileposts, which cut a few curves along the way. Excellent. We'll have lunch there, and I'll have another sixteen miles to cover in the afternoon.

I shove off, relieved to get away from the dam and our scummy launching spot. My relief doesn't last: this channel of the James is an inches-deep swamp, littered with garbage, rusted metal piping, more tires, and the wreckage of a truck trailer. It takes me close to an hour to weave through its obstacles and into the mainstream. Even there, the James is all but impassable. Rocky shallows slice the canoe; mile-long carpets of riverbed weeds clog the water, braking the boat, ensnaring my paddle, trying my patience. I paddle around one S-curve, fight my way over the weeds down a long, shallow straightaway, swing around a tight bend. Six miles below Lynchburg I paddle beneath a railroad trestle, the first crossing I've encountered, and a couple hundred yards farther on, see another canoeist fishing the shallows. He's in a solo canoe, as well, and using a kayak paddle. "How are ya?" I yell, across twenty yards of rocky water.

"Where you put in?" he asks. A skinny guy. Looks to be in his mid-fifties. Scowling.

"Percival's Island," I say. "How long before I get out of these stupid weeds?"

"Aw, it's like this for miles," he says. "I've paddled all this river. I know." He casts his line. "All the way to Norwood, it's like this. That's forty mile from here."

Near as I can tell, from looking at my maps, it's actually something like thirty-two. Even so, the prospect of hacking all that way through these damned plants is enough to make me sigh with despair. "To Norwood?" I say.

He nods knowingly. "I've paddled all this river," he announces again. "I know."

"And the water doesn't get any deeper?"

He shakes his head. "Doesn't really start to get deeper to Wingina, and that's a good fifty mile down this river." According to my maps, it's really only four miles beyond Norwood. "You goin' that far?" he asks. "You got a long way ahead of you, if you are."

"Yeah, well, I am," I tell him. "I'm going to Hampton Roads."

He laughs at me. "Then you got a *long* way ahead of you. I've paddled all this river, from Wingina to Lynchburg. Paddled it twenty times, maybe."

Let me guess, I think. He reels in his line, gets set to cast again. "I know this river," he tells me.

A couple miles downstream I sweep between the stone ruins of a long-destroyed canal dam at a place called Joshua Falls, and just below it the water starts to deepen and the paddling becomes easy. I spend most of the morning kneeling up, off the seat. Before long, I figure, I'll be standing as I cruise through flat water. I pull hard on the paddle blades, watch the canoe's tiny bow wake as I slice down river at a fast clip. Rolling hills hug the south bank, the occasional obstinate knob crops up on the north, and on both roam cattle and sheep. The horrors of Lynchburg seem far away.

In the early afternoon I spot Ian on the bank, and ground the canoe near a small dirt parking lot beside the railroad track. A couple of pickups are parked there, their owners no doubt fishing on the James. "Galt's Mill," Ian announces. He opens the wayback, and we eat our tenth lunch of car-warmed PBJs, Clif Bars and Gatorade. "There a town around here?" I ask him.

"No," Ian says between bites. "This is pretty much it." Horseflies buzz past, catch a whiff of us, circle back to investigate, lumber heavily, noisily around our heads. I slash at one with my hat. A miss.

We sweat in the intensifying sunshine; I open my second Gatorade, then a third. It'll be scorching on the water by midafternoon. The car'll be a convection oven. And there'll be no showers at day's end, I glumly realize. We're encamped, as we were last night, at the just-opened James River State Park near Norwood, which offers only primitive campsites. No conveniences but a squad of plastic privies fifty yards across a lumpy field from the tents—which, let's face it, isn't all that convenient.

We decided to camp there on the fly. While we were in Lynchburg a local mentioned this new park fifty miles downriver, and it seemed a good idea at the time to establish a base camp there that would last us for two or three nights. Of course, we lost way more time driving an hour back into Lynchburg this morning than we would have spent breaking camp somewhere else. And last night's drive put us into camp late, in absolute darkness, unable to make out any open campsites but a couple within earshot of a family get-together spread over three sites and lit brighter than high noon by hanging Colemans. We sat at a picnic table next to our tents, the trees around us aglow with hard white lantern light, drinking beer and listening to what sounded like a mass sacrifice next door.

"Man," Ian muttered. "I can't believe they haven't told those kids to shut up."

"What time is it?"

"About midnight."

"Why aren't those kids in bed?"

"I don't know, man." Ian swigged from his Sam Adams. "I'm definitely going to be wearing my earplugs tonight."

I thought I'd misheard him. "Did you say 'earplugs'?"

"Yes, I did."

"You brought earplugs out here? For sleeping in the *woods?*"

"Well, actually, Earl, I've used them almost every night since we started out," he said. He drained his beer. I reached into the beer bag and pulled out another for him as he added: "You snore."

"Yeah, I know." I waited for further explanation.

Ian shook his head. "Man, you have no idea how loud you are."

"Come on," I said. "You're in another tent. You're twenty feet away, in another tent."

Ian looked me in the eye. "I mean *loud,*" he said. "It's really pretty remarkable. I've never heard anything quite like it."

"What's it like?" I snorted like an enraged wild pig, or what I imagined one to sound like. "Like that?"

"Yeah," he said matter-of-factly. "Kinda like that. There've been a couple nights when I almost woke you up. But I knew you needed the sleep."

I drank my beer and eyed Ian in the shadowy glow from the other campsite. I'd have killed him by now, if our places were switched. He'd just gritted his teeth and screwed in his earplugs and hunkered down in his $120 Swedish pillow. He was a weird guy, no question.

Another prepubescent shriek erupted from the family compound. "Well, I've got some good news for you," I told him. "Tonight, my snoring will be the least of your worries."

Below Galt's Mill I slide through a trio of rapids alongside Pettyjohn Island, paddle around a hairpin turn that circles a steep knob on the south bank, then scrape and whoosh through more rapids at Patterson's Shoals and Wreck Island Falls and Thorn Hill Falls. This was a tough stretch of water in the days before the James River and Kanawha Canal smoothed its bumps. I find no great dangers today, however. The river's so low that the rapids have been stripped of power, and I paddle worry-free for mile on mile. My soundtrack is crickets chirping, crows cawing, the murmur of riffles and shoals. There's not so much as a railroad bridge to interrupt the afternoon's tranquility.

Then, about six hours downriver from Lynchburg, the breeze brings the unmistakable smell of another paper mill, the Greif Brothers Corporation plant at Riverville. A few minutes later I spot four rocks in the stream ahead, evenly spaced across its breadth. Perfectly spaced, I think. Who says there's no order to nature?

I've been fooled. Once past them I see that they're not rocks at all, but concrete humps. The swirls behind them aren't eddies, but jets of murky wastewater. A mile or so downriver, on one of the last bends I'll round before reaching Bent Creek, I charge over a small rapids and drift toward the south bank, where four young men are lounging on a gravel bar, fishing, drinking beer, and smoking cigarettes. Behind them is a curtain of heavy woods. Save for their lawn chairs and a large cooler they've lugged onto the bar, you'd think the woods go on for miles. There's no sign of the car that must be lurking in the trees. A day's paddle from one of the largest cities on the James, and the river has returned, at least visually, to its upland wildness. They're locals, they tell me. Come this way all the time. Feels like a million miles from anywhere, and when the sun gets too hot, all you need do is stroll into the river.

"That mill upstream," I say.

"Yeah," one of them nods.

"It mess with the water here at all?"

The guy shrugs. I describe the mysterious concrete humps. The boys on the gravel bar don't seem the least bit concerned. A couple minutes later, in fact, one of them gets up and hobbles slowly into the river until he stands thigh-deep in it. But the odd rocks nag at me. I continue my paddle, turning them over in my mind. Were they designed to resemble rocks, or was their appearance an accidental byproduct of engineering? Either way, the subtlety with which they pump their discharge into the river is spooky. The river's way low. Normally they'd be submerged, invisible. I feel as if I've seen something I wasn't supposed to. Distracted, I forget to look for Gladstone, a railroad burg crowded with houses built among gargantuan, half-buried boulders. It slides by, unseen, on the north bank.

Early in the evening I spot the U.S. Route 60 bridge about a half mile ahead, and about the same time see a teenager becalmed midstream in an inner tube. I paddle over. It's a heavyset kid, and he or she—I honestly can't tell which—is using a short canoe paddle to slash desperately at the water. The tube is spinning slowly but making no downstream progress. It takes me right back to Hidden Valley. "Hey, do you want a tow?" I yell.

The kid glowers at me. "No," he or she mutters. I look downstream to the bridge. It'll take the kid until well after nightfall to get there, assuming that's where he or she is going. "Look, it's gonna be dark soon, and you have a ways to go," I holler. "I can get you to Bent Creek in about ten minutes. You sure you don't want a tow?" I'm wondering, as I look at this kid immersed neck-high in the water, what was coming out of those concrete humps. "No," he or she grumps. "I'll be fine."

"Take it easy, then."

I pour it on. The kid drops out of sight. At Bent Creek a Game and Inland Fisheries boat ramp slopes to the water's edge just above the Route 60 bridge and just below the stone piers of a long-vanished span built in the canal days. Ian's waiting with the Volvo. We load up with beer, ice, and Gatorades at a bridgehead general store, then cruise the seven miles to camp. I tell him about the concrete humps on the way. "What do you make of that?" I ask.

Ian shakes his head. "I don't know. What do you make of it?"
"I don't know, either," I say.

DAY TWELVE

Thirty years after the river's
worst night

  At daybreak we leave the tents standing, jump in the Volvo and drive the seven miles upriver to Bent Creek, planning to rendezvous at the campsite for breakfast. A month ago, this hour of day would have been as stultifyingly close and hot as the noon to come, the sort that brings sweat-soaked sleeping bags and an exhaustion unrelieved by sleep; but now, with October coming on fast, the fields around the road are enveloped in chilled blue mist, and the wind whipping noisily into the car's open windows is bracingly cold. We pull up to the put-in, goosebumped, imbued with that achy energy that comes with a running start, unlash the canoe, slide it into the water at the foot of the ramp. Seven, eight miles, I tell Ian. A couple hours, two and a half on the outside. See you then.

Almost as soon as I push off, I see that the James has changed. Piles of sudsy, cream-colored foam glide past the canoe, some of them a foot high and crowned with a burnt-sugar sludge. Dollops of suds cover the entire river, most the size of half-dollars, others as big as hubcaps. I watch them collect in the river's bends and nooks to form scummy carpets, the bigger ones snagging the branches of low-hanging maples and ash slumped over the bank.

It is a startling way to start the day's paddle, far more jarring than the temperature. Over the past 250 miles I've traveled a river pumped with the effluent from paper mills and the treated sewage of a dozen towns, but I've not seen this—whatever it is. I pick up my pace, paddle hard, slide around sweeping curves bordered by flattening farmland. An hour later the bubbles have disappeared; the James, having shrugged off yet another in the series of indignities visited upon it by city and industry, somehow runs clear, abounds with life. I can see the bottom even when it drops to six feet down, can see the shadows of gar and smallmouth bass darting among the rocks.

And I see a head jutting from the river's surface—fist-sized, with a pointed snout, a thick neck. At first it seems a rock, one of the hundreds of dark-gray knobs and ledges that split the water's flow as I approach James River State

Park, and our campsite. But it jerks out of sight, and as my canoe passes the dimple it left behind, I see it crouched on the river bottom—a two-foot snapping turtle, a leathery bundle of claws and spikes with an eagle's beak for a mouth. Best keep my arms and legs in the boat, I decide.

At the state park I drive the canoe onto a red-dirt boat ramp and trudge up the slope to camp, and find Ian sitting on the picnic table, boiling water. We slug down a couple cups of coffee, blow through hot oatmeal, and make plans to meet at Wingina, an ancient Indian camp and vestigial town six or seven miles farther downstream. The morning has warmed. When we've broken camp and loaded the car, I'm basted in sweat, and once I've returned to the seeming cool of the water I broil: not only is there little escape from the climbing sun, but the canoe's blond plastic ricochets heat and light. Within minutes I reach a break in the left bank. The Tye River, anemic, narrow, trickles into the James between high banks. A few hundred yards upstream, I can make out the concrete abutment of a bridge carrying two-lane Route 626 over the stream.

The Tye looks powerless today. Islands of gravel, usually submerged, rise above its inches-deep water. Some bristle with saplings, evidence of the drought that's gone on for two summers now. Pastureland crunches underfoot, baked as dry as a snake's rattle. Corn is stunted. Hay won't grow.

Here the rust-red soil is parched hard, like concrete, and the streams that tumble from high on the Blue Ridge do nothing to slake it. They have no water to spare: not only is the Tye baring its bones, the Rockfish River is half its normal size. Davis Creek is so low the cows have given up on it. So low, in fact, that Tommy Huffman is praying for rain, and that might be the most telling measure of just how dry it is.

Huffman's is a modest, well-kept, red-brick house in Nelson County, the land stretching northward off the left bank. Standing on the ford below the house, it's difficult to picture it as it was one night when Davis Creek raced fifty feet deep here, when houses washed away and their pieces flew down the creek and into the Rockfish River and across Nelson County into the James.

That August night in 1969, close to twenty-eight inches of rain fell on Nelson County's clutter of apple orchards, low ridges, and broadleaf forests, the bulk of it in less than five hours. It fell so hard that the ground turned to pudding and swallowed up forests and farms. Birds drowned in the trees. In the flash floods and avalanches that followed, 125 people were drowned, crushed, or buried so deep they'd never be found.

The U.S. Department of the Interior would later call the cloudburst "one of the all-time meteorological anomalies in the United States." The Army Corps of Engineers labeled it "one of nature's rare events." The people who lived through this biblical deluge recall it in stronger terms.

The storm began two weeks earlier and thousands of miles to the east. The day was August 5, 1969, a Tuesday, and the coming trouble was announced by a weather satellite passing high over the African coast. Just west of Senegal, the craft photographed a bank of clouds over the ocean, forming an inverted V.

To the meteorologists who interpreted satellite pictures for the U.S. Weather Bureau, the clouds represented a remote worry. Dozens of such formations appear each year in the eastern Atlantic, the breeding ground for hurricanes that threaten the United States. Most amount to nothing. But the Bureau kept an eye on the inverted V as it arced westward across the Atlantic, and four days later its vigilance seemed well-placed: the clouds now sucked vast amounts of sea water into the atmosphere. The vapor rose until it cooled, condensed, and fell as rain—in the process releasing heat, which further warmed the clouds, which consequently sucked water from the Atlantic even faster. What meteorologists call a "heat engine" had started. Not only that, but the clouds were changing shape. They had encircled a column of low-pressure air, and were tightening into a knot. On August 10 they slid over the West Indies and into the Caribbean Sea, dumping heavy rain on the Leeward Islands. A day later, the satellite picked up a spinning band of rain within the cloud mass, a badge of tropical cyclones.

Twelve days after its wispy debut, the storm had intensified so dramatically that the Air Force dispatched a reconnaissance plane for a closer look. The crew returned with alarming news: the barometric pressure at the storm's center was the lowest ever measured from an aircraft, and winds there were blowing at 200 mph. Among meteorologists it was the low pressure—the standard by which hurricane intensity is truly judged—that inspired terror. This storm packed more muscle than Hurricane Donna, which had ravaged the Eastern Seaboard in 1960; than the Galveston storm of 1900, which had killed six thousand; than Hazel, and Carla, and Audrey, and Betsy, and the Great Atlantic Hurricane of 1944. In fact, a lower pressure had been recorded just once in the Atlantic, during the Labor Day Storm of 1935, in the Florida Keys. And unlike that hurricane, Camille was aimed for the U.S. mainland.

That evening Tommy Huffman was two hundred miles from the Atlantic and several times that distance from the Gulf of Mexico. He drove home from his shift fixing heaters and air conditioners for the University of Virginia, parked his pickup beside his brick rambler, and walked inside to his wife, Adelaide, and their three teenagers. Their house stood at the junction of two farm roads, and in the center of a Huffman enclave. One of the roads dived behind the house into a narrow valley, passing the place where Tommy's brother Russell lived with his wife and nine children. From there the road switchbacked up the valley's far wall into "Huffman Hollow," where two more brothers lived with their families, and another shared the old Huffman home place with Tommy's mother. The other road passed in front of the house and ran up the creek to its head. Up that way lived another two brothers, and two of Tommy's nephews who had places of their own.

The hurricane didn't come up as the family sat at the dinner table; weather in the tropics didn't count for much in these Virginia mountains. That would change in less than two days, and fifty-two of the people living along Davis Creek would die.

Nelson County slept as Camille rammed ashore at Bay St. Louis, a notch in the Mississippi coast just west of Gulfport. While the Blue Ridge night passed to thrumming crickets, and burbling rivers, and rustling trees, the hurricane obliterated houses and flattened concrete hotels, picked up freighters and tossed them ashore, peeled up interstates, snapped railroad lines. Its winds screamed at 190 mph, stirring a wave twenty-two feet tall that rolled over seawalls and into beach towns to drown people by the score. In Pass Christian, Mississippi, twelve people attending a hurricane party were crushed by their brick apartment house. A few blocks away, eleven others died in the ruins of a church. Wind and water unearthed coffins, sprung their tops, tangled their contents in the trees. Along sixty miles of the Mississippi coast, more than nineteen thousand homes were wrecked. All that remained of some towns were their names.

Camille trundled north, its counterclockwise whirl slowing. The warm Gulf water that had stoked the hurricane's heat engine was absent as the storm cut inland, and it quickly lost its breath; before it reached the Tennessee line its winds dwindled to harmless gusts, and the Weather Bureau downgraded the storm to a tropical depression.

While this happened, fourteen-year-old Warren Raines was passing another steamy summer day in Massies Mill, eight hilly miles southwest of the Huffman place. Warren's days were predictable: he stirred long after the sun had climbed high and the air turned gummy with heat. He wandered outside, pedaled his Stingray to his father's office, hung around. Carl Raines Sr. managed the Miller Chemical Company, which furnished sprays, packing supplies, ladders, and such to the county's apple industry. On occasion Warren's dad would put him to work, but more often than not, he'd be back on his bike after a while, often sharing the banana seat with his sixteen-year-old brother, Carl Jr. He had four other siblings—a sister, Ava, who'd moved off to Lynchburg, and another, Johanna, who'd just graduated from high school; a brother, Sandy, nine years old; and a little sister, Ginger, who was seven.

But it was Carl Jr. with whom he spent most of his time. They were both small for their ages, almost skeletally thin, and neither could sit still. They might mow lawns to pick up some spending money. Might work on an old Ford wagon they were rebuilding in a shed out back. Most likely, they'd wander down to the Tye River to fish, or cannonball in the river's swimming holes. The stream was only a foot or two deep and three dozen wide, but in places its bottom dropped eight feet or more. One such hole, framed by orange trumpets, mimosa, and mountain ash, lay cool and deep within a shout of the house. The Raineses' place was typical of Massies Mill: every house in town was within 250 yards of the Tye. Most of them soon would be in it, and twenty-two townspeople would be dead.

Sometime that day—Tuesday, August 19, 1969—the hurricane's remnants did the unexpected: Camille turned sharply to the east, and began to loose the load of water it had gathered on its journey from the African coast. As night fell, and the storm crossed into Virginia, a light drizzle began to fall over the Blue Ridge. The same had happened, on and off, for weeks: the region's pastures were spongy, deep emerald; thin woods had turned lush jungle.

Soon a steady shower was falling. Tommy and Adelaide Huffman headed for bed, leaving the kids to watch TV. Sleep didn't come easy: the rain started coming down hard, drumming loudly on the shingle roof. Before long the phone was out. A while after that, one of the kids came to the bedroom door to report the power was gone.

A bit later the Huffmans' white Persian cat, Bunny, came scratching at the kitchen door. She was an outdoor pet, toughened to all kinds of weather, but now she held a newborn kitten in her mouth and begged to come in. Tommy and Adelaide's daughter Anne thought the cat's behavior odd, but she opened the door.

A ringing woke Warren Raines. He sat up in his bunk bed to find that he'd fallen asleep fully dressed, minus only his sneakers. It was dark outside his bedroom window, the middle of the night. Down the hall, in his parents' room, his father was speaking to someone on the phone.

Warren jumped to the floor as his brother Carl crawled from the lower bunk, and together they trudged down the hall, sleepy but curious. They reached their father as he hung up the phone. A prank, he was telling their mother—someone saying they had to get out of Massies Mill, that the river had busted loose of its banks. He looked over to the kids. "Just go on back to bed," he told them. "Don't worry about it." As calm as Mr. Raines seemed, his family could hear that the rain had picked up, that it was striking the roof as if shot from a fire hose. "Why don't we look outside?" Warren's mother, Shirley, suggested. From the windows they could see that the road was ankle-deep. The neighbors' houses were islands ringed by water a foot deep, maybe two. Mr. Raines told the children to dress. Warren pulled on a pair of rubber boots, olive drab and midcalf-high, and headed downstairs. From the landing he could see water seeping under the front door, a puddle spreading across the oak floor.

Mr. Raines sent Carl Jr. out to start the car and pull it around front, then sent the kids outside to climb in. They had to force the porch door open against knee-deep water. It spilled over the tops of Warren's boots. A minute later, Mr. Raines put the car into gear. Even before he pressed the accelerator, the Ford's engine died. He slipped the car back into park, turned the key. The engine turned but wouldn't catch. He tried it again. Nothing. Again. Still, the car wouldn't start.

OK, Warren's father said, we'll walk. They climbed out of the wagon, stood for a moment in rain so hard and heavy it didn't resemble rain at all, seemed a waterfall. Warren's rubber boots again filled with water. He had to tuck his chin into his chest to breathe. The new plan: they'd stay on the road, which was crown-topped and built high, and walk toward the center of town. A few hundred yards away, they'd turn right and climb the hill west of Massies Mill. At worst, they'd spend the night on someone's porch. "Let's go," Mr. Raines said, and they started walking. For the first minute or two the water was only calf-deep, but then it climbed to Warren's knees, and a minute later his thighs, and as it rose it picked up speed and strength. It came up behind them and streamed across the road diagonally, pushed them forward and toward the left shoulder. They stayed close to each other, yelling back and forth over the roar of the deluge. Lightning flashed so continuously that Massies Mill was plain around them, turned hard blue-white, and the thunder was a ceaseless tim-pani roll. Over the din they heard a neighbor, Buen Wood, yelling at his wife as they passed the couple's place, telling Lola to turn the lights back on, that he couldn't see. A second later Lola was hollering to them from the porch: Y'all come on, come in here with us.

But just then the water jumped. Warren was chest-deep all of a sudden, and the water was rushing cold and muddy around him, shoving him in the back, and he was half-running, half-swimming, struggling to stay upright, grop-ing in the dark. He caught hold of a honeysuckle, just a sprig, and as it started to tear away from the bush he glanced downstream, saw his mother and sis-ters were standing a few yards away, lit by lightning, bracing one another against the current. "Catch me!" he screamed.

"Go ahead and let go," his mother yelled back. "We'll catch you."

He let go. A second later, when he reached the place where his mother and sisters had been standing, they were gone.

Until Camille, the hardest rain recorded in Virginia had come in 1942, when 8.4 inches of water fell in twelve hours on Big Meadows, in Shenandoah National Park. Three times that much was now falling on Nelson County. Along Davis Creek, the tattoo of drops hitting the shingles bled into a steady drone. At about 2:45 A.M., Anne Huffman woke her mother to report that water was dripping from her bedroom ceiling. Adelaide got up, put down a pan to catch the dripping water, and spotted Bunny in the closet. She could hear the rain outside, saw lightning flash beyond the curtains. It wouldn't hurt, she decided, if the cat stayed in the house for one night.

No sooner had she settled back into bed than she heard something outside, then heard it again. "Tommy," she whispered, shaking him awake, "I hear somebody yelling for me, hollering, 'Adelaide.'" He blinked and sat up as Adelaide hurried to the back door, and as she reached it, up staggered Tommy's brother Russell and his wife and eight of their nine kids, water streaming from drenched and heavy clothes, hair plastered flat, faces tucked into their shirts so that they could breathe. Davis Creek had come up, Russell gasped, had come up fast, and by the time he'd started the car the water was too deep to drive, and they'd had to scramble up the road. His station wagon had been carried away, lights still burning: he'd watched it go, half-sunk but moving fast down the valley.

A low rumble shook the house. Russell turned to Adelaide, asked: "What are you doing with the furnace on, this time of year?"

"I ain't got no furnace on," she replied. The sound grew, became a thousand jet fighters thundering through the hollow. The floor quivered. Windows rattled. Adelaide ran to the back door. "Oh, lands, Tommy, come here," she cried. "What's that noise? What is this horrible smell I'm smelling?"

Tommy Huffman recognized the smell immediately—disturbed mountain earth, a vaguely unpleasant odor, strong and ripe. A signal that the rain was changing the lay of the land.

Soil covering the Blue Ridge was shallow, just two to three feet from top to bedrock. When dry, each foot of earth could absorb a finite amount of water—one to two inches, perhaps. A four-inch rain would saturate a mountainside. The summer's frequent showers had left the slopes around Davis Creek sodden even before this cloudburst. Now the soil became a grainy muck, like wet cement, and it lost its grip on the hardy mountain gneiss to which it had clung for eons. In a hundred little hollows and draws around Davis Creek it began to ooze downhill, picking up speed, toppling pines and hardwoods, undermining boulders, sucking them into its flow until it had grown into a tsunami of mud and timber and stone, falling ever-faster down the mountain.

In places the debris snagged on standing trees or rock outcroppings, stacked into dams, and hundreds of tons of water and mud built behind them until they blew to pieces. The Huffmans' house quaked with each dam break that shotgun-sprayed downhill. Their roars blotted out the sounds made by the houses crushed in their paths, the cries of the people inside.

At lunchtime I reach Wingina, where a North Carolina couple, Kim Baldt and Philip Temple, stand on the bank under the highway bridge, wearing bathing suits. Ian's with them. "Hey, Earl," he yells as the canoe approaches. "These guys want to know whether it's safe to swim here."

Ian's evidently unable to answer the question himself, in light of the fake rocks I described last night. Kim and Philip watch as I beach the boat and stumble to shore, knees creaking; they look sheepish, as if they suspect the question's stupid. Before them, after all, the James rolls fast and clear, shimmering in the midday sun. Fish flip about, scales flashing. Beyond the banks, sparsely populated meadowlands stretch for miles.

But the question stumps me. I tell them that a lot of people do swim in the river here, that Wingina is on a popular stretch of the James, and leave it at that. A few minutes later, Kim wades in, waist-deep. "It's so clear!" she squeals, studying rocks on the bottom. "I can't get over how clean this water is!" I hold my tongue, and swat at yellow jackets drawn to the jelly in my PBJ, then wander into a dark grove of trees that parallels the north bank, admiring thick-trunked oaks and maples that look old enough to have witnessed the Indians who once bivouacked here, let alone all the flooding that's raked this bank in the years since.

There's been a good amount. In May 1771, torrential rains lashed the James's uplands for several days, boosting the river's level by up to sixteen inches an hour. By the time this bulge reached the falls at Richmond, it was a towering wall of water that smashed and swept away everything in its path. Cabins and farms vanished. Forests were felled. Islands were scoured. Dozens died.

Just shy of a century later, in October 1870, another freshet swamped Richmond, carrying off much of the city's riverfront. The *New York Times* reported ferry boats chugging along Richmond's downtown streets, and floodwaters in the Blue Ridge that killed fourteen people and "carried cattle and hogs before it like so many chips of wood." Another flood came seven years later, and another in March 1913. The James jumped its banks again in January 1935, in March 1936, and in September 1944. But even among these and other more recent floods in the James River watershed, what happened in 1969 stands apart.

The Tye River was normally forty feet wide and a foot or two deep as it dog-legged through Massies Mill. In the early-morning hours of August 20,

1969, it was a brown torrent that punched a quarter-mile wide and seven feet deep through the town's heart. Warren Raines clung to a weeping willow, soaking and chilled and scared out of his wits. By lightning's flashes he saw sycamores sucked from the ground by their roots, two-ton cars afloat and cruising downstream, cows wild-eyed and neck-deep and wailing with terror.

The willow sagged and slowly toppled, and Warren scrambled to the upper side of its trunk, rode it down until it stopped just above the water. Tree trunks and telephone poles surged past, snapping through the willow's branches only a few feet away. Timber beams and slabs of roof, work sheds and porches and entire garages spun by, and Warren feared that one was bound to slam into him, began to worry more about being crushed than he did about drowning. Crushed or struck by lightning, which came so fast and close that the town's destruction seemed played on a zoetrope. Bolts struck all around, thousands of them. They sounded like rifle shots.

Dawn came. In the gathering light, Warren saw that houses near the Tye had vanished. Most of those left standing on the main road were empty and mudspattered, their weatherboarding splintered, porches ripped away. Brown water flowed fast and whitecapped where the Presbyterian church had been, and streamed through the shattered stained glass of Grace Episcopal. An entire warehouse was missing from the intersection that passed for the town's center. A light shower fell. The storm, it seemed, had passed.

Still in the willow, he searched the water for signs of his father, his mother, the rest of his family. He saw none. Then, in the strengthening light, Carl Jr. appeared about thirty yards away, in the top of a tree of heaven. A johnboat headed Warren's way from the main road, neighbors inside. They took the boys to high ground as the flood waters began to recede. Where the warehouse had been, the water left behind a pile of rubble and a smashed Packard sedan veneered in slime. A dozen neighboring houses had been jerked off their foundations and squatted, warped and empty, in the mud. Castles of broken brick rose from puddle moats. And everywhere were dead fish, and dead cattle, and tremendous piles of smashed tree and house siding and furniture. The open ground seemed paved with riverjacks, smooth white stones the size of grapefruit.

They walked the main road to their father's office. Miller Chemical now sat on a bridge over the Tye, squeezed between the guardrails, blocking both lanes. The boys examined the wreckage. They found no sign of the family. They walked back across town to their house. Stormwater had crushed the family cat between the porch door and its jamb, and the animal's body was still wedged there, six feet off the ground. Inside, the refrigerator lay on its side. Upholstery was sodden, art torn from the walls, the whole ground floor knee-deep in a stinking, green-black mud.

A thumping emanated from the second floor. Warren and Carl climbed the stairs, hearts beating fast, and burst into their brother Sandy's room. Bo, the family's black lab, was sprawled on the bed, tail wagging. Otherwise the house was empty. Warren wandered the second floor, amazed at its pristine condition. The flood had dislodged a neighbor's place and spun it into the main road, where it had split the water's flow around the Raines home. The house had been in a protective eddy all night. If they'd stayed put, they'd have been fine. If they'd not received that late-night telephone call—or if they'd gone back to bed, as Warren's father had told them to—they'd have been fine.

Over the hills to the east, Tommy and Russell Huffman strode across the yard and into the Davis Creek valley, and looked down through rising mist on Russell's place. It was gone—house, cars, everything. The creekside meadow on which it had stood was stripped bare. The brothers stumbled back to Tommy's house, blurted what they'd found, and at first their wives didn't believe them, told the men they must not have walked far enough down the hill. It wasn't until they walked the road themselves that they understood what the night's rain had done.

On the mountainsides around them, white streaks gleamed in the sunlight, bedrock laid bare by avalanches. Every few minutes the earth rumbled underfoot as another waterlogged slope peeled away from the rock and slid, woods and all, into the valley. They couldn't see much of Huffman Hollow— the flooded creek blocked the only way in. It was just as well: a mudslide had carried off Tommy's forty-four-year-old brother, Robert, and Robert's wife, their three daughters, and their granddaughter. The ground had slipped at the old Huffman home place, too, where Tommy's mother lived with his younger brother, Jesse, and Jesse's family. It had spun the house around and brought its roof down. Tommy's mother suffered a deep cut on her leg, and Jesse clawed his way out of the streaming water on a guy wire that anchored a light pole.

They found three of Jesse's kids under a piece of collapsed roof, not a scratch on them. Just a few feet away was the baby bed where his youngest son slept. His bottle was still in it, but he wasn't, and he never was found. Jesse lost his wife, Lottie, and his oldest son, Jesse Jr., as well.

The family fared no better up the other road that ran past Tommy's house, that followed Davis Creek to its head. Tommy's oldest brother, Lawrence, was swept away with his wife, and the mud and rock obliterated his brother James's house and a trailer next to it. James's wife, Virginia, and his son David died in the house. His son Rodger, Rodger's wife Becky, and their son, Rodger Jr., were crushed in the trailer. Later that morning Russell learned that his boy Mitchell had died while spending the night at a friend's up that way. And in another trailer, a bit higher up the creek, James's oldest son, James Jr., died with his wife, Juanita, and their daughter, Barbara Lou. Everyone figured that James Sr. was dead, too—he wasn't supposed to have worked the night before, and they assumed he'd been home and swept away with the others. It turned out he pulled an unscheduled shift at his job. He fought his way over washed-out roads and missing bridges to get home, only to find that it no longer existed.

But before that, in the first few hours of daylight on August 20, as the storm's destruction first revealed itself to Tommy and Adelaide Huffman, as they stumbled over the heaps of debris that entombed their kin, Davis Creek was a world unto itself.

That afternoon they could hear a neighbor up on the ridge above the creek. "Is anybody alive?" he hollered. "Is anybody else alive?"

Outside their mud-splattered home in Massies Mill, Warren and Carl Raines found the Ford station wagon in which their family had tried to escape, pushed against a maple tree at the edge of the yard. The boys meandered through the town's remains, picking up clothes and furniture they recognized as theirs, and as they lugged them home neighbors stopped to talk with them. Some said they'd heard that the family was fine, that they were down at Lynchburg General Hospital, and for a while Warren and Carl were buoyed. Someone would be along to pick them up. But shortly before dark, that someone had not materialized. A family friend took them home, returned them the following morning to a town crawling with state troopers. One approached them and said, "Boys, what's going on?"

Warren and Carl answered that they didn't know. Something about the exchange cut through the daze that had enfolded Warren for more than a day, and suddenly the hope he'd carried through the flood evaporated, and in its place came a suffocating dread. "Our family's missing," he said, and he started to cry, and for a while he couldn't stop.

"Who's your closest kin?" the policeman asked. Grandparents, they told him. Their mother's people, down in Lynchburg. "Tell you what we're going to do," the trooper said. "I'm going to have somebody take you to the Nelson-Amherst line, and from there we'll get you down to Lynchburg."

So later that day they found themselves at a police roadblock in Piney River, a few miles south of Massies Mill and on the way to Amherst. And to their surprise, up walked their grandfather and their oldest sister, Ava, and their mother's uncle. "Where's the rest of the family?" the uncle asked, looking around.

The world did not yet understand what had happened at Massies Mill. "Gone," Warren cried. "They're gone."

After Hurricane Camille, the landscape had so changed in parts of Nelson County that topographic maps were obsolete. Mountain contours had shifted, riverbeds straightened or bent. Cropland lay deep under mud. Woods had vanished. Thirty years later, a watermark seven feet up the pine paneling of Grace Episcopal Church in Massies Mill recalls the night the Tye River burst in, sucked the organ out a window, and carried it to the James. In Schuyler, a power plant stands ruined, its walls felled by the rain-swollen Rockfish River and never rebuilt.

But to a surprising degree, the earth's wounds have closed. New timber has replaced the trees that flew like arrows that night. Soil again covers rock exposed by landslides. Beef cattle, corn rows, and apple orchards occupy bottomland that was lunar in its desolation. It is the storm's survivors, who lost those they loved and endured the night's terrors, that bear the deepest scars today.

Sometimes he'll hear a helicopter, and Warren Raines will find himself back under the tent in the cemetery, the coffins before him, Navy and Marine Corps choppers swooping overhead. Places around Massies Mill hold terrible significance. On the way into town, he'll point out the red-roofed tractor barn where they found his mother, Shirley. The wooded bend in the Tye where they found his father, and his big sister Johanna, and his little brother, Sandy. And down toward Norwood, where the Tye empties into the James, the riverbank where his little sister, Ginger, lay.

A Nelson County couple eventually took the boys in, and Warren stayed with them until he was seventeen. That Christmas, he moved back to Massies Mill, back into the house his family abandoned during the storm, and a year later, at Sunday school, he met Sharon. They married in 1974 and stayed that way. They have two kids.

Warren's old house still stands on the village's northern edge, plain-faced and ringed by empty lots. At the town's erstwhile heart an Oddfellows hall stands derelict, and the Masons no longer use the old buff-brick bank. The post office fell into such disrepair that the government pulled out of the building, and the tall frame general store that once dominated local commerce is empty. The only signs of its past prosperity are the rusted bottle caps and pull-tabs embedded in the asphalt out front.

At the spot where apple growers pulled off the road to do business with Warren's father, a small forest of mimosa and maple rises now, a memorial to those who died nearby. A footpath meanders among the trees and a carpet of sumac to the Tye's edge.

As for Tommy and Adelaide Huffman, they still live in the house on the promontory overlooking Davis Creek. A couple hundred yards away, silhouetted on the next hilltop, monuments to Camille's dead fill an entire section of the Oak Hill Cemetery. The Huffmans have three generations buried among them. "It took us a good while to realize just what had happened," he says.

"We were kind of in a daze, you know? I think being in that daze helped us get through it."

"Nature," he says without irony, "has a way of taking care of you."

Nelson County's 1969 downpour ranks among the most intense rainfalls in recorded American history—along with such deluges as the twelve inches that fell on Holt, Missouri, in forty-two minutes in 1947, and the thirty-four inches that pelted Smethport, Pennsylvania, over twelve hours in 1942. Camille's rain so swelled the James that a few days later the river swamped Richmond, and carried the shattered homes and forests of Nelson County all the way to Hampton Roads. Debris clogged the shipping channels.

Tommy retired from the University of Virginia, and now farms full time. He cannot remember a drought tougher on the land than this one: the ground is so dry that in place of the three harvests of hay he usually gets from his fields, he's eked out just one. Down in the valley behind the house, a few yards from the meadow where Russell's house vanished, Davis Creek seeps from a tunnel of maple, mimosa, and Judas tree. It barely clears the small pebbles on its floor. The cattle are feeding on pasture the color of sand. Wells are failing. Reservoirs are low.

Showers come now and then, but they barely moisten the topsoil. What the Blue Ridge needs is a good soaking to rescue its farms, its families.

It could sure enough use some rain.

A long, hard rain.

Late in the afternoon I round a wide bend to the left and spot, up ahead, the Route 602 bridge at Howardsville. The town dates to 1832, and during the canal days was a knot of houses and businesses clustered around a lock and aqueduct over the Rockfish River, which dumps into the James just below the bridge. Not much left of Howardsville these days—a remote crossroads just off the water, a general store on one corner. About the only outsiders it sees are fishermen and weekend canoeists who know it as a halfway point between Wingina and Scottsville, a place to camp after a few hours of leisurely paddling.

It's hard to picture the flood here, as I paddle beneath the bridge. The James's bottom, rock slabs and pebbles, is just three feet beneath the canoe. Its banks rise several feet over the water's surface. The Rockfish's mouth is narrow and overgrown, barely visible on my left. And just beyond it, incongruous but plain in the failing sunlight, is a beach—a half-moon of bright, fine sand, picnickers and sunbathers and dogs sprawled across its width. Ian is standing in its center, camera around his neck. I drive the canoe ashore, hear sand rasping on its hull, step out and take a deep breath. "Long afternoon," I sigh.

"You made good time," Ian says, then nods over his shoulder toward something behind him. "Uh, man, there's an older gentleman up there who might want to talk to you." He points toward an old fellow in a blaze-orange ball cap in a grove of trees overlooking the beach. He's leaning on a car, talking through its open window with the driver. Then he glances our way, sees me, and starts chugging downhill towards us. "He doesn't hear very well," Ian says. "I can't figure out what he's saying, exactly. He gave me a bunch of papers to read about some dispute he has with the state."

"OK," I say. "Whatever. Where's the car?" Ian points across the beach. The Volvo squats on a narrow strip of blacktop that links the rest of the planet to a Game and Inland Fisheries boat ramp off to our left, at the Rockfish's mouth. We start collecting the stuff in the bottom of the canoe, but the old guy is across the sand in no time. Well past seventy-five, to look at him, wearing a grimy short-sleeved dress shirt a size or two big, drooping dark slacks, sneakers. "Excuse me," he says. I drop the gear back into the boat and straighten up. The old man shoves a sheaf of paper into my hand. "I want you to see this," he says, "and you can see I own this land, here, and you can't park your car on my land." Mushy consonants, a mouth minus teeth.

I look at the paperwork. It appears to be an exchange of correspondence between an angry citizen and Game and Inland Fisheries. The citizen is claiming that he owns part of the property on which the state has built the boat ramp, parking lot, and approach road. The state's tone is patient and not particularly worried. I try to hand the papers back to him, but he just stands there, squinting at me. "We're just going to load up our boat," I tell him.

"Excuse me?" He fishes into his breast pocket and pulls out a hearing aid receiver the size of a cigarette pack, fiddles with its volume, gives it a whack. I notice now that wires run from the box to his ears. "We're just going to load up," I say.

"This is my land that you're parked on," he says. His voice rises to a near-shout. "You can't park there. If you're gonna use the ramp, you have to park in that parking lot." He points with a trembling finger to a small rectangle of asphalt at the ramp's top.

Ian looks over at me. "When I got here the lot was full," he says quietly.

"That car is illegally parked," our new friend tells us. "I could have it towed right out of there." He's yelling now, but smiling at me. It's weird to behold. I'm sweat-soaked, sore, and in no mood to get into a property-rights showdown with the guy. "Fine," I tell him. "We'll move it." Still holding his papers, I grab the bow of the boat. Ian picks up the stern, and we lurch across the beach. This solution fails to pacify our buddy. He sticks beside us as we slog through the sand, hollering all the while that he could have us towed, that he just might have us towed, that because we've parked on the roadside, dammit, he *will* have us towed. "You see," he explains again, "this is my land."

"We understand, sir," Ian says.

"Excuse me?" He fumbles in his pocket, evidently decides Ian's comment wasn't important. "You can't park here!"

"We'll be leaving in just a few minutes, sir."

"You saw those papers!" Still smiling.

"We'll just load up our boat, sir."

"Excuse me?"

We reach the car, drop the canoe in the road beside it. Ian jogs around to unlock the hatch. "You just wait here," the old man hollers. "Just wait here for the tow truck." I almost laugh. "Sir, look, we're going to put our boat on the car and leave," I tell him. "We're sorry we parked on your land. We didn't know it was yours."

"You can't move this car!" he hollers. Smiles broadly at me, shakes his head. "You can't move this car until I say you can move it. It's on my land!"

"Well, I'm pretty sure we *will* be moving it," I assure him. By this time the scene's attracted the interest of a couple locals, one of them a red-haired guy who looks to be in his mid-thirties. We quickly toss the gear from the canoe into the wayback, slide the paddle into the car, shut the rear hatch. We pick up the canoe and hoist it overhead, then lower it onto the roof rack. Ian opens the rear passenger door and tosses me a rope. "This car stays right here!" the old fellow yells. "I could go get my .38 and shoot out your tires!" Ian, flipping a strap over the canoe, blanches a little. "Please don't shoot us, sir," he says. I figure he must be including the Volvo in "us."

At this critical juncture the red-haired local steps forward. "Why don't you let these guys finish putting the boat on their car?" he asks the old man. "They didn't do anything to hurt you."

"They're parked on my land!" he screams.

"Well, you know if these guys came by my place on the river, I'd be happy to let them take their boat out there," Red drawls. "I'd say, 'Come on up, fellas, and have a beer, too.' He glances over at me, nods as if to say, "I really would."

"They're just canoeing on the river, is all they're doing," he says. "Now, how is that hurting you?" The old man stoops over, shakes his head. He's still smiling. "They didn't have permission to park here," he says, but his voice is lower, whiny. "This land is mine."

"I know that," Red tells him. "They know it, too. They'll probably never come back here, with you threatening to shoot their tires out. So now everybody knows it. So now let's just let these fellas tie down their boat and leave."

By now Ian and I have cinched the straps across the canoe's belly. The old-timer looks at his feet for a minute, swaying like an elephant, smiling. It's the first moment of quiet we've experienced since I hit the beach. Then he asks to see Ian's driver's license. Ian looks at me. I nod uncertainly. The landowner pulls a folded piece of paper from his pocket, spreads it flat on the Volvo's hood, and with a ballpoint pen copies Ian's name and address from the license. Ian sees this as he knots the rope at the car's front end. "Sir," he says, "please don't write on my car." Jesus, I think, this place is going to be our undoing yet. "Ian," I say, "let it go."

He can't. The old man is still writing, dragging that hard-nosed pen across thin paper. Bruising precious sheet metal beneath. "Sir," Ian booms, "please don't write on my car."

"Ian, man, c'mon," I say. "Let's just get out of here."

The old man finishes, hands Ian's license back to him. I still have his papers. I shove them into his hand, walk over to Red and thank him for his help, and we climb into the Volvo. A quick U-turn, and we're freedom-bound. I watch in amazement as the old man, still smiling, waves to us. A short ways uphill the approach road hits Route 626. A general store stands across the two-lane highway, closed but with a glowing soda machine out front. We pull into the lot, buy a couple of Dr. Peppers and drink them while leaning against the car, a few feet from a sign in the store window that warns us not to loiter. "Howardsville," I sigh, rubbing the cold, sweating can on my forehead.

"Man," Ian says.

"That was totally out of hand."

"He actually threatened to shoot us!"

I chuckle a little, and the chuckle becomes a laugh of relief and fatigue and wonder at the absurdity of what we've just been through, and after a moment Ian starts laughing, too, and we stand in the parking lot laughing like idiots for a good two minutes straight. Finally I nod toward the sign. "Maybe we ought to get the hell out of here."

"Before that old guy comes up the road after us," Ian agrees.

Down river lies Scottsville, where we rent a couple of rooms at Lumpkin's, a family restaurant and motel. After grabbing showers we reconvene in the parking lot, and drive down the town's main road to the Pig and Steak, a barbecue joint hallowed among canoeists and tubers on this stretch of the James. We gorge on barbecued pork and mountains of fries, drink icy beers, and revel in feeling clean and well-fed and in no hurry to leave. It's well after dark when we finally pay the bill and stroll farther down the main drag to the hump-backed concrete bridge carrying traffic over the river. Crickets sing along the woody banks below, their calls swelling and fading with the breeze, as we stare down at the water. It flows silent, syrupy and black, moonlight shimmering on its surface.

"Big Jim," Ian murmurs, leaning over the guardrail.

"Yup."

"Our river," he says.

"It feels that way, doesn't it?"

"Yeah, man," he says. "Like we own it."

"We do," I tell him. "We know it better than anyone, right now. It's ours."

We gaze upriver, to where the James curves sharply to the left and disappears beyond riverbank trees and the high south bank. As we do, I recall the suds dotting its surface in the early morning, the questions Kim and Philip had about the water's safety. And suddenly I'm no longer sated by dinner and beer, no longer feeling at peace. A wave of gloom washes over me. As beautiful as it looks from here, I think, this river—*our* river—is sick. Battered. Willfully so. God knows what man-made trouble coexists with its gar and alligator snappers and smallmouth bass, what perils lurk in its seemingly crystalline shallows. And we've traveled just the river's uplands. We've seen its best face. It gets worse, I realize, from here.

DAY THIRTEEN

An old carving, an old ferry, and an old town at the horseshoe bend

🦪 Hidden among the boulders and roiling rapids below the James's Goosby Island Falls is a dark slab of bedrock that bears a hand-chiseled inscription, "1774." Who the determined carver was who crouched at the head of a stormy three-foot cascade to chisel it is long forgotten, but it's there still, a hardy survivor of more than two centuries, at the tip of a tiny island that splits a remote stretch of the James in Albemarle County.

It's midmorning, little more than an hour downstream from the day's start at Howardsville, where this time Ian and I parked the car in the Official Boat Ramp Parking Lot and dashed headlong across the empty beach to dump the canoe in the water. I've spent the time since paddling through gentle bends and over small rock ledges, looking forward to reaching this little-known inscription, for it harkens to the days when a trip on the James was rugged business.

I have to stay alert while swirling through the falls, picking my way past rocks, fighting the powerful pull of the water. I reach an eddy below the island, drag the boat onto dry ground and walk a hundred feet back upstream to the island's head, eyes peeled for copperheads. Cicadas thrum from the shore. Dry leaves rustle in the gusty breeze. When I reach the island's west end I splash into the river to examine the rocks lining the narrow channel, searching for the numbers. My memory's foggy: it's been three summers since I was last on this section of the James, the only stretch I traveled before embarking on this trip. My earlier float trip bore little resemblance to the two weeks I've spent paddling my high-tech plastic canoe. My vehicle then was a batteau, a reproduction of the flat-bottomed cargo boats that two centuries ago swarmed the James to carry tobacco, iron ore, and wheat from the mountainous west to the Tidewater. Its round-chined hull, forty feet long, eight feet wide and pointed at both ends, was built of oak plank fastened with square-headed nails. It derived its power solely from the muscle of its crew. Its only steering lay in enormous sweep oars at bow and stern. Its only comforts: rough bunks shaded by a curving, Conestoga canopy of bentwood and canvas, exposed to slanting rain and patrolled by fist-sized wolf spiders.

The boat was called *The Pride of Campbell County*, and its skipper was a stocky, knickers-clad guy in his early forties named David Haney. Fifty-one weeks a year, Haney worked as a conductor on the CSX Railroad, eyeing the James from the track that hugs the river's north bank. His wife managed an after-school day care program in the couple's home in Evington, in the Blue Ridge foothills southwest of Lynchburg. Glen Shrewsbury, on the stern sweep, was a machinist. His wife, Brenda, kept their house in Forest, a speck on the map west of Lynchburg in sparsely settled Bedford County.

But each summer they ditched their modern lives, donned the calf-length britches and muslin blouses of the late eighteenth century, and joined the James River Batteau Festival, a tribute to the river and the boatmen who braved it to open the West. The festival replicates the journey once undertaken by thousands of the boats between downtown Lynchburg and Richmond. Latter-day batteaumen pole their way downriver, tie up at camps crowded with period tents, and cook over open fires to a soundtrack of tin whistles and dulcimers and bygone love songs and laments. And like the batteaux of old, the *Pride of Campbell County* and sixteen other replicas on the river that day required fast-thinking skippers, resolute crews, and a measure of luck to squeeze through the boulder fields, thump over the shoals, and blast down the chutes that the river put in their way.

For seventy years before the James River and Kanawha Canal opened to Lynchburg, batteaux dominated the river's cargo trade. Early in the eighteenth century, inland plantation owners faced the daunting prospect of delivering their crops to market in the Tidewater. The river at their feet offered the readiest solution: on it, they could ship their wares in a fraction of the time it took to negotiate the steep, stumpy mud wallows that were the roads of the day. The river provided a direct link to overseas markets, as well. Just below Richmond lay Rocketts, where river cargo could be transferred to the sailing ships that plied the James' final hundred miles to the Chesapeake Bay, and the sea.

Problem was, the flatboats and rafts then in fashion didn't stand a chance in the falls and rapids that punctuated the route. Some farmers tried Indian dugouts. They were fast, but not big enough to carry much cargo. Then Robert Rose, a traveling parson and tobacco planter with a large spread in Nelson County, figured a way to lash two dugouts together and deck them with a wooden platform. This rude catamaran was stable, reasonably maneuverable, and big enough to carry several hogsheads of tobacco. Before long folks on the river were calling them tobacco canoes. Piedmont planters found they carried a load using a third of the men needed for an overland journey, and they were cheap to use: in Richmond the platforms could be sold for lumber, and the dugouts paddled back upstream.

The parson's invention didn't stick. Central Virginia was waylaid by the great flood of May 1771, a disaster that wouldn't be equaled until Camille, nearly two hundred years later. Virtually all of the river's dugout canoes were swept away or reduced to matchsticks. Anthony and Benjamin Rucker, settlers living north of Lynchburg, devised a new craft, a wood-plank freighter pointed at both ends that crewmen pushed along by standing at the bow, jamming their poles into the riverbed, then leaning into the poles as they walked to the stern on planks fastened along the gunwales.

The James River batteau was born. Within a few years the Ruckers had been copied hundreds of times, and the river was crowded with batteaux and their three-man crews shooting the rapids to Richmond. To tobacco planters seeking self-sufficiency and low overhead, it made sense to use their own employees—in other words, slaves—to crew the boats. In Virginia's burgeoning slave economy, the batteau workforce quickly became dominated by African-Americans. They were a hardy and proud lot, strong-muscled and steely-nerved—and they comprised one of the first black professional brotherhoods in America. Frank Padget was one such batteau runner, or headman, when he took on his ill-fated mission to rescue the *Clinton* at Balcony Falls. Today a headman's image is immortalized in bronze on Brown's Island in downtown Richmond, and a batteau crewman, pole in hand, is the centerpiece of the city's flag.

At the island's upper tip I snoop among the rocks until I find the carving that Haney pointed out to me on that past trip. I'd joined the *Pride of Campbell County* for just a small portion of its eight-day struggle, and had been lucky enough to win a place with a captain who knew the river well. The numbers take the fanciful form of eighteenth-century handwriting, their serifs overstated, their curves precise. I run my fingers over the cuts, wondering how long they took to make, then splash farther upstream, looking for a date that I'd discovered in another rock while searching with Haney for the "1774." What had it read? 1802? 1806? I can't quite recall, and I can't find it today.

Instead I squat on a round-topped rock that rises just above the rushing water, and look down the path the batteaux took through the falls below. I try to imagine such ungainly wooden tubs, heavy with hogsheads of tobacco and farm produce, squeezing between the rocks. Nineteenth-century travelogues were rife with warnings of such whitewater, of hidden stumps and killer boulders. "It was with extreme difficulty that our boat could be got through with 7 hands," surveyor Thomas Moore wrote of these very rapids in 1818. "Several boats have been lost on this fall."

The same report said of Joshua Falls, just below Lynchburg and a high point of the festival's first day, "Very hard for ascending Boats & one rock which might be easily removed dangerous in descending, on which several have been wrecked & some lives lost." This was no hyperbole. Boatmen of old drowned in the floods that swelled the placid James into a run-amok beast. They were dashed against rocks. Running aground presented the gruesome prospect of being crushed between boat and boulder. Even if they escaped injury, they faced constant threats to their boats and cargo. As William E. Trout of Richmond, Virginia's foremost expert on batteau and canal travel, puts it: "Whenever you read about them, the references are not to 'boatmen' but to 'skilled boatmen.' They had to be, to go down the river when it was running at any level and not get their cargoes wet or destroy their boats—or themselves."

Batteaux dominated the river's cargo traffic until 1840, aided along the way by the construction of sluices that shot the boats around some of the tougher rapids. One such sluice survives here, just a few feet from the inscription below Goosby Island. Its rock walls are still largely intact after 224 years.

These primitive aids to navigation weren't enough to guarantee the safety of batteaux and their crews. After the Revolution the demand for smoother passage between Richmond and the hinterlands helped spur the canal's construction. Obsolete, the batteaux fell into disuse. By the time the railroad arrived, the old riverboats were rarities; by the early twentieth century, they had disappeared so completely that no one could be sure how they'd been put together.

Until 1983, when construction crews excavating the site of the James Center in downtown Richmond dug into the remains of the city's old canal turning basin. It had been filled and paved over decades before, but still contained, in the mud that once formed its bed, a fleet of sunken canal boats and batteaux. The following year a group of upriver history buffs used the unearthed boats as a model for their own batteau, the *Columbia,* and floated it to Richmond. Others followed suit, and the festival started soon after. Now, escorted by dozens of canoeists and a ragtag caravan of musicians, gypsy jewelers, and funnel-cake vendors, the water-borne parade has grown into one of central Virginia's most eagerly anticipated celebrations. Thousands of festival-goers drink in their river's history each year, getting an education rich in sweat and sore muscles and moments of panic. Stand on a batteau's prow on a misty early morning on these far-flung stretches of the James, no power lines or houses or bridges in sight, no contrails overhead, and it's easy to imagine yourself in an age when these ungainly vessels were the backbone of Virginia commerce. Do it while the 3,500-pound boat groans over a falls, and you might wonder how any commerce happened at all.

Relics of the batteau days, and of days even further back than that, abound on this stretch of river. At the rapids below Goosby Island I'm close to the site of a town, Fallsburg, that has vanished without a trace—despite a high degree of bustle, an image as an up-and-comer among riverbank towns, and its possession of a mill, grocery, shoe shop, a tannery, the obligatory saloon, a gambling house and—though it seems hard to believe—a one-mile race course. A mile downstream I paddle past the old town of Warren. Nothing remains of this settlement on the north side but a wire strung across the river that once guided a hand-poled ferry boat across the James. The old ferry itself lies weed-punched and half-buried in riverbank mud.

Just below Warren I encounter the Rock Island Falls, named for a small island dominated by a high rocky promontory on its upper end. A batteau sluice rises nearly intact from the river's low water, and I use it to paddle around the falls and the island's right side, studying the balled-up and rusted remains of a bridge truss carried here by a past flood. And a mile or so below that, I beach the canoe on the north bank to admire the Hatton ferry, one of only two muscle-operated ferries left in the continental United States. It's a throwback to the river crossings of two centuries ago, when at least 140 ferries broached the James and other Virginia rivers, and such cities as Buchanan and Lynchburg were getting their starts as ferry terminals.

The Hatton ferry is parked, idle until the weekend; the only soul around is a guy dozing on top of a picnic table outside the ferry's empty office. I wake him with a yell from the bank, only to find he doesn't work here—he's a vacationing general district court judge from the Northern Neck named Tris Hyde. He climbs off the table and tells me he's been goose hunting, and points out a dozen or so Canada goose decoys clustered at the water's edge, next to an ancient aluminum canoe. Now he's waiting, he says, for his hunting buddies to show up with their car so they can head home. He asks whether I've seen any geese on the river.

"Absolutely," I tell him. "All morning. There are Canadas all over." This is true: three or four times, while paddling around the river's languid bends this morning, I've accidentally set off explosions of splashes and honks and beating wings. He grimaces. "Haven't seen a goose anywhere," he mutters.

We stroll downhill from his picnic table to the shore, where the judge points out the ferry's ingenious system for getting people and vehicles across the two hundred-yard-wide river. It uses the James's current to supplement the muscle of its crew: the ferry is tethered at bow and stern to an overhead cable spanning the river, just like the one I passed under at Warren. Its drivers use the tethers to point either end of the boat slightly upstream, and the river shoves the diagonally positioned boat across the water like a sailboat tacking in wind. Swing the bow upstream and the ferry travels the cable from north bank to south; lower the bow and bring up the stern, and it heads back across.

"This is a powerful river," Hyde says quietly. I nod. "You come down here sometimes and you'll find stop signs, all kinds of stuff, up in the trees, left by high water," he says. "We came down one time and we found a dead cow—a dead cow, up in the crook of a tree, fifteen, sixteen, seventeen feet up." I recall the descriptions of the James swollen by Camille, and a *New York Times* dispatch I'd read describing the 1870 flood, and an immense debris pile that had washed against a bridge. "Several bureaus," it read, "a piano, tables, chairs, wash-stands, tubs, barrels, bee-hives, buckets, sofas, desks, carriages, mangled bodies of sheep and swine, mowing-machines, ladders, staircases, mill-gearing, washboards, stove-pipes, doors, window-sashes, brooms, blinds, bedsteads, cradles, picture frames, benches, and hundreds of other things, are all wedged in pell-mell with the driftwood."

"It's a very powerful river," the judge murmurs again.

From Hatton the James makes a strong leftward bend, runs straight for about a mile, then coils into a tight, horseshoe curve, reversing its course. Scottsville, the site of my planned midday rendezvous with Ian, lies on the outside of this loop. Halfway there I encounter a trio of inner-tubers—a pony-tailed, bearded fellow and two young women—floating on the James with a cooler and a tiny Labrador puppy. The tubes are almost becalmed in the water; if they're moving at all, it's at something like a quarter of a knot. The noon sun is scorching. It's going to be a long float to Scottsville.

The puppy is crawling zestfully over one of the women, whose name is Madonna, as she reads a paperback. As I pass, the dog suddenly leaps off her shoulder and disappears into the river. Without looking up from her book, Madonna reaches into the water, fishes around for what seems an eternity, and finally hoists the puppy from the deep by the scruff of its neck. "We got some liquor," the other woman yells to me, holding up a hip flask of brown liquid. "You want a hit?"

I thank her but decline the offer, and paddle into Scottsville, where I find Ian and the Volvo in a riverside park shaded by trees and aswarm with yellow jackets. The town climbing up the bluff behind us has a history inextricably linked to the James. It was founded for its proximity to the river, and in 1827 became the chief shipping point for the mountain counties behind me—Augusta, Bath, Highland, Pendleton, Rockbridge—when a forty-three-mile turnpike linked it to Staunton, and the farmers of the upper James and the Shenandoah. Each year, some fifty thousand bushels of wheat were hauled down the turnpike to Scottsville's mills, and hundreds of hogsheads of tobacco were loaded into batteaux at its waterfront docks. In 1830, the mills and the town's warehouses, strung along the north bank here, handled twenty-five thousand barrels of flour for later delivery to Richmond. An 1835 gazetteer found the place "a flourishing village," with "120 houses, chiefly of brick; one Methodist and one Presbyterian house of worship; a male and a female school, and two Sunday schools, nine general and five grocery stores, and one apothecaries shop.

"The principal manufactures are clothing, leather shoes, cabinet work, and earthenware," the publication reported, adding that the town "carries on an extensive trade in flour, bacon, butter, lard, and other products." And that wasn't its peak. With the canal's 1840 opening, Scottsville exploded. Within a decade, it was the largest flour market in the state and a station house for travelers transferring between the long Staunton plank road and canalboat.

Alas, the Civil War came. In March 1865, Union Gen. Phil Sheridan rode into town and encamped here. His ten thousand troops, among them Gen. George Armstrong Custer, briefly made Scottsville one of the biggest cities in the South. The Yankees did a number on the canal before they left, and it never really recovered. In 1881 the waterway was drained for good, and the town began a slide toward retirement, morphing into a far-flung getaway for big-city visitors, which it remains today. Among the more notable twentieth-century weekenders was Teddy Roosevelt, who built a hunting lodge near Scottsville and was often seen in town.

Local tradition holds that Thomas Jefferson holed up in a cave below Scott's Landing during the Revolution. Supposedly, his brother Randolph, who kept a big house near town, directed him to it while the former Virginia governor was hiding from the British. The story isn't hard to believe, because if there's a phrase that best characterizes Jefferson's late days as governor, it's "on the lam." The future third president was a great man with a powerful brain and an incredible range of interests, but he was no soldier, and he spent a good bit of time simply *running*. I can't verify the legend, however. Below Scottsville I'm standing on my knees, neck craned to see beyond the CSX tracks on the left bank, and I see no caves, no rock shelters, no nothing.

A short while later, clouds slide in from the west. Rain starts to dimple the river's surface. Thunder, more annoyed-sounding than threatening, rumbles overhead. I study the banks, ready to beach the canoe and run for cover if bolts start dropping, but none come. The rain dwindles to a heavy, chilled damp. After the morning's heat, it's sweet relief.

Late in the afternoon I paddle past another old batteau sluice at Seven Islands, an archipelago of low isles and countless rocks on a wide curve of river that occupies most all of its floodplain. The stone around me is dark and algae-slimed, imbued with a silent, sullen wisdom, with the energy an object acquires simply by witnessing the passage of years, the lives lived in its proximity.

I wonder whether the carver of the "1774," fast-forwarded somehow to this place, this day, and out of sight of cities and people—particularly people in inner tubes—would detect that more than two centuries have passed since he left his mark. A few things might give it away, I figure. But not immediately. Then I catch a movement in the corner of my eye and turn to see a bald eagle, head and tail glowing in the rainy gloom, leap from a tree on the James's edge and flap silently downriver.

DAY FOURTEEN

On which puny-brained geese outsmart us, and the fist of an angry God swings oh so close

Ballooned with mammoth, artery-clogging Lumpkin's breakfasts, Ian and I pack our gear, empty the rooms, and stagger to the car, bound for the boat ramp at Bremo Bluff. We pull onto State Route 6, which wends its way to Richmond on the looping path of an ancient Indian trail, enjoying the bright coolness of the early morning sun, the damp blast of wind buffeting the Volvo's interior.

We lose a few minutes when we spot an old fire tower off the highway and set out to climb it. Its height might give us a vantage to eyeball Bremo, a rose-brick manor with massive Roman porticos that lies off to the south of the road, invisible behind acres of creased pastureland and heavy woods. The house is reputed to be among the most beautiful in America—not a surprise, seeing as how Thomas Jefferson's notations were all over the plans for the building. Those plans burned up in an 1894 fire at the University of Virginia, but not before Jefferson was widely credited with the mansion's design.

Bremo has an interesting history going for it, too. It was built by Gen. John Hartwell Cocke, who was among the South's most vociferous critics of slavery in the years between the Revolution and the Civil War; he called the arrangement "the cancer eating upon the vitals of the Commonwealth," and in one 1832 letter wrote, "I have long and still steadfastly believe that Slavery is the great cause of all the chief evils of our land, individual as well as national." Cocke lived just long enough to see Virginia and the rest of the Confederacy pay a steep price for disagreeing with him.

Unfortunately, the tower's on private property, the base of its staircase papered with "No Trespassing" signs, and nobody's home in the adjacent house. For a couple minutes we discuss climbing it anyway. What's the worst that could happen? Injury? Not likely. Arrest? Well, maybe. We lose our nerve. We drive on to Bremo Bluff, on the river's north bank, where we stop at the post office to mail postcards. It's a snug hamlet of restored Sears mail-order houses and sparkling cottages, with a ready source of income: the stacks of a huge power plant loom just to the east.

Across the John H. Cocke Memorial Bridge, on the James' south bank, all signs of prosperity evaporate. No Bremo mansions dominate the high ground overlooking the river. There are no bright bungalows, no fat paychecks. The south side of the bridge seems on the brink of abandonment. A gasoline station turned antique store is a hollow cinder-block shell ringed by weedy, broken concrete. Buildings of wood plank warped and frayed with neglect lean, staggering, beside the road, courting complete collapse at any moment. One long-empty house has been reclaimed by scrubby forest; only its gingerbread-trimmed gables are visible through an embrace of vines. "Good God," I mutter, flipping through my packet of maps, "what's the name of this place?"

"New Canton," Ian says, steering the car through the decay.

"Huh," I reply. "Well, let me tell you, if this is *New* Canton, I'd hate to see Old Canton."

"Wow, look at that!" He points at an old commercial building that is leaning drunkenly over the road. We glide past it in silence, half expecting it to topple. "I've gotta come back here and make some photographs," Ian says. "This place is a wreck."

Half an hour later I'm paddling around a long, slow bend to the left, a broad floodplain around me. Beyond the plain, steep bluffs rise in the crook of the bend. Over on the south bank, the hills are far less dramatic. Well, why not? I think. The James's left bank has always had the breaks—most of the money, most of the power, most of the people. The Jamestown party chose the north bank, and it stayed the preferred side among planters staking off grand plantations upriver, and among Richmond's founders, and among the canal builders pushing west. The canal spawned towns on the north bank and the railroad more, while the south stayed wild, unpopulated. It remains so, relatively speaking, even today: New Canton, forlorn as it seems, is among only a few settlements on the central James's right bank. The last one back was—what?—Bent Creek? That's a stretch of essentially undeveloped waterfront more than fifty miles long.

Years ago, a man named Parke Rouse Jr. published a book called *Below the James Lies Dixie* that suggested the Southside—Virginia's long, agrarian belly, sandwiched between the river and the North Carolina line—has more in common with the Deep South than it does with the rest of its state. Along this stretch of the James, that rings true. Stretching away from the south bank is territory that resembles the north side decades ago: an essentially cityless expanse of pine forest, cotton patches, and tobacco and peanut fields, its population underpaid and simply housed, suspicious of outsiders and resistant to change.

On a long straightaway I glide past a pair of overgrown islands. I'm peering through the scrawny maple and ash that crowd them when I hear the sounds of a downtown traffic jam, far off. It takes a second to figure out that they're coming from above me. Canada geese pass overhead in ragged chevrons, necks straining, wings flapping urgently, two dozen of them hurrying south. I pause my paddling to listen to their distant honks. Their haste seems a little premature: it's a breezeless morning, muggy, the sun furnace-hot, just as it has been almost every morning since I set out from the Hevener farm. I've just begun the day's work, and already I'm a sweaty mess in the canoe, T-shirt soaked, my grip on the paddle slick and uncertain. What could press the birds to fly deeper into the heat, on a day like this?

The straight section of river is miles long. Each crawls by. The sun rises to mid-sky. My paddling slows. I thump over a couple sets of small rapids, encounter shallows that almost ground the canoe, but experience nothing that can take my mind off the heat. The high ground on both sides of the water seems to press closer. The air tastes like steam from a pressure cooker. Then, around a gentle bend to the right, a concrete bridge materializes, and I actually yelp for joy. Ian's standing on a boat ramp just above the crossing. I ram the canoe ashore and stagger onto the ramp, weak-kneed. "Am I glad to see you," I croak. "It's like the sunny side of Mercury out there." He nods knowingly. "It's about like that in the car, too." I see that his shirt is as rank-looking as mine.

We leave the canoe by the water's edge and walk uphill to the Volvo, swing the hatch up and lean against the back bumper while guzzling drinks. They do little to take the fire out of the day. But before we've finished our first PBJs, Ian notices that clouds are moving in from the northwest, dark and gray, bloated-looking and hanging low. The sun disappears. Shadows disappear. The wind picks up, blows little dust devils around the top of the boat ramp, sends an empty cigarette pack skittering, and the temperature drops ten degrees, maybe more, in the space of two minutes. You can smell rain coming. "This could get exciting," I say.

Ian, between chews: "What do you want to do?"

"I don't know. I'm not thrilled by the idea of a lightning storm."

"You see any lightning?"

I watch the sky for a full minute. I see no flashes, hear no rumbles. "Let's keep going," I tell him, "and just plan to meet every half-hour or so, in case it turns ugly." I nod across the river, to the far side of the bridge. "You check out Columbia?"

"Yeah," he says. "Not much to it."

Sure enough, the burg across the way is not much of a town. Situated on the James's north bank at its junction with the Rivanna—a wide, powerful stream that arcs far to the northwest, past Monticello and Charlottesville—Columbia is an old train station, a few unpainted and deeply weathered country store buildings, and a sprinkling of houses along Route 6. But a lot has happened here. In the canal's heyday, this was an important wayside, and the canal's junction with a second man-made waterway heading up the Rivanna. During the Revolution, it was known as Point of Fork, and in the namesake point—the sharp wedge of land formed by the rivers' confluence—Americans kept an ammo dump, which they abandoned to the British after a wily Redcoat commander had his small force build a huge number of campfires near the town, tricking the revolutionaries into thinking that the whole British army was massing there. Before that, boatmen knew this place as the Forks of the James. In those days, maps had the James River end here: cartographers called the river I've paddled since Iron Gate the Fluvanna, and its waters, combined with the Rivanna's, created the big river below. And long before that, this place was called Rasawek, and was reputedly the chief city of the Monacans, a much-feared Indian tribe that controlled the riverside turf from the Blue Ridge to the Falls of the James at present-day Richmond.

It may have been the Monacans who built a great burial mound along the Rivanna north of the present-day University of Virginia in Charlottesville, which Thomas Jefferson explored and described in his writings. Burial mounds once dotted this part of the Piedmont, as they did the whole state west of the Fall Line. Most were near old Indian villages; a few marked the locations of battles. All were situated to offer the best view of the surrounding scenery. "I have gone through cemeteries laid out in serpentine walks and embowered in roses and shrubbery," wrote a nineteenth-century commentator who used the pen name "Montanus." "I have read epitaphs chiseled deep in the snow-white marble; but never have I seen the place which I thought more appropriate as a resting-place for the dead than the spot were [*sic*] the mounds . . . are located."

Unfortunately, a good many fell victim to amateur archaeologists like Mr. Jefferson. In September 1901, Edward P. Valentine of Richmond dug up a grass-covered mound four and one-half feet tall and sixty to sixty-four feet in diameter near Hays Creek, a tributary of the upper Maury in Rockbridge County. He found hundreds of well-preserved human skeletons inside, snugly arranged and curled into fetal positions. Valentine took some pictures, then boxed up the skeletons and hauled them back to Richmond. They remained in the collection of the Valentine Museum for decades. Other mounds were discovered along the Cowpasture in Bath County—five in one bend, another a ways off that was thought to contain one to two hundred bodies. Still another rose from beside U.S. Route 11, in the Valley north of Staunton. They and dozens of others are gone now, those not picked apart by looters destroyed by field plows, as was one of the Bath County sites. "It is now almost worn down to a level," Montanus reported in 1850, "and the earth is black and rich from the dust of man."

"It is a levelling age we live in," he lamented. "The grasping desire for land, which seizes on the Indian's home, will not spare his grave, when he is gone."

Our first rendezvous comes at a washed-out bridge three miles downstream. Ian finds the bridgehead on a narrow county farm road and hacks his way to the water's edge as I approach, pushed by a strengthening tailwind. The sky has continued to darken. Clouds are low and racing. "What do you want to do?" Ian asks. The vanished bridge's concrete pillars loom around him.

We're silent for a minute, listening. No thunder. "It's seven miles to Cartersville," I say. "That's two hours of paddling."

"A long time to be on the water with a storm coming up."

I glumly nod my agreement. Rain wouldn't bother me in the least—actually, compared with the heat that's dogged me through the day, it'd be sweet—but should lightning start shooting around halfway between here and Cartersville, I'd be in trouble. We inspect the maps, looking for a closer take-out. There isn't one. "Thing is, we can't quit for the day with so little paddling behind us," I say. "Let's keep going. We'll meet in Cartersville."

"OK." Ian stands up. "Two hours."

"Make it an hour and forty minutes," I tell him, pushing away from the bank. "I'll pour it on."

Halfway to Cartersville the rain comes. It's over quickly, but it's so intense that it dumps a couple inches of water into the bottom of the canoe. Still, I hear no thunder. I paddle on. The rain stops, and I bake dry in the sunshine and heat. At Cartersville, another south bank settlement at a bridge crossing, the threat of bad weather seems passed: clouds still roll over the river, but they're several shades lighter than those that came before. Ian and I decide to press on to West View, a remote boat landing on the north bank in Goochland County, about five miles farther.

An hour later I'm paddling comfortably along a series of wide bends through flat farmland and forest when I suddenly notice that I hear no cicadas in the trees, and no cricket chirps, either. The gnats that usually hover in low clouds over the water have vanished. No birds fly by. The river is utterly, eerily silent. I glance over my left shoulder and gasp. A huge thunderhead is swooping down on me, its crown towering thousands of feet skyward, its innards swirling, wispy tentacles hanging from its bottom and curling around the treetops, the cloudbank's entire mass the color of charcoal. It's like seeing the heavens ball up a fist.

At that moment a blast of cold wind practically upends the boat. The trees on both banks rustle loudly, then start swaying, and the air fills with dry leaves. The temperature plummets. I have just enough time to paddle into the lee of the left bank before the rain comes all at once, in buckets, so hard that the big drops smacking the canoe's bottom sound like a drumroll. The drops are cold. Waves sweep over the James, and a foglike mist springs from the water. Darkness descends.

The rain intensifies, pelts so hard that now the world around me disappears. I can see nothing of the right bank; can make out the left, just fifteen yards away, only as a dim ghost. The river ahead merges with the mist and the darkness so seamlessly that I seem to be paddling toward a dense, gray wall. A johnboat roars past on my right, the sound of its motor consumed by the hiss of rain hitting the river, its fisherman driver watching dispassionately as his wake slams into the canoe's sides. He and his boat vanish in seconds. I peer through the fog to the north bank's spectral trees, strategizing: Where do I go when the lightning starts, as it seems sure to do? Where's safe? With growing alarm I realize there's no sanctuary off the river. Beyond the bank's four-foot bulwark of rust-colored soil is nothing but flat, treeless pastureland.

So, my heart beating fast, I keep paddling. The wind seems to blow in every direction at once, sometimes punching straight down on me from the clouds. Whirls of dead leaves circle the boat. Water fills the canoe's bottom— one inch, then two, then three, then four. Then, far ahead, a pair of headlights pierces yellow through the storm's bruiselike gloom. It's Ian, using the Volvo as a lighthouse, and I point the boat toward the beams, put my head down and paddle like mad.

I find him standing on the West View boat ramp, water cascading off his hooded jacket, legs and socks and boots sodden. The car's lights are the only clue to its presence just a few yards away. We have to yell to hear each other over the rain's din as we dump water from the canoe and strap it to the roof.

Sitting in the car a few minutes later, soaked and cold, the windows fogging around us, I pull my maps from my drybag and see that the boat ramp is tucked behind an island, and that the James' main channel flows on the island's far side. Had Ian not guided me to safety, I'd have surely paddled to the island's right, past the narrow channel to West View. God knows how far I'd have paddled before realizing my mistake—or what we'd have done about it.

DAY FIFTEEN

On which the expedition escapes State Farm in a hell-for-leather dash

West View is still a mass of puddles as we pull up in the Volvo, bleary-eyed after a tough night in camp. We had a hell of a time finding a campground anywhere near the river, even considered doubling back to Scottsville to hole up for a third night at Lumpkin's. Eventually, though, we spotted a commercial campground on the map, about fifteen miles south of the James, and steered that way. The choice seemed auspicious: halfway there, we pulled into a gas station to fuel up the wagon and found that its convenience store boasted not only an impressive array of foreign beer, but a Taco Bell. Loaded up with gasoline, Harp, and about ten pounds of fast food, we rolled on through the dark bottomland.

The campground was a big place, sparsely occupied by motor homes and travel trailers parked on gravel pads cut diagonally through a forest of maple and pine. The combination store and office at its entrance was closed when we arrived, so we passed it by to nose slowly along narrow drives that curved over swells and sags in the terrain, squinting through the gloom for some sign of a tent site. There were none; all of the spaces we found seemed designed for motorized camping. All were floored in rock. After a couple orbits around the place we wound up back at the office, where this time we found the campground's manager, a meaty guy in his fifties, waiting in a Jeep. We followed him into the building, waited as he turned on the lights and took up a position behind the counter. "We need a tent site," I told him.

"There are plenty out there. You have your pick of the place." He spread a map of the campground on the counter before us. "OK," I said, leaning over the map, "where, exactly, are they?" He didn't seem to understand the question. "All of these," he said, a finger drawing a circle around the whole camp. "They're *all* tent sites."

"Well, the ones we saw seemed set up for motor homes," I said. "They were gravel."

"It's soft," he replied.

"Soft," I repeated. "The gravel."

"Fine for tents," he nodded. "People put up tents here all the time." He looked up from the map. "What did you expect?"

"Grass," I shrugged.

He cocked an eyebrow. "You can't have people camping on grass," he declared.

"Huh?"

"Well, sure," he said. "You have tents on the grass all the time, the grass dies. I don't know of any campgrounds that let people do that."

I felt like giving him a list. Instead, with the hour getting late, I paid the man and walked with Ian back to the car. "This sucks," Ian muttered.

"Yup. We're in for a long night." I'd left my window rolled down. Now I opened my door, and in the dome light's glow beheld a massive orange house cat crouched over the Taco Bell bag, its jaws wrapped around a chicken burrito. Ian and I started screaming as the cornered animal darted into the driver's seat, then back over the food, then froze, head whipping back and forth between us. Finally it sprang past me into the dark, skittering on the parking lot's loose pebbles. "Damn it!" I hollered. "That thing ate half my dinner!"

Ian groaned. "I don't know about this place," he said. "We have to camp on rocks, and now this. It doesn't bode well."

Not for nothing did he worry. Full of beer and those portions of our meal the cat didn't finish, we repaired to our respective tents to discover that the "soft" gravel felt like beds of nails. Sharp chunks of rock poked through my sleeping pad, insinuated themselves between my ribs, jabbed my hips and already-sore shoulders. I shifted the mattress a half dozen times, trying to find a smoother rectangle of floor, and finally gave up and drifted into a fitful sleep.

It's a relief to get back to the river. We lug the canoe across West View's red mud, and are collecting the smaller gear from the wayback when a pickup pulls up, a trailer behind it loaded with a small bass boat. The truck's bearded driver rolls down his window. "Where's the best place to put in if we want to get near the State Farm?" he asks.

State Farm is a half day's paddle downstream, and the home of a sprawling quiltwork of penitentiaries and prison farms along both sides of the James

(EARL SWIFT PHOTO.)

IAN, FRESH FROM A CLENCH
WITH HIS SWEDISH PILLOW, GATHERS
HIS WITS TO POUR HOT WATER
FOR COFFEE.

in Goochland and Powhatan counties. "You planning a breakout?" I ask. The guy slumped in the pickup's passenger seat, a squirrelly looking, unshaved character, doesn't so much as smile. The thought enters my head that maybe I have too big a mouth. The driver chuckles, though. "No," he says. "Just heard that there are some rocks in the water there that are good fishing." He produces a state highway map, on which the James is a narrow, featureless blue line, and State Farm a small dot. "They're somewhere around here," he says. His fingertip covers a dozen square miles of territory. I fetch my own set of maps from the car, flip through them to State Farm, find a stretch of rocks and rapids that begins a mile below the prison complex and continues for two or three miles. About eighteen miles downstream from here. "That'll probably be it," I tell him. I point out one midstream boulder that's actually named—Tom Rock, for an unfortunate boat captain who apparently ran into it twice, long ago. The driver studies my map for a long minute, then thanks us. We watch the pickup leave, creaking over the potholed mud.

I turn to Ian, the maps still open in my hand. "You know, there's not a heck of a lot between here and there, in terms of our getting together," I tell him. "Looks like we've got eleven or twelve miles before the first decent place to meet." He examines the chart, agrees that a bridge crossing at Maidens looks to be our best bet. "OK," he says. "I'll just plan to be there in three hours or so."

"Good deal," I say. "What are you gonna do in the meantime?"

Ian sighs. "Maybe try to sleep in the car for a while."

Half an hour later I round a gentle bend to the left presided over by Rock Castle, a lofty outcropping on the north bank. Small islands appear, ringed by dark, gumdrop-shaped boulders. The James widens slightly, its depth decreasing as it does; soon the water is only inches deep in places, crisscrossed by hidden sandbars and humps of gravel. A mile and a half below Rock Castle I scrape along the right bank, and rolling farmland that in the early nineteenth century was a busy little village called Jefferson, now faded without a trace. Six miles farther, I pass the unfortunately named Lickinghole Creek. I slow as I do, peering into its mouth to an old canal aqueduct that spans its width. The structure is one of Goochland County's treasures, a seldom-seen but often-painted blend of strength and delicacy; framed by creekside trees, it vaults Lickinghole in a low, long arc, a sharp departure from the more vertical, conservative spans elsewhere on the canal route.

I cross the river to the creek's mouth, fighting bottom that grinds against the hull all the way, and float motionless at the confluence for a few minutes, staring at the light-colored, hand-cut stone shaped somehow into this graceful work of art. Who were the men who built this? I wonder. How long did it take them? I often marvel during interstate drives at the scale of roadbuilding, the mountains chopped and streams bridged and tunnels dug to get a highway through uneven country. The interstate highway system is America's answer to the pyramids, an accomplishment so monumental that it almost defies understanding. But modern highways are built of concrete and steel, materials that make for speedy progress. An interstate hundreds of miles long can be surveyed, graded, and paved in under a decade. Not so an undertaking like the James River and Kanawha Canal, every mile of which took an army of pickaxe-swinging laborers months to carve from the James's left bank, and every stream entering the river required an aqueduct of carefully chiseled stone. The workers in the canal's first digging crews embarked on their westward odyssey with no expectation that they'd finish their work inside of a decade, nor even that they'd personally see it finished at all. It was an endeavor taken up by generations.

Could we do it today? In this age in which personal fulfillment has become a buzz phrase, in which instant reward for minimal labor has become an American expectation, do we remain capable of tasks like building the JR&K? Could we embark on a job like building the Vatican's great basilica, St. Peter's, which involved more than a hundred years and generation on generation of workers, many of whom didn't see it started or finished but nonetheless labored through the decades between? I doubt it. As technology has boosted the speed with which we've accomplished our aims, our patience has dwindled, and with each new convenience, each new advance, that patience shrinks further. We become less capable of living without our conveniences, and far less tolerant of delays in our gratification. Heck, since the advent of personal computers I've come to look back on my college career, which ended not very long ago at all, with something like awe. How on earth did I peck out all those term papers on a *typewriter*?

I push away from the creek's mouth and paddle into a long bend to the right, and a few minutes later hear the bass throb and clatter of a CSX freight train invisible beyond the trees. The real beauty of the Lickinghole aqueduct, I realize, might not be its graceful curves but its utility, for unlike all but a handful of American highway bridges its age, it's still in use. The same stonework that once carried packet boats across the creek now carries trains. In fact, it's carried coal and freight by rail for twice as long as it carried the canal.

Little more than a mile below Lickinghole Creek the James bends sharply to the right, and I find myself facing a strong, cool headwind that ruffles the shallow water and turns paddling into a wearisome fight. The canoe slows; the paddle's blades act as air scoops as I lift one while slashing at the water with the other. On the curve's outside bank is a scattering of houses called Cedar Point on my map. It marks an interesting stretch of the JR&K, for here Richmond-bound canal boats left the man-made ditch, passed through two locks and traveled for five miles in the James itself, pulled by mules on a towpath hard against the river's edge. The train tracks, true to the towpath's old bed, hang close to the water on a high embankment.

As I paddle slowly against the wind, the river seems to grow shallower. I run aground repeatedly, and, tired and cursing, take to half-standing in the boat in an attempt to better see the underwater obstructions ahead. It does little good: no clear path among the sandbars and clumps of submerged vegetation presents itself, and I kneel back down and hack at the river's feeble flow, thumping on rock and sandy bottom. By the time the Michaux Bridge looms into view, marking my rendezvous with Ian, I'm spent. A Game and Inland Fisheries boat ramp slopes down the right bank just above the bridge, and I cut diagonally across the river to reach it. But as if to give me one last slap, the James throws up an impenetrable chain of sandy lumps. I grind so hard onto one midriver that I can't dislodge the boat without getting out and giving it a shove. Seconds later, I'm hung up again. Disgusted, I crawl out of the canoe and splash ankle-deep across half the river's width, pulling the boat by its bow. "This wind is killing me," I mutter when I've reached Ian.

He nods sympathetically. "That water looks pretty slow, too."

"It is," I say. "I gotta take a break. How far to the next decent take-out?" Ian pulls a map packet from his back pocket, unfolds it, marks off the miles to the next boat ramp, at a place called Watkins Landing. "Thirteen miles, give or take."

"Thirteen miles," I repeat. "I definitely have to take a break. There's just no point to paddling against this wind." As I speak, a gust sweeps the boat ramp, lifting a cloud of grit from its concrete surface. The sky is heavily clouded. It feels far later than early afternoon. Rain seems a distinct possibility. "Well, let's do that," Ian says. "We can go into Goochland, file our stories from yesterday, get some lunch, and see what the wind's doing when we finish."

"Sounds like a plan."

With that, we load the canoe onto the car and motor over the bridge to the Goochland County seat, a town of small houses and strip malls strung along the roadside. It's a peculiar little place, dominated as it is by the prison industry: off to the left, as we head into town, is the entrance to a women's prison. Just across the river, in Powhatan County, is a big reformatory for errant boys. And three miles downstream are two sprawling penal farms, one on each side of the James and linked by a low, one-lane bridge. We invade the *Goochland Gazette*'s small storefront newsroom, borrow unoccupied desks, and unfold our laptop computers. Ian transmits his pictures back to Norfolk, then offers to drive a dozen miles to snag lunch. "Absolutely," I tell him. As he heads out the door, I add: "Watch out for cats."

I work on my story. Ian returns. We eat. I finish my story. I struggle for half an hour to get the modem in my laptop to converse with the computer back in Norfolk, succeeding after a dozen attempts. Four hours have passed when we finally leave Goochland and drive back over the Michaux Bridge.

The bridge crossing coincides with a place on the map—just a locale on the north bank these days, rather than a town—called Maidens, a contraction of "Maiden's Adventure." Supposedly it took its name from an episode way back, in which the Monacan Indians still frequented these parts and captured a young white man whose honey swam the river to rescue him. I haven't been able to find any reference to who she was, if she existed, nor what became of her beau, but it's true enough that the Monacan Indians had a town on the James's south side here. Ian and I put the canoe in the water with plans to meet at the low State Farm Bridge, and to decide there whether to push farther. I paddle away from the bank into a four-mile stretch of almost straight river, and pick my way over the rocky remains of the Maiden's Adventure Dam, where canal boats, having completed the river trip from Cedar Point, re-entered the JR&K for the final twenty-seven or so miles into Richmond.

The State Farm Bridge lies less than a mile below. As I near it, I make out the Volvo parked under a knot of trees on the right bank, maybe a hundred yards upstream of the bridge's south end. As I draw closer, its headlights flash several times. Ian appears on the shore a moment later. "Hello, Earl," he brays.

"Are you completely nuts?" I yell. "Good God, Ian, you're in the middle of a huge prison complex, and you're flashing your lights?"

He laughs dopily. "Uh . . . oh, yeah."

"They're gonna probably send an army of screws down here," I say. "You've probably got 'em thinking we're part of some huge breakout."

"I should have thought about that," he says breezily. "Breakouts by canoe probably happen all the time."

I start laughing. "Man, don't expect me to bail your sorry ass out," I tell him. "I've never seen you before." The canoe hits the shore, sticks. Ian's standing on the lip of a four-foot bank. "So how's the wind?" he asks.

"I can't believe you. But better—the wind's better. It's died down a little." I look at my watch. It's 5:30 P.M. "We have about two hours of light left."

"And how far to go?"

I check the map, use the railroad's mile markers to estimate. "Ten miles. Maybe a little more."

He grimaces. "You're gonna have to fly."

"I would," I say, and as I do I suddenly feel exhausted. We could quit for the day here, I think, go find a decent campsite—someplace without rocks—and set up before dark. Actually have an hour or two to kick back. Our last moment of relaxation was at the Pig and Steak, back in Scottsville, which seems ages ago. "Let's not do this," I say. "Let's bag it here."

Ian nods, and I stand up on my knees, stretching. Before I start out of the boat, though, I get to thinking more. If I don't tackle the ten miles now, I'll have to do them tomorrow. Right now, tomorrow's a short day, something we've consciously arranged so that we can rest up before the day after tomorrow, which'll bring me into the rapids in downtown Richmond. The choice, then, is to wear out tonight or face the prospect of a long, tiring day tomorrow, when I can less afford to be wiped out. "On second thought," I sigh, "never mind. I've got to keep going."

Ian nods again. "OK," he says. "But are you gonna be able to make it by dark? That's a haul."

"I don't know," I tell him. "Probably not. You better give me some extra stuff, just in case. I'm going to need my headlamp. And better give me a T-shirt, and my fleece jacket, and my boots. And some Clif Bars." Ian disappears beyond the bank and returns a minute later, arms full. "I don't like this," he says, handing down the jacket and T-shirt. "I don't like this at all. What do I do if it's dark, and you haven't shown up?" I open my dry bag, stuff the clothes inside, reach up for the headlamp. "Stay there," I say. "Don't panic. If it gets really late, tent up at the boat ramp. I'll keep paddling unless I absolutely can't go on, which I don't think'll happen. But if it does, I'll sleep in the boat, and get going again as soon as there's some light."

"Man." He tosses down the Clif Bars. I shove them in the bag, burp the air out of it, roll its top, and clip it shut.

"You have your maps?"

"Yeah," he says, pulling them from his pocket.

"The river doesn't look bad," I say, studying my copy. "Some rapids a mile or so ahead. Past that, it's a straight shot. Just make sure you're at the boat ramp when I get there, OK?"

"OK," he says, folding his maps. "When should I start to worry?" I pole myself off the bank with my paddle. "Four hours," I say. "If I'm not there in four hours, I'll probably be sleeping on the river."

A minute later I glide beneath the State Farm Bridge, a ribbon of concrete that lacks any amenities, including guard rails. Below it I pick up my pace. A race is on. A half mile down I spot what appears to be an animal far ahead on the water—a humpbacked creature, bright white and moving fast. I'm squinting, trying to make it out, when its sound, a phlegmy whine, catches up with it. The animal is the rooster tail of a powerboat, only the second—after the johnboat in the rainstorm last night—that I've seen on the river since Lake Moomaw, more than 250 miles upstream. I pass the gasoline-powered anglers a short time later, still now, lines out, in the trees on the right bank. We wave silently as I pass and enter a wide, rapids-flecked bend, the water again only inches deep and choked with weeds. A rock garden rises around me at the head of a small island, the spaces between the stones narrow, other rocks lurking just below the water's surface.

The James swings to the left, winds into a tight turn around a promontory on the north bank. More islands, more rock, but the water deepens, and as I paddle I notice that it runs so clear that I can make out tiny shells on the sandy bottom, four feet down. Two dozen miles from the biggest city on its banks, and you'd never know it. Fish, tawny and speckled, dart around down there, and one paces me for a full minute. The banks are forest and field unbroken by road or house.

Boulders stud the river. Some tower, dark gray and mottled, six feet out of the water, driftwood collected at their feet. A regiment of them loom two feet or taller. All are round-topped and smooth like skulls. Around them, water purls empty in the yellow light of early evening. The only sound is my plunking. I ghost past elderberry blossoms nodding on the bank, beneath drooping sycamore limbs, a light tailwind nudging me on. The channel splits, the main veering right, around a low, long island. Pleasant Island, or Pleasant's, is an impenetrable tangle of thick forest and weedy vine, part of a broadening floodplain. The railroad, like the canal before it, veers away from the river here, hugs the edge of the higher ground at the plain's edge. A little ways downstream, the plain's so wide that the tracks are half a mile from the left bank.

Halfway down the island I see a small power skiff among the rocks ahead, two fly fishermen aboard. It turns out to be the same pair who asked for directions back at West View this morning. I decide not to stop to chat; the sunlight's color is deepening, and the dark forest around me seems to be thickening by the minute. But when I try to get by with a hello on the fly, the bearded fellow stops me. "You've come a long way," he says.

"Yup," I say. "About nineteen miles."

"Where you headed tonight?"

"Watkins Landing."

"Same here. Guess we'll be heading in pretty soon."

I say goodbye. He wishes me luck. Then, as I put the paddle in the water, he says: "By the way, how far are we from Watkins Landing?"

I take my paddle back out. "About seven miles," I tell him.

His eyes widen. "Seven miles? *Seven*?"

"Well, yeah," I nod. I pull out my maps, count off mile markers, mentally correct the distance according to how faithfully the railroad follows the streambed. "Six or seven."

He looks thunderstruck. "So, are we gonna be able to make it by dark?"

Wow, I thought. He's in trouble. He's asking a guy in a *canoe*. "I don't know," I tell him matter-of-factly. "There's some doubt about that, for me. But you guys should have no trouble." I nod toward his outboard motor. He shakes his head. "I've got a motor," he says, "but I don't know if I should use it."

Downstream, rocks wait in profusion, ten underwater for every one that juts from the surface. I can see what he means. It's often tough work to get the canoe through this kind of water. I can't imagine what it would be like to take that skiff over the ledges and among the boulders. Once dark descended entirely, you'd be clueless about whether you could put the boat's motor in the water. Without a really powerful spotlight, you'd be helpless. Even with a light, going downriver in the dark would be slow and frustrating. There's a real good chance, I realize, that these guys are spending the night on the James. They're lucky the weather's mild.

Time's running short now. I paddle steadily, taking no breaks, and soon churn past Sabot Island, so named because French Huguenots settled nearby thought it resembled a shoe.

The Huguenots were reluctant arrivals on the right bank in 1700. Their immigration to Powhatan County had its beginnings fifteen years before, when Louis XIV of France revoked the Edict of Nantes, which had formally tolerated Protestants. They now had to embrace Catholicism, and they weren't allowed to leave France. These orders didn't go down easy, and a slew of Protestants fled the country despite them. Thousands wound up in England, where they were officially welcome but strained the local comfort level, as any refugee population will, until someone eventually had a bright idea: Why not ship some willing Frenchmen to the Virginia colony?

So it was that a shipload of Huguenots stepped ashore in Hampton, and into a nasty bait-and-switch. The French were merchants and tradesmen, a citified bunch untested by life in the wilderness, but had made the rough Atlantic crossing under the impression that they were bound for a relatively safe chunk of territory south of present-day Hampton Roads. Fertile land waited there that even a neophyte could farm. It was nestled close to the colony's population centers. Most of the Indians had been chased off. There, they figured, they'd built a self-sustaining piece of France in America, a settlement where the French culture persevered and Protestantism flourished and money was made. Things looked sweet. This wasn't fantasy, for the King of England, William III, had explicitly directed Virginia's lieutenant governor, Francis Nicholson, to settle the French on the Virginia-Carolina line in Norfolk County, today the city of Chesapeake.

This, Nicholson ignored. The French got the word in Hampton that they weren't bound for a laid-back existence near the coast, but for the western frontier. Planters downstream of here were keen to see this part of the James colonized, figuring that occupation of the trackless wilderness a few miles above the falls would serve as a buffer against Indians. The coastal tribes had been decimated by this time, but venturing into the wilds this far out was a dicey proposition. One man, in particular, pushed to get an outpost going—William Byrd, a large landholder and among the colony's powerful, sought settlers to move into the site of an abandoned Monacan town, once the tribe's chief village, Mowhemencho, on the James's south bank at Watkins Landing. As long as the possibility of an Indian attack existed, Byrd would have a hard time attracting settlers to his properties downriver from the Indian village. He had a second incentive to settle the Monacan town site: he had the nearest mill and supply house. The settlers would have to come to him for their provisions. He'd make out well.

The change in plans made the French unhappy—deeply, deeply unhappy. But there was nowhere else to go, and a lot of them were too sick with dysentery to fuss much, and returning to England wasn't an option—they'd pooled all their cash, and it had gone fast. So, filled with dread, 120 of these businessmen, shopkeepers, and manufacturers embarked upriver.

Their first sight of home wouldn't have been a happy one. The Indian town site's open ground had given way to saplings. Its core was a sad collection of collapsing huts and a large stone that had played some role in ceremonies. Otherwise, they were among only river and dense forest a long, long way from France.

Once the shock wore off a little, the Huguenots whacked away the brush, paced off streets, built rough huts for themselves. They cut a road twenty miles eastward through raw country, paralleling the James to a creek below present-day Richmond, where William Byrd's mill stood. Later in the year another 150 French arrived in the neighborhood, staking out a settlement along the river a few miles below the Indian village.

Then winter came. Their first crops were planted, but wouldn't yield food for months. Flat broke and hungry, the settlers sold their weapons, clothes, and few household possessions to eke by. Even so, starvation loomed. Rescue came from Lieutenant Governor Nicholson, who'd gotten them into this mess in the first place. He told the colony's House of Burgesses that he found the town so deplorable that without aid "at least till they may reap their next crop they must inevitably perish." The colony's counties coughed up enough money to enable Byrd and Benjamin Harrison—both of them among several generations to bear their names, and to complicate history with a lot of Roman numerals—to obtain provisions for 250 settlers.

With that bailout, Manakin Town, as it was called, was over the hump. The following summer the settlers built houses, cleared fields, harvested their crops. By 1702 a visitor found the place robust and lush. "Things that are grown are there in such abundance that many Englishmen come a distance of 30 miles to get fruit, which they mostly exchange for cattle," Francis Louis Michel reported. "Gardens are filled there with all kinds of fruit. . . . The cattle are fat because of the abundant pasture." Three years later, Robert Beverley wrote that the French were making cloth and taking a stab at winemaking. "The last year they began an Essay of Wine," he noted, "which they made of the wild Grapes gather'd in the Woods; the effect of which, was Noble strong-bodied Claret, of a curious flavor. I heard a Gentleman, who tasted it, give it great Commendation."

Darkness is almost complete as I round a gentle bend to the left and see, far ahead in the gloom, three gleaming rooster tails crisscrossing the river. I paddle up to the ramp as Ian, walking to its edge, bellows, "Well done!" We walk the canoe to the car among a bunch of young wet-suited guys loading Jet Skis onto trailers. None of them speaks French, and the reason lies in the rapid decline of the Monacans.

Manakin Town was laid out around a central square on the James's edge, the Huguenots planning to leave the village each morning to work their outlying fields, but to live together to better put up a fight, if the occasion arose. Close to three hundred people lived in the town at its height. But as the Indian threat passed, the farmers tired of their commute, and one by one took up permanent residence in their fields. With the population's dispersal, the drive to create a French culture here lost its critical mass. Marriages to the English watered down the stock, and in time the Huguenots became indistinguishable from the other Americans around them. In 1747 half of the sermons preached in the parish church were in English. Four years later, two-thirds of them were, and by then the village was deserted. A few elders still spoke the mother tongue, but with their passing, Manakin Town had disappeared.

As we walk up the ramp, one of the Jet-Skiers asks where I began the day's paddle. West View, I tell him. "West View!" he gasps. "You came from West View *today*?"

I did, I say. "Shoo," he replies, "that's a long way."

In truth, I don't feel at all tired, despite the fact that I've paddled pretty much nonstop for—how long? I look at my watch. It's 7:40. I've covered ten miles in just over two hours. Besides that, it's actually been a pretty average day. I've been pulling twenty-five-mile days or even more since Salt Petre Cave. It's a good thing we're as far along as we are, I think. I can't keep this up.

Ian is clearly relieved that I've survived the trip from State Farm. He proposes that we celebrate by loading up on fast food and beer, as a change of pace. I point out that we've got a pile of freeze-dried food in the wayback, but on reflection, decide that tacos sound pretty good. We cruise through the night to our next campsite, Pocahontas State Park in Chesterfield County, about fifteen miles southeast of the boat ramp and just south of Richmond. We find food and beer on the way, and at the park find a lovely campground of tall pines and large, well-groomed tent sites. We make a couple loops through the woods in the Volvo before selecting a deep, flat site close to the bathrooms and showers, but shielded from their light by a screen of trees and shrubs. We toast the day with cold Sammies, and as we cram our mouths with nachos and burritos, I realize that those fishermen never turned up at Watkins Landing while we were there, and that it was stumble-around dark by the time we left. I wonder how they're making out.

DAY SIXTEEN
On which our faith in all things Swedish is tested

❧ Our journey down 325 miles of the Jackson and James rivers has been studded with milestones, points along the way by which Ian and I have measured our progress. The McClintic Bridge, where we first found water deep and wide enough to canoe, was one. So was Iron Gate, where the Jackson met the Cowpasture. Balcony Falls. Lynchburg, the first major city along the James's banks. This morning promises to bring the most exciting yet: I'm to put the canoe in at Watkins Landing, roughly eighteen miles west of Richmond, and paddle into the capital.

So Ian and I bound out of our tents and into the post-dawn chill eager to hit the water. We load up the car, strap the canoe to its roof, hop in and . . . sit. The trusty Volvo's engine turns over, catches for a moment, and dies. Ian turns the key again. Once more the Volvo, its odometer now reading 277,400 miles, growls to life, then sputters, then stops. He tries again. Same thing. "Come on, baby," he mutters. He turns the key again. Again, it won't catch.

"Maybe it's just cold," I offer. Ian refuses to accept this possibility. This is a car made in *Sweden,* he says. Built to start in the Arctic, in temperatures far more extreme than the overnight low we've just endured, which was all of fifty degrees. "I think I know what it might be," he says. He'll need to get to his spare parts, which are stashed back in the wayback, under the carpeted floor. We get out, open the hatch, empty the cargo hold until a pyramid of gear dominates the campsite. Armed with an odd-looking electrical relay, his tools, and his repair manual, Ian disappears under the hood. I can hear him sweet-talking the car, cooing to it, calling it "baby," between grunts and turns of his screwdriver.

Twenty minutes later, he steps away from the wagon and approaches me with a grave face, looking like a doctor meeting with relatives after a difficult surgery. "I've done all I can do," he says. "If this doesn't fix it, I can't fix it out here."

"OK," I say. "Let's try it." Ian climbs behind the wheel, takes a deep breath, closes his eyes, and turns the key. Nothing happens. "Well, I don't see that we have a choice," I tell him. "Let's get it towed. Maybe, if I can get someone to take the canoe back to Watkins Landing, I can get some paddling in while you're getting the car fixed."

"That'd be great," Ian says. He uses his cellular phone to call directory assistance, and has the operator read him the list of local Volvo dealerships. We passed one of them on the way to camp, not too far back. He gets its number, calls, arranges the tow. Reluctantly, we take the canoe off the roof and unpack the rest of the gear, stashing the loose stuff in the tents.

While we're waiting for the tow truck, I look around our Chesterfield County campsite, marveling that we've gotten this far. As wonderful as our odyssey has been, it's been punishing, as well. The canoe, resting in the weeds beside the car, has been stained brown by the river, dented, scraped, and deeply gouged by its rocks. The equipment piled around it is scuffed and muddied. I'm sunburned and windchapped, sore-shouldered and bloody-kneed after two weeks of paddling. Ian is cultivating his first beard, with troubling results.

We tell each other several times how lucky we are that the car chose to break down here, rather than in Eagle Rock, or Indian Rock, or way up on the Jackson at Mustoe. How far would we have been from a towing company in any of those places? And if we'd found one, how many dozens of miles would we have been from a mechanic with the parts and know-how to fix an old Swedish station wagon? We decide that car trouble anywhere upstream, aside from perhaps Lynchburg, would have been a bona fide disaster. As it is, we're inconvenienced. We'll lose a little time that we'll simply have to make up downriver. We say all this, and we try to mean it. But lurking behind the words is an unspoken fear: that the Volvo's dead—and with it, our trip.

The tow truck arrives, and Ian disappears with it ten miles into the Richmond suburbs. He leaves the cellular phone with me, and I use it to call the paper's capital bureau. Is there anyone there, I ask, who might be able to drive me and the canoe to the put-in? A reporter, Holly Heyser, says she'll be happy to meet me, and thirty minutes later she pulls up to the campsite. Her car, however, is a microscopic Toyota Paseo, with a roofline that looks shy of three feet long. No way will it carry the canoe; I find myself wondering whether the car might fit inside the boat. She returns an hour later with her boyfriend's shiny black all-terrain vehicle, but I judge its factory roof rack a little too delicate for the task at hand.

Just as it begins to look as if we'll have to scrub any paddling for the day, the phone rings. It's Ian, who reports that the dealership has found the problem—an arcane component with a three-part name that, translated from the Swedish, roughly means "exorbitant parts and labor costs." They'll have it fixed in a few minutes, he says. He'll be back in camp within the hour. I turn off the phone and howl at the trees.

By the middle of the afternoon we're back at Watkins Landing. The ramp is empty of Jet Skis, the slow green river beyond it, quiet. The only other person around is an old guy backing his truck down the concrete slope, easing a trailer into the water. His bass boat floats just offshore. "How'd the day go?" I ask him.

He winces, shakes his head. "Just some little smallmouth," he says, "just little things—seven, eight inches long."

"That's weird," I say. "Yesterday I saw tons of fish here, just a little ways upstream. Big ones." He stares at me. "Really," I tell him. "I could see them all along Pleasant Island. Could see them right from the canoe. I had one follow me for a while."

"Oh, you can *see* them," he huffs. "But the water's so clear, *they* can see *you*."

I push off. Within minutes I'm again gliding among squadrons of fish, and, just as the old fisherman complained, the water's so clear I can make out individual scales on their backs, flashing iridescent as they dart from shade to sunny river bottom. Were it not for my maps, I'd not know that I'm close to the James's largest city. The river seems to run as clear here as it did back Wingina, or Glasgow, or Buchanan. About the only clue that Richmond approaches is the current, or the lack of one. The water, stopped downstream by the Bosher Dam on the city's west side, is impounded in what amounts to a long finger lake. The going is slow, against a steady wind that seems to nail me full in the face, no matter what direction the curving river takes me.

Farmlands peek, low and golden, from behind a thin curtain of riverbank trees. I lean forward on my knees, stretching to see beyond the shores, hoping to catch a glimpse of whatever might remain of the coalfields. I see nothing. They're out there, though: the ground west of Richmond is broken by mines and water-filled shafts. As unlikely as it seems, this low piedmont was home to America's first commercial coal operation.

Coal was first mined here, in fact, before Richmond was laid out as a city. The simple operations of 1730, when the frontier was not long past this section of the James, soon grew into a bustling industry involving several companies, hundreds of miners, and shafts seven hundred feet deep. The coal was so plentiful and easily had that wagon wheels supposedly churned it up in their ruts. Other places had more coal, particularly western Virginia and Pennsylvania, but the fields here were close to a big river and quick ocean access, and could sail the fuel to other eastern cities. The bigger fields didn't catch up until railroads came along.

Deep underground the miners, mostly slaves, chipped at unstable rock walls, slogged through black water, breathed a gritty mist. The ceilings fell in. Water could suddenly, silently, fill the galleries. Loose coal and coal dust could spontaneously burst into flame. A persistent fire forced the Black Heath Pits, one of the busiest of the early mines, to close off the burning tunnels in 1788. The fire smoldered for thirty years.

Explosions were the greatest fear. One nineteenth-century observer wrote of a methane gas detonation "of the most fearful character" that rocked the Black Heath Pits. "Of the 54 men in the mine, only two, who happened to be in some crevices near the mouth of the shaft, escaped with life," he reported. "Nearly all the internal works of the mine were blown to atoms. Such was the force of the explosion, that a basket then descending, containing three men, was blown nearly 100 feet into the air. Two fell out, and were crushed to death, and the third remained in, and with the basket was thrown some seventy or eighty feet from the shaft, breaking both his legs and arms." Another explosion at Black Heath, in 1839, killed forty-five men; another in 1844, eleven. And that field was typical. The president of the Maidenhead Pits lamented "a terrific explosion" in 1842 that killed thirty-four men. "Some of the dead men, the flesh charred on their bones, held their shovels in their hands," he noted.

These disasters killed not only men, but mules—some of the mines incorporated underground stables for the animals needed to haul trams of coal to the shafts. "Some of them," an 1843 visitor wrote, "remain below for years, and when carried to the strong light of day, gambol like wild horses."

By the time that writer made his visit, the mines close to Richmond were tapping out, which prompted the mining companies to venture farther west and south and to link the new fields with short rail lines. These productive new mines provided the fuel that fired Richmond's Tredegar Iron Works, which were to the Confederacy what Krupp was to twentieth-century Germany. Without the pits, the Southern struggle would have been brief.

Things slowed down after the Civil War. In May 1883, the end was near: that month the Norfolk and Western Railroad pulled into Norfolk with its first shipment of coal from western Virginia. To this day, though, the Chesterfield County flag depicts a coal miner leaning on his pickaxe, a pine tree behind him, a river at his feet.

The James's seeming cleanliness above Bosher Dam today is heartening, when you consider that the mines were among the first industrial polluters along this part of the river. Two miles downstream I start encountering the first signs of the coming metropolis. An occasional riverfront home appears through the trees, and farther along, the sound of a high school sporting event drifts in waves from somewhere to the south, a blend of cheers, muffled drums, and braying horns.

Now the south bank begins to fill in. I pass a small marina, an American Legion post, a chain of homes with pontoon party boats lashed to the riverside. Soon the homes emerge from the woods to command the waterfront, lavish, new-looking places with landscaped gardens. Another gentle bend, and I reach Richmond proper. Ahead, buoys jut from the river, warning of the dam beyond—a deadly obstacle of stone and concrete, 880 feet long and ten feet high, built to funnel water into the JR&K Canal for the waterway's final nine miles to the downtown waterfront. A concrete fish ladder is under construction at the dam's north end, a long-awaited device that enables shad, striped bass, and other migratory fish to reach upstream spawning grounds. Unfortunately, there's no such contraption for boaters. As I near the dam I blow my whistle, and hear Ian holler back from the shoreside trees to my right. I find him perched on the edge of a lawn just a few yards upstream of the drop.

"I had to talk my way in," he says as we haul the boat onto the grass. "I'm not sure the woman who owns the house believed me when I told her why I needed to get back here." I look at the big, well-manicured home that dominates the property, then at Ian. We haven't showered since Scottsville, and we both look it. He's sheened in sweat and grime. His T-shirt is befouled in ways that usually trigger the declaration of a Superfund site. His beard has achieved a ragged, well-scratched, heat-rashed funkiness. And he's looking pretty respectable, next to me. "She's probably calling the cops," I say.

Ian studies me for a moment. "I think *I* might."

We lug the gear across the yard to the Volvo, which Ian has parked in the driveway, then return for the boat. The homeowner, a young, athletic blonde, wanders out of her garage as we lash the car to the roof. She evidently decides that we're no danger and brings us a bunch of sodas, which we guzzle on the spot. The car starts immediately, which prompts an exchange of high-fives. We hit a fast-food joint, load up with something like eighteen dollars' worth of grease, and drive southeast across suburban Richmond to Pocahontas State Park, where we toast our luck with a couple of beers.

We've reached a big milestone. It doesn't spark a celebration, per se—just relief, that it wasn't the journey's last.

DAY *SEVENTEEN*
Risky business in Richmond

❧ When Captain Christopher Newport left England for the New World early in 1607, he and the 103 souls in his command were fortified with the advice of their bosses back home. "Do your best Endeavor to find out a Safe port in the Entrance of Some navigable River making Choise of Such a one as runneth furthest into the Land," the advice ran. Once they did that, they were to discover whether the river they chose sprang from mountains or a lake—for a lake might well have a river running from its far side to the East India Sea.

So it was that Newport and his fledgling colony, among its members a stout, bearded adventurer named John Smith, sailed into the mouth of the Chesapeake Bay, and struck up a broad, powerful river they found there to a marshy peninsula. And that within days of its landfall on what it dubbed Jamestown Island, the colony dispatched a party up the river it called the Powhatan. And that just one hundred miles from the great river's mouth, the explorers were halted by an unexpected, and unwelcome, spectacle: where they had hoped to find a lake, they were confronted instead with a noisy tangle of whitewater and granite where, as Smith put it, "the water falleth so rudely, and with such a violence, as not any boat can possibly pass." Newport, Smith, and company had reached the Falls of the James.

No greater obstacle has confounded navigation on the James River than the boulder-strewn rapids at present-day Richmond, where for six miles it gnaws through the last vestiges of an ancient volcano on its drive to the sea, its waters split and squeezed into a chaos of chutes, cascades, and swirls within sight of downtown's skyscrapers. No city on the planet has such a natural wildness in its heart. The James tumbles 105 feet in this noisy, foam-flecked obstacle course, careens through some stretches of whitewater rated Class IV, even Class V—and in one place at high water, the absurd Class VI.

On top of nature's perils are those of man, for here the river is laced with broken dams, bridge piers, slabs of concrete, iron pipes, gnarled daggers of torn rebar. Arms and legs and skulls have been shattered on the rocks and submerged hazards lying in wait below the ledges and dams. Canoes have been split, bent, wrapped into doughnuts. And many a swimmer has drowned in these falls, where hydraulics can suck the strongest underwater and spin him in place. The Williams Island Dam, an innocuous-looking concrete weir that zigzags from either side of its namesake island to the James's banks, has by itself claimed eleven lives.

So it's with grave trepidation that Ian and I eyeball the river at the Pony Pasture, a riverside park above the rapids that overlooks an archipelago of dark boulders and rock slabs stretching far from shore. Dragonflies dart among these tiny islands. The morning sun winks on the water, reflects off hundreds of small, mirrorlike puddles in the stone. I consciously note that it's a beautiful scene, but feel nothing but edgy. Today's the big day, the last great hurdle before flatwater, the place where the waterway we've followed for sixteen days and more than three hundred miles finally, violently, displays the strength it's gathered on its journey from Hightown. The last rush before the river becomes a tidal arm of the Chesapeake. And I'll soon be in the middle of it, fighting rapids that dwarf all those that have come before.

We rock-hop thirty yards out toward the river's middle, find it passing slowly, quietly, peacefully. Too peacefully: the river's silence, its denial of any clue as to what waits just downstream, hints of menace. More than hints, actually. "You scared?" Ian asks, as we stand on a ledge, staring down into the languid, almost syrupy James.

"Half to death," I tell him.

Long before setting out on this trip, I'd read enough about the James to know that Richmond posed its toughest challenge. The falls here make those at the Balcony seem mere ripples. A week or two before Ian and I set out to find the source of the Jackson, I called my friend Lillie Gilbert, owner of Wild River Outfitters in Virginia Beach, and asked whether she could recommend a guide to help me pick through the Fall Line's rock gardens and rapids. She answered without hesitation. "Floyd Baker."

"He knows the river?"

"He knows it as well as anybody," she said. "He's very good." She gave me his number, then offered to have Floyd bring me a paddle better suited to rapids-running than my skinny-bladed touring model. "He's a little scary-looking," Lillie advised. "He's got a shaved head, and a goatee. But he's a sweetheart." So I called Floyd and won his agreement to meet us in Richmond to guide me through the falls. Shortly after we leap the rocks back to shore, he pulls up in a mini-pickup. As he parks, I see that under the truck's shell is a plastic kayak, a tiny, playtoy-seeming thing with a stubby snout and a pinched tail. Next to my canoe, it seems suicidally small. Floyd gets out, thick-chested, strong-armed, bald head gleaming. He does, in fact, look a bit scary. He shakes my hand. "We're mighty glad to see you," I announce.

"Yeah, man," Ian agrees.

Floyd doesn't say much. He glares at me. He glares at Ian. He glares at my canoe. He clearly has doubts. We pass a few minutes of awkward small talk, during which Floyd eyes the James and proclaims it the lowest he's ever seen.

Then he hands me my loaner paddle, changes into his wet suit, cradles his kayak under an arm, and leads the way to the rocky shoreline. He shimmies into his blue speck of a boat while Ian and I struggle to lower the canoe to the water, then pulls on his helmet and straps it under his chin.

I reach for my own helmet, never worn, its bright red plastic unscuffed. I have to pry it open to clear my ears, then pull it snug. The foam inside grips my skull as tightly as talons, and only a little more comfortably; within seconds my temples ache. Still, it beats slamming bare-headed into a boulder at twenty miles an hour. I buckle the strap under my chin, and we shove off.

Right away, Floyd points out places that testify to the water's low level. We're surrounded by bent-back rocks normally submerged, thousands of them. "Usually can't see that one," Floyd says as we paddle through the barely riffling water, and I recall Hope Zollman using almost the same words back at Balcony Falls. Floyd points out another: "Water's usually up over that one." And another: "I've never seen that before."

We head downstream in the river's middle, a hundred yards from either shore, the water's speed building around us. It is a bright, blue-sky morning, the sun intense, a cool breeze whispering from the south, but the shallows command our attention. We scrape our plastic hulls on riverbed rock, scoot and pole the boats over sand bars, notice Canada geese standing in the middle of rapids that normally run fast and strong and a couple of feet deep. The water remains startlingly clear, seemingly clean enough to drink. There just isn't much of it.

"With every foot of water," Floyd tells me, "this becomes a different river. At five feet it's one way; at six, completely different. I've seen people run it when it was up twenty feet, and the water covered the parking lot back at the Pony Pasture.

"Today will be something new for both of us," he says, "because I've never run the river at this level before."

The Powhite Bridge looms overhead, and we sloop down a few quick bumps—the Powhite Ledges, a mild warm-up for the craziness to come. A little farther on, we hook right around a rocky shelf and slide down a fast-moving chute at the Choo Choo Rapids, named for a tall, arched railroad bridge overhead and created by a blown-out dam. In a second I'm catapulted from standstill to sprint. The canoe flies smoothly over a chain of standing waves as I paddle furiously.

Floyd flips his kayak around effortlessly at the bottom, tucks it into an eddy. I grunt through the turn behind him. As I do, I'm aware that the canoe is doing everything I ask of it, and I detect a foreign sensation spreading through me: relaxation. I'm suddenly at ease. My new-found dexterity is the work of my loaner paddle, which has oversized blades that I can dig into the water with far more bite, with which I can swing the canoe's nose around with speed and control. Plus, of course, there's Floyd, who leads the way through each set of rapids, plays my Sacajawea among the thousands of rocks that dot the river.

My calm doesn't last long. At one rapids I somehow catch the bow against a boulder and the canoe switches ends at the lip of a three-foot drop. I shoot a hand out to hug a rock on my right, and hang there for a minute, facing the wrong way, unable to paddle against the current, unwilling to risk a backward run, poised at the brink of disaster. Floyd, having already descended the falls in the traditional, facing-forward style, studies my situation from the flat water below. "You're going to have to let go," he advises. I look over my shoulder. The falls is a steep, gushing braid straddled by boulders, a dogleg to the left at its bottom. "There's nothing else you can do," Floyd says.

It seems certain that I'll dump the boat on the way down. If somehow I don't, I'll slam into the rocks lining the dogleg and surely flip there. I reflect sadly that I've been undone by a rapids rated only a Class II. Child's play. But Floyd is right. There's no way out but surrender. I crouch as low as I can in the boat, lean forward to grab the front thwart bracing its gunwales, and pull my other hand from the rock. Instantly the canoe tilts over the lip and free-falls backwards down the hole. Then, perhaps two seconds later, I realize the rushing water has steered me through the dogleg and onto the flat. Floyd is laughing, shaking his head incredulously. The toughest rapids so far, and I've run it with no hands.

At the rapids called First Break the James pours through a hole blasted into the concrete Belle Isle Dam by Hurricane Camille, creating a muscular spigot of water twenty feet wide. We eye the stream from above the break for a minute or two, trying to choose the best spot to hit the cascade's lip. The decision made, Floyd attacks the rushing water, swoops downward, drops almost out of sight—I can just see his helmeted head from where I wait in the canoe. He waves me on, so I plough into the foam. It shoots me downhill as if from a slingshot, the canoe riding butter-smooth and nose-high over a spine of standing waves to the shoreline of Belle Isle.

This half-mile-long, rock-ringed oval of land is littered with the remains of its busy history: Floyd and I beach the boats and drag them high and dry on the island's sloping granite fringe, stepping over chunks of slag left over from an old furnace, then hike up the bank and into the trees and past an algae-choked pond that fills the bottom of a long-derelict quarry. We walk a broad, well-tamped path through sun-dappled forest, side by side with the ghosts of a Confederate fort, a crumbling concrete power plant, antebellum mills. And a Rebel prisoner-of-war camp. In the summer of 1862, the Confederates began housing captured Federal officers at Libby Prison, a converted warehouse on the north bank, and the Union's enlisted troops here at Belle Isle, on four well-guarded, fenced acres of sand at the island's lower end.

It was not a happy place. As many as six thousand Northern soldiers were crowded on the grounds. The best accommodations were canvas tents, and at times a third of the prisoners didn't have even those. Death by freezing claimed many. In the fall of 1863, a Red Cross–style outfit called the United States Sanitary Commission started shipping relief from the North—clothing, food, shoes and such—with the Confederacy's permission. It helped for a while, until a captured Union general coordinating the handling of the shipments in Richmond wrote a letter suggesting that the commission slip cash into cans marked as preserved fruit, for use in bribing guards. The Rebs tightened the cuffs. Shipments were carefully inspected. The flow of goods to Belle Isle slowed to a dribble. Before long, starvation started to consume the place. Eventually, the Confederacy decided to relocate the prisoners, and Belle Isle was shut down after having housed more than twenty thousand men in its two-and-a-half years. The POWs were taken to a new prison—in Andersonville, Georgia.

Sunbathers squint at us as we step out of the trees and onto rocks at the island's north side, still wearing our helmets and life vests. The river forms a rushing panorama around us, roaring as it races among thousands of soft-shouldered rocks on the streambed. Beyond the boulders, a sheet of water spills over the Hollywood Dam, a diagonal obstruction that shunts the James's middle toward its north side. Beyond the dam rises the old canal's towpath, and past it, the river's high bank. And on top of the bluff I can see the white marble monuments of Hollywood Cemetery.

There's nothing left of the prison on the island behind me. But up there, at Hollywood, Civil War memories remain far more intact. Walk among the cemetery's knolls, beneath holly, oak, and magnolia, and you find Southern troops unnamed and buried dozens to a grave. "Gettysburg," one granite slab reads, the open turf around it home to nearly three thousand dead. Nearby, another stone stands sentry: "Unknown." Farther off, a third: "Seven Pines Unknown." And beyond that, "Unknown Soldiers from Shields Woods." Grids of small numbered headstones sprout from the hillside below, but most of the eighteen thousand soldiers interred in Hollywood's Confederate section rest as they died before the Federal guns—together, a sea of faceless gray, cells in a collective ideal more than individual men.

It was among these Rebel graves that one of America's earliest Memorial Day ceremonies was held. Here that widows and mothers erected one of the South's largest monuments to its fallen. And it's the Southern dead, as much as the two American presidents buried within the walls, that have made the graveyard a tourist destination. Hollywood is consecrated ground. The Arlington of the Confederacy. A shrine to the Lost Cause. Meander through the 135-acre cemetery today, and you'll hear defiant grief rustle through the trees as surely as the breeze off the nearby James. Not far from the Gettysburg dead stands a memorial to Charles Harris McPhail of Norfolk, who died at twenty-five "while gallantly charging the enemy at Malvern Hill." He was "a brave and faithful soldier," the stone reads, who "here makes his last bivouac with thousands of other martyred sons of the South who sleep around him." Across the grounds, on the bluff overlooking the rapids, a bronze Jefferson Davis stands larger than life atop an epitaph that stubbornly labels him "An American soldier, and defender of the Constitution." "Faithful to all trusts, a martyr to principle," the pedestal reads, alluding to an argument lost in four bloody years of war. "He lived and died the most consistent of American soldiers and statesmen."

Hollywood was a dozen years old when the Civil War erupted. By that time it was already home to a president, Virginia native James Monroe, whose tomb is enclosed in a twelve-foot Gothic revival cage on the cemetery's riverside uplands. After the war, sculptures and verse unrelated to the fighting quickly studded the grounds. Today they account for more than fifty thousand of the roughly seventy thousand graves at Hollywood, among them some of the cemetery's best-known memorials.

But the war is never more than a few yards away. Near Glasgow's grave is that of Maj. Gen. J. E. B. Stuart, the swashbuckling Confederate cavalryman. Sharing a grassy circle with President Monroe is the monument to President John Tyler. The simple, forceful obelisk makes no mention of Tyler's status as the only ex-president to renounce his country and join a foreign government (he died just before taking a seat in the Confederate Congress). And Matthew Fontaine Maury, whose role as a Confederate naval officer was eclipsed by his fame as the "Pathfinder of the Seas," shares his headstone with his second son, John Herndon Maury, who was "Captured near Vicksburg, January 27th, 1863, and lies in an Unknown Grave." George Pickett, who lost his division at Gettysburg in the charge on the Union lines that bears his name, is buried here, too.

Finally, in the heart of the Confederate section, amid legions of marble monuments withered by wind and rain, a ninety-foot pyramid of granite looms over the platoons of fallen Rebs, a headstone for the unidentified. It is an imperfect but curiously compelling monument, its stones rough and unpolished, like the men they honor, and held in place only by the slabs around them. Stand at its base, peer up at its peak, and if the wind's up, and blowing through the magnolias, you might mistake their rustle for a snare drum's drumming, far away.

Whatever Richmond has become in the 135 years since the Civil War's end, it remains the capital of the Confederacy. You could parachute blindfolded into most American cities these days, and wander for hours without figuring out where you were, so alike have they grown in their profusion of strip malls, chain stores, and assembly-line architecture. But that wouldn't happen in Richmond; all around town you encounter physical clues that history was writ large here. On Monument Avenue, massive statues of the South's heroes—and, incongruously, one of tennis player Arthur Ashe—rise from high pedestals and circles of carefully tended lawn. Downtown, tours snake through the White House of the Confederacy, Jefferson Davis's residence during the war. Next door the Museum of the Confederacy honors the memory of a cause still held sacred by a large number of southerners. Within sight of Belle Isle, the ruins of the Tredegar Iron Works, the arsenal of the Confederacy, stand in red brick on the north bank. Outside the state capitol, an elegantly simple Roman revival edifice designed by Thomas Jefferson, a stone George Washington strikes a heroic pose on horseback. The Confederacy adopted this depiction of Washington as its national seal, evidence of its belief that in defending states' rights, it was true to the intent of the Founding Fathers.

There's something beyond the physical about the place—a quiet mourning, a palpable sense of tragedy. A Yankee visitor might be tempted, on seeing Monument Avenue and witnessing the quiet reverence of docents at the Davis mansion, to conclude that Richmond is stuck in the past. He might be right, too. But how many other American cities can lay claim to the kind of history Richmond has seen? How many other cities have survived the indignities Richmond has suffered, can say they've been burned, violated, and shamed in two wars? That twice their populations have abandoned their homes and run for the hills?

Richmond's years as the Confederate capital, and its fall to a long Union stranglehold, would take an entire book in themselves to recount. Suffice it to say that by the time the War Between the States opened, Richmond was a century and a half old, and had acquired the trappings of a sophisticated, modern metropolis. That during the war its people lost everything, were widowed and orphaned and practically starved. And that by the war's end, it was a smoking ruins, torched by its own troops and inhabitants as the Yankees pushed into its streets. A Currier and Ives print of the city's April 1865 evacuation depicts throngs of Richmonders streaming over the Mayo's Bridge, an updated version of which still crosses the James, while fire devours homes, warehouses, and factories behind them. It's not pretty.

Far less frequently recalled is the city's first abandonment, in January 1781, when nine hundred British troops under the brilliant turncoat Benedict Arnold sailed up the James to a couple dozen miles below here, then marched on the capital. Gov. Thomas Jefferson called out the militia, and if the soldiers had dug in for a fight and opened up on the Redcoats with cannons, Richmond might have put a serious dent in Arnold's movements, perhaps even stopped them cold. But what few troops responded to the governor's call never fired their artillery, and they turned tail when violence seemed imminent. Jefferson busied himself trying to move the revolutionary government's arms, supplies, and records upriver, then got out of Dodge, a good percentage of the city's white population right behind him. Meeting no resistance, Arnold's men raced through Richmond to Westham, on the north bank near the present-day Williams Island Dam, and burned a foundry, a magazine, a boring mill, and several houses there. They dumped five tons of American gunpowder into the water, destroyed a pile of government records, and carried off five cannons that Jefferson had ordered hidden in the James. They broke into warehouses, and split open casks so that "liquor ran in streams down the gutters, and cows and hogs partaking freely, were seen staggering about the streets." Then they marched back east. It was not America's proudest moment: in just forty-eight hours, Arnold's small force had marched far into enemy territory, invaded and ransacked a city of eighteen hundred inhabitants, and returned to its boats without losing a single man.

Four months later, in early May, the Virginia General Assembly abandoned the capital for Charlottesville. As Jefferson's term as governor wound down in the closing days of the month, the assembly was poised to investigate his behavior in the face of the British invasion; one legislator, George Nicholas, introduced articles of impeachment against the governor for incompetency. Fortunately for the future president's reputation, the British headed for Charlottesville, and the legislature had to run before it could act on the matter. After Yorktown the lawmakers dropped the investigation, instead extending the governor their thanks. They didn't applaud his military prowess, however.

Echoes of war wouldn't be the only things to give the city away to the blindfolded skydiver. There is, of course, the James, which Richmond shows off with wild enthusiasm. Thirty years ago, the Fall Line was a cesspool, clogged with raw sewage and industrial filth that collected in the eddies behind its rocks. Today, it is a playground, the city's getaway, clean and clear and the centerpiece of a remarkable park that hugs the river's south bank and includes Belle Isle. On a sunny Sunday, the rocks and pools and swimming holes are busy with splashing children, lounging couples, solitary readers. James River Park is arguably the best-conceived and naturally blessed fusion of urban parkland, water, and raw beauty in the country. And the ruined dams and discarded stone bridge piers breaking the water only add to its appeal, standing as reminders of the great and terrible things that have unfolded on this little stretch of river.

Floyd and I boulder-hop along Belle Isle's north shore, and stride across a ledge that sweeps upward, like a sailboat's bow, to a pinnacle of granite overlooking the sharpest, toothiest rapids on the Fall Line. Today, with the river so dry, Hollywood Rapids is a dangerous blend of unstoppable force and im-movable stone. A heavy, racing tongue of water spills into a chute walled with boulders and met at its end by two other rocks, hard-edged and deadly. Miss-ing them requires a hairpin turn while moving at high speed.

"You normally don't even see those," Floyd says of the rocks. "And you sure wouldn't want to get up against them. If you make a mistake here, you're going to get hurt." I stare at the roiling water, mesmerized. Its speed, its mass, its power, are daunting enough. The rocks—and the gymnastics it would take to miss them—are another matter entirely. "Can it be done?" I ask him. I know the answer—kayakers run Hollywood all the time—but at the moment, I can't understand how. He pauses a moment, cataloguing the maneuvers necessary to stay alive, and concludes, "It's probably doable."

"Could I do it?"

"You?" Floyd asks, looking at me. He scowls. "No." Well, I think, that set-tles that. "Me?" he adds quietly. "Probably not, today."

We portage the boats around Hollywood.

Downriver the James is all but blocked by an island and dozens of rocky satel-lites that 300 million years ago were parts of a huge vat of magma. The molten stone filled a chamber deep below a chain of volcanoes that stretched across eastern Virginia. The volcanoes died. The magma cooled. Eons passed. Lashed by wind and rain, the volcanoes gradually wore away, until finally nothing re-mained but their stony heart—the magma, now hard metamorphic rock called Petersburg Granite. Since then, the granite has eroded, as well, particularly here in the falls. The rounded boulders that stud the James, and the river's rock floor, are its ruins. They make everything about the seemingly permanent, rock-solid city around us seem transitory indeed.

The rock splits the wide river into two narrow channels. One, just off the north bank, becomes a ramp of whitewater called the Pipeline. Maybe 150 yards long in all, it sends the James stair-stepping down a closely spaced succession of drops, saving the biggest for last. Getting through Richmond means get-ting through the Pipeline, so Floyd and I beach the boats a few yards upstream, climb onto a concrete riverbank pipe for which the falls is named, and walk along its top until we're looking down on the worst of the rapids. It's a crazy swirl of splashing and pounding, of surface whirls and bubbling. The rapids' smallest braids are as big around as oaks, and the roar they make as they smack onto the unyielding rock is a disquieting baritone. The James indeed, falleth so rudely, and with such a violence, here.

Ian's been waiting for us. He is ashen-faced. I can find nothing to say to put his mind at ease. Just a few minutes ago, as Floyd and I neared the shore for this reconnoiter, I ran the canoe head-on into a boulder so hard that I was thrown into the boat's nose. Slamming my gut into the front thwart was the only thing that kept me from sailing overboard. And now this. I am doomed. That's it: I'm doomed. No way am I going to get through this laughing. I turn to Floyd, who is intently eyeing the water as he leans on a railing installed atop the pipe for just such activity. "I believe this is where I'll eat the river," I tell him.

He grunts. "Let's hope you don't eat too much of it." We stand in silence for a couple of minutes, taking in the wild ride waiting below, then get down to strategizing. Floyd points out each step of the staircase, notes each rock that interrupts a straight shot down, comes up with a plan: we'll hit the top midstream, move slightly left as we slide over the second drop, veer over to center-right for the third, go straight down the middle for the big one. All of which sounds simple, except that the river is outrunning a rocket sled. It'll all come so, so fast. "Look," Floyd says. "You do what you can do. Try to follow this course, but don't worry too much about where you hit it.

"The important thing is to keep your boat straight," he says. "Keep it straight. If you're pointed even a little off to the side, you'll get into trouble. Just hit it straight-on, and let's see what happens."

I may be overly sensitive, but his tone seems a little less confident than I'd like. It seems to say: "It's been real."

We climb back into the boats. Floyd pushes off, heads straight into the current, zips down the first drop. I watch his helmet bob out of sight below the lip of the falls, take a deep breath, and shove myself away from the bank. I've been in some tight jams on this trip, I remind myself. I tackled rapids alone, miles from help, hours from rescue, back when I could barely steer the canoe. I've fallen over waterfalls backwards at least twice. I survived those damn spiders. All that, and I haven't dumped since Gathright. I can do this. And if I don't, how bad can it be? Ian and Floyd will be there to fish me out of the drink.

Sure, I'll probably wipe out. But maybe, I think, I can do as Floyd says, just keep the boat straight enough to get near the bottom, before I do. I paddle into the current, determined not to fishtail, resolute not to spin. I'm so busy concentrating on getting the canoe square with the lip of the rapids that my anxiety evaporates. The current grabs, starts to suck me toward the brink, to swing my bow to the right. I dip my paddle in the water, the bow snaps back around and the boat sails over the edge.

It hangs bow-high for a moment. Then the canoe tilts nose-first and slides down a frothy, dancing, deafening tube of water like a sled on hard, smooth ice. I don't even notice the rocks as I bound over the second and third drops; the only color I see is white. The big drop at the bottom brings a wave of cold water over the bow and onto my chest. I dig my paddle into the water and swing the canoe into an eddy beside Floyd. "You did it!" he hollers, sounding truly surprised.

"Yeah!" Ian screams from the pipe. "Yeah!"

I let loose a whoop, loud and long, and laugh uncontrollably for a minute. Then, my wits somewhat collected, Floyd and I paddle downstream, over a couple of smaller falls, and cut diagonally across the river toward the south bank.

"You guys must have built up some good karma on this trip," he tells me as we glide through the water, "because today you got through some things you had no business getting through, really." I think about this for a minute. I can't recall anything particularly generous we've done—that I've done, anyway—but the notion that I've had some unseen assistance in the falls doesn't seem far-fetched. "I guess that's true," I say.

We near a concrete boat ramp, our take-out. "You did OK," Floyd says. He pauses, then adds: "But don't try doing this by yourself."

I promise him that I won't.

DAY EIGHTEEN

In the wake of the first European settlers—and against the tide

Ancarrow's Landing, mid-morning: Ian and I stand on a concrete parapet overlooking the river, which flows green and sluggish on an outgoing tide. The James's edge is cool and leafy, its surface calm; our vantage offers no hint that we've bounced through a sun-baked canyonland of industrial towers, storage tanks, and hissing pipes to reach this old boat-building site on the right bank, just a mile or so below downtown Richmond. We are surrounded by industry, a hodgepodge of gravel pits and rusting water towers, tobacco barns and cigarette factories and sewage-treatment plants. A half-mile behind me, traffic on busy Interstate 95, the East Coast's principal north-south highway, follows the river southward. The interstate's whooshes and rumbles are constant, the backdrop to all other sound.

Last night, after treating Floyd to a barbecue dinner near the Pony Pasture, we drove back to Pocahontas State Park and celebrated. We'd cleared the

KIDS FROLIC ON A RIVERBANK TREE
AT DUTCH GAP—A SCENE
NO DOUBT PLAYED OUT HERE
FOR GENERATIONS.

thorniest obstacle of the journey, we figured. The Falls of the James were behind us. In fact, all the falls on the James were behind us. Ahead lay easy paddling on bumpless tidal estuary, and just a hundred miles of it—less than a third of the distance we'd already traveled. We toasted our success with a six-pack of Sam Adams, and a decision to sleep in until eight o'clock.

Now I have the twinge of a headache, and with it has come the suspicion, slight but nagging, that we've celebrated too soon. Jinxed ourselves. Maybe it's the boat ramp's industrial soundtrack, which lends a weird foreboding to the bright, idyllic scene before us. Maybe it's the realization that a hundred miles, easy paddling or not, is a mighty long way—going upriver, it's clear back to Howardsville. Maybe it's the water's powerful laziness, which for some reason reminds me of pacing tigers at the Norfolk zoo. Maybe I drank too much beer. "Looks a lot different," Ian says, peering down at the water.

I have the maps open. "It does," I agree. I notice something depicted in the charts that I haven't seen up to now: navigation markers. Lights. "Look at that," I say. I show him the map. He nods. "Like I said."

We lug the canoe down the concrete boat ramp, arrange to meet for lunch a few miles downstream. While we talk, the head of a large turtle silently breaks in the water, hangs motionless for a couple beats, and jerks beneath the surface with a glop. A minute later, when I climb into the canoe and dip my paddle, I'm amazed to see that its blade is visible four feet down. Somehow, despite its meanderings through the largest city on its banks, despite its role as a catchment for city and industry, the James has reached the tidewater looking clean and fresh.

It is, of course, much less healthy than it looks. Stormwater runoff, farm runoff, chemical nasties, and sewage have persistently plagued this part of the river. The oil, gasoline, and grit on Richmond's streets are carried by rain into the storm sewers, and from there straight into the James. Old combined sewer networks—built before standard practice sent street runoff to one pipe, and sewage through another to a treatment plant—now dump both into one pipe, and during heavy rains, straight into the river. The James here is overfertilized. The sewage hits water already tainted with farm fertilizers that spill down upstream riverbanks every time it rains, and with the chemicals that feed suburban lawns and golf courses, forming a nutrient stew that algae love to eat. The algae gorge and multiply, and as they do they suck the oxygen from the water. Fish and other animals have a hard time of it. Richmond has embarked on a sewer upgrade that should eliminate the last of its old combined sewers, but as I push off the ramp and paddle away from the bank and its overhanging trees, they're still in use. I resolve to stay in the boat.

In its first few miles below town the James has carved a long, tree-lined straightaway that runs almost directly south, and some of it, like Ancarrow's

Landing, could be mistaken for rural stretches far upriver. But the trees thin in places to betray tank farms, quarries, and warehouses, smudged smokestacks, and a conveyor belt fogged in gray dust, dumping coarse gravel into a barge tied to the right bank. The sounds and smells of the city drift over the water. The interstate swings closer and stays there, so that the chorus of accelerating trucks and swooshing cars grows louder.

The day's first half-hour takes me past Rocketts, the old deepwater wharves that long ago served as Richmond's commercial link to the outside world, now pretty much undistinguishable from the rest of the riverfront. I hug the left bank as a tugboat grunts past, headed upstream with an empty gravel barge. The barge's blunt front end ploughs up the channel, creating a curling wave ahead of the craft and a broad wake that radiates toward the banks in parallel ridges, the first of them two feet high. The canoe rocks violently when they hit.

Away off the bank once stood the village of Powhatan, populated in 1607 by an Algonquian tribe under a chief named Parahunt. The village was part of a vast confederacy of tribes that occupied all of coastal Virginia, and that answered to Parahunt's father, the emperor Powhatan. It was a powerful, no-nonsense nation, thousands strong and growing: through war, threats, and alliances, Powhatan had absorbed an ever-expanding chunk of the Mid-Atlantic. His empire, in other words, bore some resemblance to 1607 England, and his people to the small party of men that stopped to see Parahunt en route to the Falls of the James.

Christopher Newport, John Smith, and the rest of the party had followed their sponsors' "Instructions by way of advice" after pulling into the Chesapeake, had found a big river and traveled it inland to a place with deep water and defensible terrain, and there planted an outpost. They weren't a jolly bunch. The ocean voyage had been way longer than expected, the discomfort of those aboard three little ships made worse by backbiting and accusations and craziness. The expedition's leaders were constantly at each other's throats. Little seemed to get done in any sort of reasonable time. And the town site they picked was a buggy swamp ringed by brackish water. After unloading the boats, they'd split into three groups, one to build a fort, another to get fields cleared and crops planted, the third to explore. So it was that twenty-four of them headed farther upriver in a shallop on Thursday, May 21, 1607, a week after arriving.

Over two days they rowed thirty-four miles upstream, meeting some friendly Indians from the Arrohattoc tribe. One offered to map the river ahead on the ground, using his foot. Capt. Gabriel Archer offered him a pen and paper instead, and despite the fact that the Indian had never seen nor held either, he whipped out a serviceable map with them.

The next morning the newcomers moved five miles farther upriver to the Arrohattoc village. A big party ensued, during which the chief, or *werowance,* was announced. By this time the English had heard of Powhatan, and assumed that the arriving chief was the big guy himself. Actually, it was Parahunt, whose village here, just below Richmond, was named for the emperor and was among his nation's key bastions against the Monacans, the coastal Indians' enemies. The party ended, the English pressed on farther upstream, took on half a dozen Indian guides, and discovered the falls. They scouted them briefly, then doubled back to spend the night in the river, probably not far from Ancarrow's Landing.

The English must have been pretty pleased with themselves, at that point. They'd enjoyed an auspicious reception from the chief they thought to be Powhatan. The river beyond the falls, daunting though the rapids were, promised a route to the Pacific, the Eastern Sea. And when Newport tried to send his six Indian guides back to their village, one named Navirans was so eager to stay that they let him. The next morning the English threw a banquet ashore for their Indian hosts, during which Parahunt and his men stuffed themselves on pork and slugged back a fair bit of hooch. Amid all the partying, Newport mentioned that he was keen to hike a ways beyond the falls. Parahunt arranged to meet him at the rapids.

Shortly after the shallop dropped anchor at the eastern edge of what's now downtown Richmond, Parahunt appeared with objections to Newport's plan. The Monacans lived out that way, and were his enemies. Besides, he said, the mountains upstream of the falls were far away, too far away. Not wanting to sour his new friendships, Newport deferred to the chief. Before the captain left, though, he had his men erect a cross inscribed "Jacobus Rex 1607" on a midriver islet. This unhinged the Indians a bit, but Newport explained that the cross represented Powhatan and himself, bound together in friendship.

Headed back downstream, they passed this place again, exchanged waves with Parahunt and his people, and floated on to visit Arrohattoc, whose chief was nursing a hangover. The next day they sat down to a banquet in the village. At one point in the festivities, the chief asked the English to fire a musket. The villagers were so terrorized by the gun's smoke and fuss that some of them visiting the shallop dived overboard. Still, the prospects for life in the New World looked bright. Newport and company left Arrohattoc on pleasant terms and, with Navirans as their guide, cruised the next day to visit an Indian queen's village on the right bank, then farther down the James to a wide stretch of river where they met the chief of the Pamunkeys.

And there things started to go bad. The chief was a half-brother of Powhatan named Opechancanough, whose mouthful of a name—it's pronounced *opy-can-can-oh*—has been the bane of Virginia history students for nearly four hundred years. Opechancanough invited the captain to spend the night, which carried the promise of another friendship forged. But when Newport and the chief wandered off together in conversation, some of the English, protective of their boss, followed. Opechancanough threw a fit over this evidence of mistrust, and booted the foreigners out of his village.

The mood along the river changed abruptly. The next day—Wednesday, May 27—the English landed at Jordan Point and were surrounded by Indians, whom Navirans told to rustle up some fish for the visitors. They did so, but something about the encounter spooked John Smith and some of the party's other members—particularly when, the fish delivered, Navirans unexpectedly quit the expedition and walked off. The English raced back to Jamestown, where their hunches were confirmed: the day before, they learned, two hundred Indians had swooped down on the unfortified town, killing a boy and wounding eleven men. That, as it turned out, was a rather mild omen of the days to come.

I paddle past the invisible site of Powhatan village and down the straightaway. Around me is the beginning of the coastal plain, the shelf of low bottomland and swamp that makes up much of the Eastern Seaboard. Here the bedrock of the Piedmont plateau slopes downward, and is covered by a thickening blanket of sediments, much of it deposited by the James and the other rivers cutting east toward the shore. By the time the James reaches its mouth, at Hampton Roads, the sediments are two thousand feet thick.

Close to two hours into my paddle, the straightaway ends in a sweeping leftward curve, dominated by a hundred-foot-high palisade called Drewry's Bluff. Ringed by wetlands, the bluff commands an expansive view in every direction, an attribute that wasn't lost on the Confederacy. Southern troops dug an earthen redoubt on top of the heights, and garrisoned it through most of the Civil War with naval artillerymen, marines, and army regulars. They also armed it with the South's biggest naval guns, arranging them in a long line along the clifftop, pointed downstream. A mile below Drewry's, a second palisade, Chaffin's Bluff, lines a hard river bend to the right, returning the James to a southward course. The Rebs installed guns on that high ground, too. Any ship bound for Richmond had to pass this strategic pinch point—a dicey proposition even for heavily armored gunboats.

The Federal navy learned this the hard way. On May 15, 1862, a squadron of ships chugged up the river, intending to lob shells into the Confederate capital from just below the falls. The gunboats were led by the ironclad *Monitor,* fresh from its famous duel with the Confederate *Virginia* in the Battle of Hampton Roads. But between Drewry's and Chaffin's bluffs the Union force found the river's deep water obstructed by several sunken wrecks, placed there to slow any marauders. Before they had time to pick a route through the snags, Drewry's big guns opened up. In the four-hour firefight that followed, the *Monitor* was virtually useless: her turret gun couldn't be pointed high enough to target the bluff-top southerners. Smacked around fiercely by a Rebel crossfire, the ships turned tail.

I paddle past a wide creek mouth in the right bank. Just south of it the bend begins, and I start yelling for Ian. The fort itself is perched close to the cliff's edge. Grass-covered earthworks, worn by nearly fourteen decades of rain and wind, enclose open lawn and an encroaching forest. From the top of the battlements you can see the James stretching downstream at point-blank range. It's no wonder the Federal navy didn't try a second run on Richmond.

The war offered more comfort to the soldiers stationed here than it did most Confederate troops. The fort usually had coffee, tea, and sugar, and the men built a village in which to live. "I would like you to see Drewry's Bluff and the big cannon down there," a southern army officer, Charles Minor Black-ford, wrote his seven-year-old daughter in August 1864, "big enough for you to almost crawl into. The breastworks there are very high and they have little rooms in them in which the powder and shells and shot are kept so they may not be injured either by rain or the shells of the enemy. The fortifications are all turfed which makes them look much nicer than any you have ever seen. The soldiers live in small cabins, all of which are whitewashed, and they have beautiful walkways between them and flowers and grass to make them look better." Richmond diarist Mary Boykin Chestnut called the fortification "our Gibraltar." The army officers on post usually called it "Drewry's Fort" or "Fort Drewry."

What no one associated with the installation ever called it was the name that's given for the place on my 7.5-minute quad map from the U.S. Geological Survey, which is usually a reliable authority on such things. The map, like many postwar references to the redoubt, calls it "Fort Darling." The name is a Yankee invention, one that was being used shortly after the battle with the gunboats, and may have had its start as a code name. By August 1862, "Fort Darling" was being thrown around enough by the Union government and northern press that the *Richmond Daily Dispatch* felt the need to put its foot down. The paper complained that month that "the Yankees, in all their allusions to our batteries at Drewry's Bluff, have applied to them the name, 'Fort Darling'" This name, the paper suggested, "should be forever ignored in the Confederate States."

I beach the canoe on a narrow strip of mud and black sand at the bluff's base, and peer up through overhanging trees and dense brush growing from its vertical face. "Ian!" I holler. From a long way off I hear him answer. It takes me a minute, as he yells on, to find his face in all the viney tangle. Finally I spot him four stories up, standing on the edge of a crumbly precipice. "Can you get down here?" I shout.

"I don't think so," he says. "There's really no path down. It's just a straight drop."

"Well, I'm hungry," I say. "I'm ready for lunch." I pull out my maps. Down-river, almost to the bend at Chaffin's Bluff, is a narrow break in the right bank that opens into a squarish lake. A road dead-ends at the lake's edge. I can't tell from the map, though, whether there's any way to reach the road. "Try get-ting to the lake," I yell. "I'll paddle in off the river, and if you're there, we'll eat lunch. If you're not, I'll keep paddling. At worst, we can meet four miles farther down." Ian waves. His head disappears beyond the cliff's lip.

The beach below Drewry's Bluff has its own distinguished Civil War history. I paddle now where the C.S.S. *Patrick Henry* spent most of the war's last three years as the classroom, dorm, and administrative building of the Confederate States Naval Academy.

The ship was a side-wheel passenger steamer on the run between Rich-mond and New York when it was seized at the outbreak of hostilities. The Norfolk Navy Yard transformed the ship into a twelve-gun troublemaker with a 180-man crew. Just after the Battle of Drewry's Bluff, the converted liner was assigned academy duty, and its first class of 106 won appointments. Classes began in October 1863, with two graduates of the U.S. Naval Acad-emy running the place, and 59 Annapolis midshipmen in the student body. The minimum standards for admission were a bit loose: the ranks included a twelve-year-old.

Aboard the *Patrick Henry* were classrooms, mess decks, drill space, and hammocks; some midshipmen slept aboard, some in cabins up at the fort. Even so, the academy couldn't accommodate all of them, so they were rotated among the school, other shore billets, and duty aboard the Navy's ships. The time away from campus was something like a modern college internship, only you got shot at.

I paddle down to the opening in the bank, find the lake flat, featureless, hemmed by skinny trees and waterlogged bottomland. Across its surface, per-haps a quarter mile away, I can make out a gap in the trees where the road must end. It's empty, and stays that way. After waiting ten minutes for the Volvo to appear, I spin the canoe around and head back through the lake's shallow mouth to the river. As I turn downstream, I notice a carefully tended spread across the James—gleaming white, tree-shaded house and outbuildings, all with green roofs; a dense lawn; a heavy-duty riprap fairing along the water's edge. And a flower bed, mid-yard, planted so that its red and green blooms form the initials "JD." The "J" takes the form of a cowboy boot. It's Jimmy Dean's place—as in Jimmy Dean the Texas-born country singer-turned-sausage maker. The flowers replicate his sausage company's logo.

Our fallback meeting point is a park and public boat ramp on a hard left bend in the river, next to a mammoth Virginia Power plant. I share the miles approaching the bend with a crowd of powerboats. They whine past at highway speeds, carving deep trenches in the river's middle, creating steep-sided shock waves that slap noisily against the banks and turn the canoe into a carnival ride. They multiply as I pick my way among the blackened stumps of ancient piers, through a five-mile series of gentle curves. The power plant soars from the right bank, plunging the bended river into a shady twilight. Humming loudly, it shows off a fretwork of catwalks and gratings and exposed pipe.

Just below, I spot the busy boat ramp, and beyond it, Ian standing on a gravel beach backed by dense woods. The river appears to branch, one leg heading north, off to the left, the other continuing straight ahead. I have reached the Aiken Swamp–Dutch Gap Cutoff, descendant of the oldest canal in America. The cut is just under a mile long, and snips through the necks of two oxbows that looped so radically they almost formed a figure eight. Imagine a billowy letter S, reversed so that it faces to the left. Now draw a straight line linking the letter's head and tail. That pretty well mimics the canal's path.

It started as a far less elaborate ditch, shallow and narrow and just a few hundred feet long, at the present canal's lower end. In 1611, some 350 stouthearted, heavily disciplined English settlers from Jamestown led by Thomas Dale, a wheel in the colony, established a city just below here on the river's south side and called it Henricus. It became home to the first hospital in English America, its name a mix of the poetic and prosaic, Mount Malady. Also to the first library. And, though it never opened to students, the first chartered university.

Dale used a Dutch technique to help palisade the settlement. The English dug a moat across the base of the neck on which the town was sprouting, and erected a paled fence behind it. Settlers took to calling it Dale's Dutch Gap. Eleven years later, Henricus and most of the surrounding countryside were wiped out in an attack organized by Opechancanough. Whether the Gap slowed the Indians down is kind of moot.

It certainly slowed things down for Benjamin Butler, however. In May 1864, the Union general led a huge amphibious force up the James, disgorged his troops downriver from here, and poised for an attack on Richmond or Petersburg. And poised. And poised.

Butler was loathed by the Confederacy, mostly for his supposedly brutish behavior while commanding the occupation of New Orleans. He wasn't easy, in fact, for his own lieutenants to like: balding and paunchy, ruddy-faced, he spent a lot of time screaming at his subordinates. He also had the habit of winking in conversations, which struck many as creepy. Now, with the power in his hand to win far greater infamy, he sat. His attack never materialized. He busied himself with building defenses, so that soon his force was dug in behind an unassailable earthworks. It was not the signature of an attacking army;

the Confederates recognized that Butler wasn't going to strike, and used the time he bought them to erect a well-defended line of redoubts around Petersburg, the supply center for the capital. Those Southern fortifications became keys in the later siege of the city. They may have extended the war by months.

Big on construction projects, Butler also attempted to build a true canal through the oxbows at Dutch Gap, figuring it would give federal ships a shortcut around Southern guns on the bends. The plan didn't offer a heck of a lot of utility: Drewry's Bluff still remained upriver. Nonetheless, the general saw his soldiers move fifteen thousand cubic yards of soil with little more than shovels, harassed all the while by Rebel sniper fire. By war's end, small boats could work their way through the ditch, but not much else. After the war, the Union Army's blood and sweat became a gift to Richmond shippers: dredged and widened, the canal shaved more than seven slow miles off trips to and from the city.

I weave my way among jockeying boaters to the gravel beach, where I nose the canoe ashore and follow Ian up to the Volvo. We load up on bread, peanut butter, jelly, and Gatorade and hike back down to the water's edge, where we watch a trio of shirtless boys shinny up a big sycamore, clamber out onto a bare branch overhanging the river, and jump. The scene could be from any time in the river's European history, I think—1620, 1776, 1865. God knows how long a rope has hung off that branch. Then a cigarette boat thunders by at dangerous speed, bow slapping the water with rhythmic whacks, a roostertail fifty feet high in its wake.

I plough through wake-mussed water after lunch, and as I dip my paddle I notice that its blades now vanish a few inches from the river's surface. The clear-running James has turned a murky brown. Off to my left is the upper oxbow severed by the canal. It's now called Hatcher's Island, and appears to be a marshy thumb more water than land. To my right is the remnant of the lower bend, Farrar's Island. On its edge, at the canal's eastern end, is the site of old Henricus.

The town site is on a point ringed by fly-ash ponds, a bare-tree swamp where blue herons congregate, and a large tidal lagoon, and is home to a partial palisade, a watchtower, and a small cottage. Interpreters in seventeenth-century costume tend an impressive herb and vegetable garden within the walls, do seventeenth-century chores, and answer tourists' latter-day questions. It's a somewhat sanitized picture of the real deal. The inhabitants of the original city didn't shower regularly, as their present-day imitators do. Nor did they get regular dental care. Nor have a sanitary means of dealing with the grim volume of sewage that 350 hard-working colonists produce on a daily basis. Nor enjoy the benefits of all-temperature laundry detergents. It was a base, diseased, and lousy existence.

But it beat Jamestown. When Thomas Dale arrived in the colony's first city, he found it wholly unfit for duty—strafed by malaria-bearing mosquitoes, boggy, ill with its own waste, and susceptible to Spanish attack, a constant worry among the English. Not only that, but its occupants were listless zombies who passed time bowling while their settlement crumbled around them. Within days of his May 1611 arrival, Dale cruised up the James to this place, "a high land invironed with the Mayne River, near to an Indian Town called Arrahattocke—a convenient strong, healthie and sweet seate to plant the new Towne in." He returned that September with his 350 helpers to establish the place as the westernmost outpost of the English-speaking world. The men quickly built defenses around the neck and fenced off the fields of corn around it, and in time got around to digging the Dutch Gap. A visitor found that the defended city had "three streets of well-framed houses, a handsome Church, the foundation of a better laid (to bee built of Bricke), besides store-houses, watch-houses and such like."

Dale wasn't an easy boss. A lifelong professional soldier, he demanded utter obedience from his men, and should they fail him, in even the smallest way, they could count on an almost perversely harsh punishment. Twenty-one civil and moral wrongs, among them blasphemy and speaking badly of the leadership, were capital offenses. Uttering "unlawful oaths" would get you a dagger through the tongue. And should, God forbid, a settler come to see Indian life as preferable to this perpetual lock-down, Dale ordered him chased down and killed. "Some he apointed to be hanged Some burned Some to be broken upon wheles," one contemporary reported, "others to be staked and some to be shott to deathe." Thomas Dale practiced a particularly harsh brand of tough love.

It's not surprising that Dale found Jamestown in such disarray when he pulled in. In fact, it's a bit more surprising that he found anyone left alive in the settlement, for the place had seen tough times in the nearly four years since Newport led his tiny force upstream in the shallop. Crammed into a triangular log fort, subsisting on brackish river water, the Jamestown pioneers had succumbed by the hundreds to illness. The nastiest, perhaps, was an epidemic of fevers, swelling, and "flux"—the sudden and deadly discharge of bloody fluids from the body—that appeared within weeks of the first group's arrival, and may have been a combination of typhoid and beri-beri. By the autumn of 1607, nearly half of the colony was dead. Those who survived lived in fear of the Indians and squabbled among themselves. The leadership behaved idiotically. Tempers frayed. The colony's council deposed one of its own, George Kendall, who was eventually executed, and tossed their first president, as well. They elected in his place one John Ratcliffe; the villain of Disney's *Pocahontas,* in reality he had little time to do any damage.

That December, Capt. John Smith, a hirsute, tough fireplug of a guy whom

Disney turned into a blond leading man, led an exploring party up the Chickahominy River, which enters the James just above Jamestown. They paddled into an ambush. All of the men with Smith were slain, and the captain avoided death only by grabbing an Indian and using him as a shield. Within minutes, that defense was useless: he was surrounded by two hundred warriors under Opechancanough. Captured, facing execution, Smith mesmerized Opechancanough with his compass and a discourse on the earth and its place in the universe. It's a puzzle how he communicated such complex concepts to the chief—Smith, after all, didn't speak a lick of Pamunkey, and Opechancanough may have known all of a half dozen words in English. Somehow, though, the captain so impressed the chief that he was treated like a rock star. Well-fed and fussed over, Smith was marched hither and yon through the swampy countryside for a few days, then presented to the emperor.

Powhatan, Smith wrote, was "of personage a tall well proportioned man, with a sower looke, his head somewhat grey . . . his age near sixtie, of a very able and hardy body to endure any labor," and "with such a grave and Majesticall countenance, as drave me into admiration to see such a state in a naked Salvage." What followed has been hotly debated by generations of historians. To hear Smith tell it, Powhatan ordered him dragged to a pair of large stones and his head laid against them, while several Indians prepared "to beate out his braines" with clubs. All of a sudden, the King's daughter—a little girl of ten or eleven named Matoaka, but whom the world knows as Pocahontas— "got his head in her armes, and laid her owne upon his to save him from death."

That doesn't ring true to a lot of folks. Smith was the only English witness to the incident, and Pocahontas had been dead for years before a full account of it saw print. Besides that, some historians have questioned Smith's descriptions of earlier exploits—his claim, for instance, that while in Eastern Europe he beheaded three Turks in staged battle, was sold into slavery, murdered his master, donned the dead man's clothes, and rode to freedom. Whatever. Americans have chosen to embrace the story, tall tale or not, and it ranks among the nation's great myths, prominent in the literature and folklore that define Americanism.

Maybe, just maybe, full-scale war with the Indians was avoidable at that point; Smith was released, and traded successfully with the tribes for a while. But other English bartered foolishly, screwing up the rate of exchange between the colonists' trinkets and Indian corn to the point that the price of groceries became extravagant. Driven by hunger, the settlers took to simply taking the food they needed. By late in 1608, Smith had explored the upper Chesapeake and met some of Powhatan's enemies, and armed with a new understanding of the empire's vulnerability, became more aggressive in his dealings with the "Salvages."

Relations spiraled downward. Early in 1609, Powhatan broke off talks with the English. Smith, his power compromised by the colony's internal politics, strove to reinforce his authority with the local tribes by training a band of guerilla fighters and leading it on strong-arm visits to Indian towns. During a call on the Pamunkeys, he held a pistol to Opechancanough's head until the tribe coughed up enough corn to save the chief's life. Powhatan was not about to put up with such nonsense. The emperor's territory was already under pressure, with ocean to the east and enemies to the north and west. The last thing he needed was a bunch of unpredictable aliens raising hell in the heart of his holdings. His people started looking for an excuse to fight.

And God knows, the English provided it. With the arrival of a resupply convoy in August 1609, Jamestown was suddenly filled with newcomers hostile to Smith. He responded by dispersing them far from the town to establish new settlements—a strategy that, given the personalities involved, was guaranteed to end badly. English captains George Percy and John Martin and a hundred colonists set up camp near the villages of the Nansemonds, sent messengers to the Indians, and lost their cool when the men failed to return. They raided the Nansemond towns and "burned their howses, Ransacked their Temples, Tooke downe the Corpses of their deade kings from their Toambes, And caryed away their pearles, Copper, and braceletts, wherewith they doe decore their kings' funeralles." Things were no better up the James, where Francis West settled 120 men in a flood-prone fort near the falls. In mid-August 1609, Smith arrived on the scene, found the fort wanting, and forced Parahunt to sell him the village of Powhatan. West's men moved in and behaved like hooligans, beating up the Indians, stealing corn, and trashing homes.

Payback was ugly. The Nansemonds encircled the English in a siege that claimed nearly half of the expedition, and Parahunt's men killed at least fifty of West's over several months of raids. The scattered English beat feet to Jamestown, and John Smith sailed for England, having been maimed in a freak gunpowder explosion on his way back from West's outpost. Now, without their one real leader, the settlers awaited their fate.

Their prospects seemed to brighten momentarily in mid-October 1609, when Powhatan sent fresh meat to the fort with the promise of a pile of corn. But the following month, when John Ratcliffe showed up in Opechancanough's neighborhood to take delivery of the food, an ambush waited. Two-thirds of his fifty-man force was killed. Ratcliffe, captured, was tied to a tree. Indian women used mussel shells to skin him alive.

Not long after, Francis West sailed to the Potomac and successfully traded for corn with Indians there. But the English queered the deal, turning on their potential allies without reason and hacking a good many of them. Then they sailed for England, leaving Jamestown without food or friends.

Winter came, and with it a misery so intense that every hardship and terror the settlers had so far endured seemed laughably insignificant. Powhatan's bowmen surrounded the fort, and stuck there for six months, killing anyone who ventured outside the walls. Inside, starvation gripped the garrison. When the fort's food stores dwindled, colonists ate their hogs, dogs, and horses. When they ran through those, they caught and cooked rats. And when that didn't ease the pain in their guts, they ate their dead and "Licked upp the Bloode" of the wounded. Some didn't wait for death before digging in: one colonist killed his pregnant wife, chopped her up, and salted her; he threw their baby in the river. When the siege lifted, Jamestown was in ruins. Two out of three Englishmen were dead.

Just below Henricus I reach a wide confluence, where the oxbow that earlier arced off to the left rejoins the river. I paddle across this wide, choppy expanse of water and back into the James's natural channel. A half mile farther on I glide beneath the high-rise span of the Interstate 295 suspension bridge. Another mile of power boat-churned water, and I reach the head of a second artificial cut through this section of river aptly nicknamed "the Curls"—but not before the water changes, becomes slow, difficult to paddle. I wonder, at first, whether I'm just tired, and not getting as much glide out of each paddle stroke. But even when I dig in and try muscling the boat faster, it seems unwilling to move. It takes me a few minutes to realize that it's not me, but the river itself: for the first time in the trip, I've encountered a foul tide. Ian was onto something this morning: this is a different river from the one that tumbles into Richmond.

We pull the boat from the water on the south bank and head back to Pocahontas State Park. It's our last night in this comfortable bivouac; we load up most of our gear as night falls, then make plans for a long strike down the river at first light.

DAY NINETEEN

What's that smell?

Well before sunup, Ian and I strike the tents and pull out of our campsite at Pocahontas State Park. We waste no time: high tide's on the way. Yesterday afternoon made clear that the lower James will be less a river, in the traditional sense, than a sloppy, wind-raked finger of ocean. Not only are its banks already veering apart—the James is close to a quarter mile wide now—but for half of each day the tide robs it of a single-minded drive it has displayed since spilling from the rock pile in Hightown: to run downhill. To reach the sea.

It vacillates here, takes two steps forward, one back, and repeats this dance step all the way to Hampton Roads. Putting the canoe in the water at high tide will give me roughly six hours of good paddling on a current moving with me, hurrying me downstream. If I'm on the water when the tide turns, however—after low tide, when it starts coming back upstream—hard, frustrating work will ensue. Svelte as the canoe looks, against the incoming tide I might as well be driving the Hoover Dam downriver. The reversed current will brake the boat's glide between my paddle strokes, blunt my speed, cloud my disposition.

It's just past dawn when we get back to the river. I push off from the right bank and paddle into the Jones Cutoff, the second of three canals sliced through the oxbowed Curls. Marsh dominates the left bank, low woods the right. Soon the sun rises to hover just over the river, tingeing its languid surface with gold, warming the tops of the maples and oaks on its flanks. A cool, light breeze wafts in from the west to nudge me gently downstream. The only sounds I hear are those of the paddle's blades dipping into the water, and droplets flung from the blades as I pull them back out. I'm alone. After yesterday's gasoline-powered madness, the peace is entrancing.

But as I traverse the third cut, at Turkey Island, the sylvan morning ends. A gust brings a whiff of something familiar, but distantly so, from deep in the past . . . High school. Biology class. Dissections. *Formaldehyde.* I paddle on, and a blue steel tower emerges from the trees on the south bank, along with tall braids of shiny, curlicued pipe. The smell becomes almost overpowering. Ah, I think to myself, I must be near Hopewell.

For the better part of a century this industrial city at the James's wide confluence with the Appomattox River has advertised its presence with each breeze. The unhappy recipients of its message can live twenty miles away or more if the wind's blowing right. It has been a city of chemicals since its founding in 1915, when real estate types auctioned five hundred lots they'd drawn off in corn and peanut fields just outside the gates of an enormous guncotton factory. The E. I. du Pont de Nemours Company soon operated the largest plant of its kind on the planet, and by year's end Hopewell—named for an old estate at the confluence—was a boomtown of thirty thousand, its main street lined with hastily thrown-up stores and saloons, its population quartered in rickety frame houses, tents, and tarpaper shacks.

Some people called it "The Wonder City." Actually, the only wonder was that its citizens didn't kill each other as fast as they pulled into town, for with its run-amok growth, Hopewell became a scene from the Wild West, its men-folk packing pistols as they strode the plank sidewalks. Shootings were common. Gambling was rampant. "Disputes were quickly settled by the trigger," one newspaper account reported. "During one night alone the coroner had six killings to investigate. Faro, keno, poker, crap paraded hand-in-hand with bootlegging, prostitution and kindred vices."

With America's entry into World War I, the population blew to forty thousand. Then the fighting ended, and the jobs did, too. DuPont closed the plant, and Hopewell's population plummeted almost as quickly as it had risen. By 1920, it was a village of thirteen hundred. The town had location going for it, however. Lying as it did at the confluence of two big rivers, with railroad lines and highways linking it to the country's interior, it was ideal for big industry. Other companies moved in, chemical companies, so many that in the decades that followed, little Hopewell became the self-proclaimed "Chemical Capital of the South." Motorists encountered road signs emblazoned with the boast as they reached the city limits. Prosperity didn't come cheap: the town grew ugly, an eyesore of snaking pipes and steam and stink. Hopewell residents laughed off the price they paid for steady jobs with jokes about the stench, calling it—as the residents of just about every industrial hellhole will—"the smell of money." Until 1975, when they stopped laughing and started pulling down road signs.

That July, state officials shut down a tiny factory in a converted Hopewell gas station after learning its employees were contaminated with Kepone, a wickedly toxic and long-lasting ant and roach killer, thought to be linked to liver cancer, as well as skin, eye, and neurological damage. The pesticide had been developed by the Allied Chemical Company in 1949, and Allied had stewed up batches of it in Hopewell from 1966 to 1974. After that, it had been made for more than a year by the Life Science Products Company, a small outfit run by former Allied employees.

The state moved in when some of Life Science's workers started suffering tremors and chest pains. Not long after that, investigators found Kepone not only in the company's small building but in the air, the soil, and well water around it. And then came a truly terrifying revelation: Life Science Products had dumped thousands of pounds of the stuff into Hopewell's wastewater treatment system—and through it, into the James. The state banned fishing and crabbing on the lower James for thirteen years. The *New York Times* called it "one of the great environmental disasters of the century."

The toxin didn't go far after leaving the town's pipes. Tons of it settled in the mud on the river's bottom, where it was layered ever-deeper beneath the silt the James carries from farms and mountainsides upstream. Dredging the Kepone out of the river was not much of an option: environmentalists feared that it would kick up clouds of the pesticide, enabling it to travel farther down-river to the fish and crabs of the Chesapeake, and the cities of Hampton Roads. So it stays on the river's floor. It might last hundreds of years down there.

In the Turkey Island Cutoff I paddle past a tiny ferry parked on the right bank, the only link to the Presquile National Wildlife Refuge on Turkey Island it-self, off to my left. The island's a soggy, paisley-shaped piece of ground, swamp covering all but a sliver of it; the ferry is idle now, the low bank around it empty. Beyond the island, among sycamores, maples, and gravel pits on the north shore, stands a lonely monument to the great flood of May 1771—the deluge thought to be the worst ever on the James, at least until 1969. Its stone reads: "The Foundation of this Pillar was laid in the calamitous year 1771 When all the great Rivers of this Country were swept by Inundations Never before ex-perienced Which changed the face of Nature And left traces of their Violence that will remain for Ages." The obelisk stands at the flood's high-water mark, something like forty-five feet above the river's normal level. I estimate that dis-tance up the sides of riverbank trees, try to picture forty-odd feat of water over my head. I'm not up to it. It seems impossible.

The river curves sharply right, and as I paddle southward the right bank cuts away to form a small bay at the mouth of the incoming Appomattox River. Suddenly the James is more than a mile wide. The breeze stiffens. The flat water turns to a foot-high chop. I shove my way through it, paddling steadily, cut-ting across the bay's mouth toward the land at the Appomattox's far side.

City Point is a sharp horn curled upstream, high bluffs rising from its river-front. I cross the wide water briskly and grind the canoe ashore on a sandy beach at their feet, slip off my life vest and pull the boat onto dry ground. To my right, a footpath curves around the point; to my left, perhaps seventy-five yards off, is a parking lot. Cars, pickups, and minivans, a dozen in all, are widely spaced throughout it. I head left. Ian's supposed to meet me somewhere on the point, but we've not specified where. I find no sign of him or the Volvo in the lot; its few occupants are sitting on their truck hoods or standing in the sand, staring out into the river. So I hang around a while. Ten minutes click by while I pace the asphalt. Should I go on, I wonder? Would he know to meet me downstream? I decide he wouldn't: The river's big here. He'd worry. He'd stick.

Roads head in two directions from the water's edge, one of them uphill to the top of the bluff and a manicured historic site. I hike that way, past well-tended old homes built on the hillside, and arrive at the clifftop and another parking lot. An expanse of cloudless, bright blue sky greets me. Strong sun-shine. No Volvo. Twenty minutes have passed, during which the tide has been rolling out. I'm getting antsy. I walk back down to the parking lot at the beach, again find it missing Ian and his car, and return to the boat. Another five minutes go by. Where, I think, would Ian be most likely to go—here, on the water's edge, or up at the historic site? Where would he expect to find me?

The boy's thinking can be odd, I reflect. Chances are, he'd drive to the high ground, and stand at its edge yelling my name like he did at Drewry's Bluff. If I were to walk down the footpath to the right, I'd get below the historic site and might hear him. Along the way, I pass a chain of placards explaining the point's history. Its most notable adventures came during the Civil War, when it was the port for the Union siege of Petersburg, not far up the Appomattox. The ground I walk was a tremendous wharf and railroad terminal, hastily thrown up to receive and dispatch tons of supplies to the Federals trying to cut off Richmond's supply center. A couple minutes on the path takes me around the horn and out of sight of the canoe, and for a moment I consider going back, suspecting that he'll pull into the beachfront lot while I'm off down the shore. I decide to walk on for another minute. Across the water, on the Appomattox's far bank, Hopewell's smokestacks burp exhaust into the atmosphere. If that's the smell of money, I think, there's an abundance of cash in the air this morning.

The minute up, I stop and holler: "Ian!" And to my surprise, I hear back: "Earl!" I can't see him beyond the brush sprouting from the bluff, so I shout directions to the boat. "I want to get out of here," I add. "The tide's running." He's pulling into the lot when I round the path near the canoe. I watch him park and climb out of the car. "Man, that was lucky," he says as we near each other.

"No kidding," I tell him. "Good to see you." We shake hands. "Look," I say, "I need to get going. You have your maps?" He pulls them from his pocket, unfolds them. From City Point the right bank falls into a deep bowl, its far side curving up to another finger poking into the current more than two straight-line miles away. Jordan Point. A lift bridge of silvery steel shoots 4,463 feet from its tip to the left bank. "Let's meet there," I tell him, studying my map.

"Looks like there's a marina on the point."

"Cool. I'll see you at the boat ramp."

Off City Point's eastern shore lies a fat marshy island. I cruise past it in shallow but broad water, skirt past a dozen little islets of mud and cordgrass, rock in the wakes of powerboats that have finally joined me. It's early, just eight o'clock, but feels far later—perhaps because I've already lost a third of the tide. Or maybe because the day's already steamy. A haze seeps from the river, smudges its surface, erases the line between water and low shore. I'm nearing Jordan Point before its details start to sharpen, and I can make out the rooftops of the marina, the highway riding the peninsula's spine and launching onto the Benjamin Harrison Bridge.

I paddle close to the shore beneath the bridge's brawny latticework of girders, listening to cars hiss overhead, and round the point into the marina's protected lagoon. The ramp waits beside a big racing boat that's tied up in front of the place's store. A couple of guys are clambering around on the monster, talking to sunburned, big-bellied fellows up on the dock. The sight of the canoe seems to kill the conversation. They stare as I gingerly nudge the boat's hull to the ramp, rotate ninety degrees to settle parallel to the concrete.

Up on dry ground I stop, stretch my back, have a look around. It was here that John Smith and his colleagues sensed the Indians were up to something late in their first reconnaissance up the James. It doesn't look much like an Indian camp now: The parking lot and marina store are busy. Traffic passes on the highway. The old Hopewell–Charles City Ferry dock rises from the riverbank a few yards off, a relic of river crossings before the bridge's completion in the mid-1960s. But somewhere around here, perhaps right where I stand, Navirans announced he was hitting the trail, the English got spooked, and there started the long months of trouble that culminated in the "Starving Time."

Understandably, Jamestown's survivors were eager to blow out of the colony after the siege. They were getting ready to do so when up sailed the colony's boss, Thomas Gates, who'd been shipwrecked for a good while on Bermuda. Gates took one look at the mess that England's proud North American colony had become and decided that evacuating was, in fact, the thing to do. He, his men, and the survivors packed up and left. Jamestown was abandoned.

Then came one of those crazy pieces of luck on which history turns. As the battered colonists sailed gratefully downriver, they met a flotilla of English ships headed the other way, led by Lord De La Warr, Virginia's new governor. De La Warr turned the fleeing settlers around and returned them to Jamestown, bringing along a lavish store of food and equipment, a pile of weapons and a force of hardened soldiers. The day was the turning point in England's colonial experience, the juncture at which Jamestown moved from weary helplessness to a stern, military efficiency. De La Warr enacted a new code of behavior, called the "Lawes Divine, Morall and Martiall," that put the screws to anyone disobeying God or country. Shortly after, he launched an offensive against the Indians.

In July 1610, the English killed twenty friendly Kecoughtans in what's now the city of Hampton. In August they struck upriver, burning a Paspahegh town; George Percy, leading the attack, reported, "we fell in upon them putt some fiftene or sixtene to the Sworde and Almost all the reste to flyghte." When one of his lieutenants brought him the Indian "queen," her children, and one warrior, Percy "taxed him becawse he had Spared them his Answer was thatt have-ing them now in my Custodie I might doe with them whatt I pleased.

"Upon the same I cawsed the Indians head to be cutt of," Percy wrote. "And then dispersed my fyles Apointeinge my Sowldiers to burne their houses and to cutt downe their Corne groweinge abott the Towne." The English weren't winning any more congeniality awards than they were spelling bees. They killed the captured Indian children by "Throweinge them overboard shoteinge owtt their Braynes in the water." The queen's demise was a little less complex: Percy simply ordered her stabbed to death.

More English raids followed, during which the colonists killed men, women, and children, cut down corn, wrecked villages. They waged a ruth-less war founded on the principle that to steal corn meant not having to grow it, and not having to grow it meant devoting fewer men to agriculture and more to kicking tail. In 1611 Powhatan struck back. A Lt. Puttock was on duty one day in Jamestown's blockhouse, a key bastion where the peninsula joined the north bank, when Indians started taunting him. Puttock eventually lost his temper and charged the unseen enemy with his entire complement of about twenty men. Hundreds of warriors let fly their arrows; the English didn't have time to fire a shot. Had the Indians immediately attacked the main settlement, they'd have caught it unawares and inflicted major damage. But they let out a wild war whoop, which brought fifty musketeers running to the blockhouse. Their fire drove the Indians off.

The door was closing on Powhatan's opportunity to erase the colony. That May Thomas Dale arrived, stiffened the already lethal "Lawes Divine, Morall and Martiall," and got everybody busy renewing attacks on the surrounding tribes. Heavily armored, the English were already doing well in battle when late that summer another 250 or so hand-picked, all-business troops arrived. It was that September that Dale established Henricus. For the first time, the colony had real muscle.

Ian pulls into the lot as I circle the marina store, trying to work the hob-ble out of my knees. He strolls up with a wave. "We're almost out of Gatorade," he says. "Why don't we get some cold ones here?"

"That'll work," I say.

"How's the paddling going?"

"Good," I tell him. We step into the air-conditioned store and gasp. When I've basked in the cool for a moment I add: "The tide's making a big difference."

"Great, man. Where do you wanna meet next?" We grab a half dozen drinks out of the cooler and walk to the counter, where a grizzled ancient mariner is running the register.

"You have your maps?"

"Yeah." He pulls the folded wad from his pocket, flattens it on the counter. We pay the man for the drinks as we consider the map's depiction of the river ahead. Another big, round bay is carved from the James's south bank below Jordan Point. Its far side is a knob of land called Maycocks Point; another couple of miles beyond Maycocks, the bank thrusts toward the river's middle, creating a sharp turn around an old plantation, Flowerdew Hundred. I step off the distance between here and there with my fingers. "About seven miles," I say.

"You think you can do that by the time the tide turns?"

I nod. "Should be able to. We can have lunch at Flowerdew."

"Sounds good."

We're about to turn for the door when I spot a stack of tide tables on the counter. Their cover depicts Garvey Winegar, outdoors writer for the *Richmond Times-Dispatch*. He's wearing a safari jacket and a Panama hat, holds a fishing rod, and has a smile on his face that suggests gastrointestinal discomfort. It's clearly a posed studio shot. "Nice picture," Ian murmurs. On the card's flip side is the table itself, along with a list of points along the James and, for each, the adjustments to the table necessary for an accurate tide reading. The math involved is a struggle, but we take a couple of copies with us.

Back on the river, a fresh load of Gatorade in the cooler behind my seat, I start across the bay scooped from the right bank. This one's so big it has a name—Tar Bay—and swells the James to two miles wide. My course takes me straight from Jordan Point to Maycocks, a mile from either shore. Power boats whine past far down the bay, looking gray and fuzzy in the haze. Others thump by in the river's main channel, off to my left. Farther that way, on the north bank, stand the famous James River plantations, a chain of eighteenth-century riverfront mansions. As I paddle, one of the biggest, the Shirley Plantation, is nearly behind me, dominated by a mammoth cube of a house, its double-hipped roof crowned with a giant pineapple. Off my port bow lies Berkeley, home of the Harrisons. The first of the family to live there was Benjamin Harrison III, attorney general and treasurer of the colony; next came his son, Maj. Benjamin Harrison IV, member of the House of Burgesses; that Benjamin Harrison's son, the fifth Benjamin Harrison, member of the Continental Congress and signer of the Declaration of Independence; the fifth's son, William Henry Harrison, ninth president of the United States; and William Henry's grandson, Benjamin, the twenty-third president. Farther downriver, almost straight off the bow, lies Westover, which vies with Bremo for America's best-looking house. The plantations were practically independent nations in Virginia's colonial days, their populations of slaves, farmhands, and artisans self-sufficient and linked directly to Britain via the river. Each plantation had an extensive wharf on the James that enabled ships to deliver European goods and load Virginia tobacco. Each had little use for middlemen.

A third of the way across Tar Bay's mouth I reach the first in a necklace of sandy, cedar-studded islands that span half of the big water ahead. I hug them gratefully, struck by their Robinson Crusoe wildness and beauty; though small and rising just inches above the high-tide mark, they look shady and comfortable. I bounce the canoe from island to island, straining to make out something of Berkeley on the far bank. I'm not much interested in the mansion itself, which dates from a time long after the Indian menace had passed. But I am intrigued by President William Henry Harrison, for he was key in ending the fight that our old friend Cornstalk took up against settlers on the Appalachian frontier. In fact, Harrison's success in fighting the Shawnees was a big part of his campaign for the presidency.

After the Revolution, the Indians kept up their attacks on white settlers west of the Alleghenies, until a fed-up George Washington finally dispatched Gen. Josiah Harmar to attack the Miami, Shawnee, and Delaware villages near present-day Fort Wayne, Indiana. Harmar failed to pry the Indians from their land; if anything, they stepped up their attacks. Washington ordered Gen. Arthur St. Clair to force the Indians to say uncle. St. Clair marched into Shawnee territory with two regiments of army regulars and militia. Their morale was poor. Their training was poor. Their equipment was poor. And on November 4, 1791, their health followed: some twelve hundred Indians attacked the encamped army just before dawn, killing half of St. Clair's army, something like seven hundred men, in under four hours. It was the single greatest defeat of the U.S. Army at the hands of the Indians, who suffered just twenty-one dead and forty wounded.

Washington was no doubt losing his patience, and now dispatched an even bigger army into the Ohio. Its boss, Gen. Anthony "Mad Anthony" Wayne, trained his troops for two years. When he finally moved on the Indians in August 1794 his forces vastly outnumbered the foe, whom they met in a forest littered with trees felled in a recent storm. Fallen Timbers, as the battle became known, was a major success for the infant republic. Afterwards, a good many of the Ohio Indians decided their continued existence depended on a negotiated peace with the encroaching whites. In 1795 a council was held at which many Indians accepted a treaty clearing the way for whites to settle a big chunk of the Ohio country.

Not all the Indians, however. An exception was Tecumseh, a leader of the Shawnees—the chief who, as a child, lost his father to Andrew Lewis's militia at Point Pleasant. Tecumseh had fought against Harmar and St. Clair, and at Fallen Timbers, and was convinced that the Indians could hold off the westward-advancing Americans if the tribes could set aside their differences and make a united stand in the Ohio country. He was joined in this vision of a Midwestern Indian nation by his younger brother Lauliwasikau, who in 1805 claimed to have visited the spirit world and received instructions there: the tribes should shuck the white man's ways that they'd embraced over the past half-century, should turn their backs on alcohol, should embrace the customs and lifestyles of their forefathers. Other Indians took to calling this self-described seer "The Prophet," especially after he correctly predicted a solar eclipse in 1806.

Two years later the Shawnees' neighborhood was getting crowded with white settlers. Tecumseh, The Prophet and their followers retreated west into present-day Indiana, where they founded a city on the banks of the Wabash River called Tippecanoe. The settlement, nicknamed Prophetstown, quickly expanded as Indians loyal to the cause of a united front arrived and stayed. Whites got nervous. Prophetstown had the smell of an uprising about it. Tecumseh was gone on a recruiting trip, and The Prophet in charge, when William Henry Harrison put together an army and marched on the town in 1811. He and his troops encamped a short ways off.

Centuries later it's tempting to lament what followed, in the same way one might complain about a boxing match that ends in the first round. Had The Prophet gone on the defensive, his town's warriors could have held off Harrison's thousand-man army for a good while. Had he sought peace, he might have avoided a fight altogether, and preserved Prophetstown for a future showdown. But The Prophet had taken to believing his own press. He was convinced that he could cure the sick, and that his magic would protect his warriors in battle. Before daybreak on November 7, 1811, he and an army of 450 rushed the American camp.

The Battle of Tippecanoe was a bloody affair. Sixty two of Harrison's soldiers were killed on the spot or died later, and nearly twice that many were wounded. The fight went to the whites, however: when the attacking Indians noticed that The Prophet's magic hadn't protected their gunshot colleagues, they fought with a little less abandon; before long, they simply ran for their lives. Harrison marched into unprotected Prophetstown and burned it down. The Tecumseh Confederacy was through.

Despite my efforts, I see nothing of Berkeley as I cross Tar Bay. The James here has grown too wide to make out much at all on the left bank. But this is a good place to recall a tribute to the Shawnee written by Capt. John Stuart, a veteran of the battle between Andrew Lewis's militia and Cornstalk's warriors at Point Pleasant.

> It was chiefly the Shawanese that cut off the British army under General Bradock, in the year 1755, only nineteen years before our battle, where the General himself, and Sir Peter Hackett, second in command, were both slain, and a mere remnant of the whole army only escaped.

It was they, too, who defeated Major Grant and his Scotch Highlanders, at Fort Pitt, in 1758, where the whole of the troops were killed and taken prisoners. After our battle, they defeated all the flower of the first bold and intrepid settlers of Kentucky, at the battle of the Blue Licks. There fell Colonel John Todd and Colonel Stephen Trigg. The whole of their men were almost cut to pieces. Afterwards they defeated the United States army, over the Ohio, commanded by General Harmar. And lastly, they defeated General Arthur St. Clair's great army, with prodigious slaughter.

I believe it was never known that so many Indians were ever killed in any engagement with the white people, as fell by the army of General Lewis, at Point Pleasant. They are now dwindled to insignificance, and no longer noticed; and futurity will not easily perceive the prowess they possessed.

Off Maycocks Point I notice the outbound tide is slowing. Paddling becomes a slog. The canoe, sprightly just minutes ago, seems thick, deadened. I've miscalculated the time it would take me to reach Flowerdew, or misunderstood the tidal charts—whichever, I've run out of easy going. I'm grunting along below the point when I notice a flash on the bank, perhaps a half mile away. At first I figure it to be sunlight bouncing off the chrome of a turning car. But a minute later another comes, bright and quick. Then another. Then a fourth. Soon it's clear that it's a signal: flashes are coming every few seconds. I turn the canoe toward them.

It takes me a full fifteen minutes to close the distance enough that I can see Ian standing on a short pier that sprouts from the foot of a sloping lawn. A picnic shelter—it's too big to qualify as a gazebo—stands nearby. A house looms above. I ease the boat ashore and step out. Ian pulls the canoe by its nose onto dry ground. "I saw your signal," I say. "How'd you make those flashes?" He reaches into a pocket, pulls out a rectangular mirror. "The Volvo's vanity mirror," he says. "I unscrewed it from inside the glove compartment."

I'm stunned by his resourcefulness. Ian shrugs. "I wasn't sure I'd be able to get near the water up at Flowerdew. And I could see you were a long way out." I shake my head. "So how'd you know I'd see it?" We walk toward the Volvo, which is parked at the foot of a long, sinuous drive up the hill and behind the house. "I just kept aiming it at you," Ian explains. "I had no other way."

"Awesome," I say. "And you timed it perfectly. The tide's already turned. I'm crawling along out there." We make several PBJs, grab a couple of Gatorades, and walk to the picnic shelter. "Where are we?" I ask. Ian points behind him with his thumb as we sit at the concrete's edge. "I met this guy, the son of the owner, out on the road. Asked him directions, and he offered to let me down here."

"Wow," I say.

"Yeah," Ian sighs. "It's quite a spread."

We eat. Before long a pickup appears at the top of the drive and rolls to a stop beside the Volvo. Its driver is a lanky, curly-haired guy who looks to be in his mid-thirties. He nods hello and saunters to where we sit, eyeing the beached canoe on the way. "Hey again," he says to Ian.

"Hi," Ian replies, then turns to me. "This is the guy I was telling you about." We shake hands. "How far are you gonna try to get today?" he asks, nodding toward the boat. According to the maps, from here the James curves left around the point at Flowerdew Hundred, then back to the right and into a three-mile straightaway, then horseshoe bends to the left around a massive peninsula that juts from the north bank—Weyanoke Point. On the point's far side the river runs straight for another long stretch and hooks around a peninsula on the south side. Below that point—a watery knob called the Kennon Marsh—is another eighteenth-century plantation, Brandon, and beyond it another, Claremont. "It'd be nice to get that far," I tell our host, pointing to the black rectangle denoting the Claremont manor.

He seems shocked. "*Claremont?*" he gasps. "That's a right long way, to Claremont. You might be able to make it, but it'll be dark." It doesn't look that far to me, really, but I return to the map to find an alternative. On the near side of the same peninsula is another plantation house, Upper Brandon. "Maybe Upper Brandon, then," I tell him.

He nods thoughtfully. "Yeah, you should be able to make it to Upper Brandon," he says. "How far have you come so far today?"

"Far end of the Turkey Island Cutoff."

"Well, then, sure. You'll get to Upper Brandon." With that, he jumps back into his truck and takes off. We finish our sandwiches and lounge for a few minutes in the picnic shelter, until Ian stands and slowly walks our empty Gatorade bottles over to the car. On the way back he stops in the middle of the drive, staring down at his T-shirt with apparent disgust. "God, I can't believe I'm still wearing this shirt," he mutters. "I meant to change it the day before yesterday."

"It's pretty repulsive, all right," I agree. "What, did it just slip your mind?"

He wipes his hands on the shirt's already grimy fabric. "Yeah," he says. "I guess I forgot."

"It's a wonder that guy let you down here, looking like that," I tell him. "You look downright Hopewellian."

"It is pretty amazing."

"So: Are you gonna change shirts?"

Ian looks at me as if the thought hasn't occurred to him. "Nah," he says, shaking his head. "Not much point, this late in the day."

Slowly, wearily, I paddle around thin Windmill Point and into the Three-Mile Reach, the Flowerdew Hundred plantation unseen beyond a tree-fringed sandy beach on my right. The first windmill in America was built there, on land staked out as the Jamestown settlers gradually pushed upriver in search of fortune and some elbow room. To my left, the big Weyanoke neck droops south. As I reach its point I cut across the river, hugging the north bank for a few minutes. Here, where the water narrows to less than a half-mile wide, Union troops under Ulysses S. Grant built the world's longest pontoon bridge to the James's south shore, which they crossed to begin their siege of Petersburg. Sassafras grew here in the colony's early days; an Indian word for the plant gave the point its name. Beyond Weyanoke, the James broadens again, and I cut diagonally across its mile-wide course, hoping to trim the time and effort that hugging the bank requires. It's slow going, however: the tide pulls relentlessly at the canoe. Boat wakes slam me, and a southerly wind whips up two-foot waves that attack from my right. It takes me an hour to wallow to the river's far side, where I again see a series of flashes on the water's edge. Ian is standing on a shallow beach framed by willow oaks. This time, he's used his camera's big, battery-pack flash gun to summon me.

I could push on, but I'm whipped, and we've a long drive to our next campsite. The only practical one we've found is a big commercial campground at Jamestown, which we decide will require our driving back to Jordan Point, crossing the Benjamin Harrison Bridge, then taking State Route 5, the Pocahontas Trail, a long way down the river's far side. Actually, if we had a brain between us, we'd see that driving down this side of the James and taking the round-the-clock ferry from Scotland Wharf to Jamestown is a much faster route. Alas. We lack that brain.

We can't see the red-brick Upper Brandon plantation house as we drag the canoe from the water; it's hidden behind boxwoods, magnolias, and oaks, and further buffered by acre upon acre of farm fields at its back. We load the boat onto the car and set off to find the plantation's caretaker, worried about getting back on the property at first light. After driving long, narrow farm roads among vast, flat fields of corn, we find our man and a handful of young longhairs gathered around the back of a pickup, ramming black powder into a muzzle-loader. The caretaker, preoccupied, tells us we shouldn't have any trouble. We thank him and leave.

Back at Jordan Point, the marina's looking a bit different. Cars are jammed into the lot, along with a tractor-trailer advertising beer. Among the people swarming the place are several young women representing the same beer company in shorts and curve-hugging T-shirts. After nineteen days on the river, I'm nearly staggered by the sight of them. Ian, less impressed, pesters me into the store to load up on Gatorade and beer. We push on.

On the far side of the bridge we turn down Route 5 and cruise, windows down, stereo cranking REM, around gentle bends on sun-dappled two-lane road, falling into shallow dips in the low, alluvial terrain. We pass Sherwood Forest, the home of President John Tyler and reputedly the longest frame house in America, at three hundred feet or more. We cross the Chickahominy River on a narrow bridge enclosed by crisscrossing girders. Finally, after driving for an hour, we pull into the James River Campground.

A high hangar of a building encloses the camp store and office and a barnlike rec room. As we near the door we pass a row of newspaper machines. I'm startled to see a headline blaring that Hurricane Mitch has smashed into the Gulf Coast and is now headed for Central America. Our trip has been oddly incommunicado, despite our having talked to the newspaper's editors every day. When I've asked people in the newsroom what's been happening, I've sought, and they've given me, run-downs on goings-on in the office and around Norfolk. Otherwise, I've been clueless about events around me. The headline's a wake-up: the world has been busy while I've been on the water.

Before even looking for a campsite we jump into the big outdoor swimming pool. The sun's low by now, the air cool, the joltingly transparent water icy cold. We swim, gasping, for about twenty minutes, then shiver our way back to the Volvo and roll slowly across a wide, flat shelf of bottomland that comprises most of the camping areas. Travel-trailers are scattered about, many of them supplemented by awnings and lawn chairs that suggest their owners have been here a while and aren't leaving anytime soon. But at the campground's far end is a sharp, wooded rise, and at its peak is a cluster of tent sites overlooking the river and Jamestown's ferry pier. We choose a dirt-floored site and pitch the tents as darkness falls.

Afterward we drive into Williamsburg, a few miles north, file our stories at the College of William and Mary, and pick up some fast food. We eat at a blufftop picnic table by the light of the candle lanterns, ferries loading and unloading on the river below us, kids sneakering by in the dark, playing tag. Four teenagers are circled around a campfire a few sites away, faces glowing saffron and orange, the trees above them breathing with the flicker of the flames. Their boom box is droning heavy metal. Between songs we can hear the low murmur of conversations in the campsites around us. It feels good to have company.

DAY TWENTY

On which we find Jamestown not at all
like that Disney movie

❧ Morning comes at Jamestown. Ian and I crawl out of the tents shortly before sunup and cook a breakfast of coffee and oatmeal at the picnic table, shivering in a chilly wind that sweeps across the river and into the campground, talking over the whoosh of our stove's blue flame and the chattering of the trees. As we pore over the maps it now becomes clear that taking the ferry is much quicker than driving all the way back to the Benjamin Harrison Bridge. With little time before the tide tops out we load up the car and, leaving the tents pitched, head for the pier.

The ferryboat *Williamsburg* is loading as we drive the long concrete dock. We thump aboard over a thick steel ramp, follow the crewman's signals to a parking space near the bow, and get out to walk the deck under the boat's spotlights. The air is heavy with dew, the wind blasting from the south dense and gusty and buffeting the gunwales. Soon a guy on shore lifts the ramp away. With a shudder and a burp of black smoke, the *Williamsburg* glides away from the Jamestown terminal and turns downstream, seagulls hovering over its wake.

An automobile ferry has crossed the James here since 1925, and today the crossing is the only round-the-clock public ferry in Virginia. Four boats carry tourists and commuters on the fifteen-minute voyage from Jamestown to Surry County, often carrying full loads. Not this morning, though: only fifteen or so vehicles are arranged around the ferry's thin stalk of a superstructure, which flares two stories up to a broad indoor passenger lounge and, another deck up, matching wheelhouses at each end. The bow on this vessel is the stern, as well, and vice versa. We run downriver with the following wind, as the sky rapidly lightens from dark purple to a sullen gray. As Jamestown Island slides by to our left, the ferry makes a right turn toward the river's middle and ploughs through heavy chop for Scotland Wharf. It's a relatively smooth crossing on this wide, heavy boat. But I wonder: what in God's name is it going to be like in the canoe?

We ease into the Scotland ferry terminal, find a longish line of cars waiting to board for the return trip. The settlement is built on a bluff, which the narrow lane away from the pier climbs to settle on a flat, essentially curveless route toward Route 10, the river road back to Upper Brandon. Along the way we pass the entrance to Smith's Fort Plantation. A long, straight drive leads to the Warren House—also called the Rolfe house—a two-story, four-room, seventeenth-century place, symmetrical, three narrow dormers spaced evenly along its steep roof, a pair of windows on either side of the centered front door. Behind it a ways, back on the bank of Gray's Creek, are the remains of a fort built by the English within a couple years of Jamestown's founding. They intended it as a defense against Spanish and Indian attack, a refuge if the main settlement got into trouble.

Locals will tell you that an underground passageway leads from the house to the fort, and I've met some who insist that they've been in it themselves. One old-timer told me of a shaft dropping from a second-floor closet that was said to be a connector to the tunnel. The shaft is there, all right, but it dead-ends at the base of a chimney. It doesn't link up with any passageway to the fort, if such a thing ever existed—and come to think of it, that would be a pretty unlikely arrangement, anyway: who'd build an underground tunnel that starts on the second floor?

The house got its name from Thomas Warren, who for years was believed to have built it in the mid-seventeenth century—a belief recently disproved by experts who've dated it to the eighteenth. The house's other name refers to another early occupant of the property, either John or Thomas Rolfe. Both hold unique places in the Jamestown story: John married the Indian princess, Pocahontas; Thomas was their son.

In 1612, in the midst of the shifting war between the burgeoning English settlement and the tribes allied under Powhatan, Capt. Samuel Argall of Kent, mariner and explorer, arrived on his third trip to Virginia as skipper of the *Treasurer*. On a winter trading visit to the Potomac he fell in with some old Indian friends, and early in 1613 persuaded them to help him kidnap a visiting daughter of Powhatan's. Argall's friends lured Pocahontas aboard the *Treasurer*, and the captain sailed off with his prize. Pocahontas was held captive for a year, much of it at Henricus. A preacher there converted her to Christianity, and the princess, now about eighteen, caught the eye of a tobacco planter from across the James, John Rolfe. They were married at Jamestown in April 1614.

Their wedding ushered in a long peace. For the first two years of their marriage the new couple lived along the James, where they were joined by a baby. He was a year old when he, his father, and his mother—now going by the name of Rebecca Rolfe—traveled to England in the spring of 1616, crossing the Atlantic aboard the same ship on which Pocahontas had been kidnapped. From this inauspicious start the trip became a triumph. Pocahontas charmed England's elite, wowed the Queen, and apparently spurred the King to launch a charity for the establishment of an Indian school in the New World.

Unfortunately for just about everyone associated with Virginia, Pocahontas fell ill. Rolfe moved her out of London's bad air to Brentford, a few miles down the Thames, where, while convalescing, she laid eyes on John Smith, whom she hadn't seen in more than seven years and believed to be dead. After she recovered from the shock, she and Smith talked at length about old times.

Neither would return to Virginia. Pocahontas, her husband, and their baby boarded the *George* for the trip home, but ended it only twenty-two miles down river, when her illness forced them to put in. She died and was buried in Gravesend. Thomas Rolfe remained in England after his mother's death. As a young man he moved back to his homeland, where he owned what's now Smith's Fort Plantation.

We're late getting on the water. By the time I push off from the beach, the high tide's close to two hours old, and the day's already shaping up as a hot, sticky mess. We pull out our maps as I float a few yards off the bank, sweating before I've paddled a stroke, my life vest heavy and damp around my gut. Three miles or so downriver, Upper Brandon's sister plantation, Brandon, hugs a bluff above the James. We could meet there, we figure, but what would be the point? With the tide sliding fast toward the bay, I have to make the most of the next four hours. I'll have no time for unnecessary stops.

A few miles below, Claremont rises from a terrace overlooking the river. Our maps depict a small settlement on the riverbank nearby. "I'll head there," Ian says, "and if you're doing OK, and making good time, and don't want to stop, you can just keep going. If you need something, though, that's where I'll be."

"Good deal," I say. "And if I don't pull in there, we can just figure on meeting at the Scotland ferry pier."

"That's a long way," he observes.

"Yeah, it is," I agree. "But it'd be nice to get that far before the tide turns." He waves and jogs back up the bank toward the Volvo, and I start up the lumpy peninsula. Within minutes the broadleaf trees along the bank dwindle, and the sandy bank turns to mush. Cypress trees and blackwater spring up in their place. The Kennon Marsh is so densely wooded that snaking a boat through it looks impossible, and the few visible patches of water unbroken by trunks are clogged with the cypress trees' knobby knees. Even the early-morning sun, hanging low and bright beyond the marsh, pushes its way only tentatively into the watery thicket; a few yards from its edge a gloaming descends that deepens to full darkness at the forest's heart.

I pause at the marsh's fringe to peer into its gloom, wondering whether a person could walk clear across it on the cypress knees—they stud the water that densely—when a silent flurry of motion overhead catches my eye. I glance up to see a huge bald eagle launching from a treetop directly above me. This mile-square point of soupy land, on this busy curve of river between two great cities, is the unlikely home of one of the Lower Forty-eight's great bald eagle nesting grounds. From near-extinction the birds have rebounded by the dozens here, and today nesting pairs crowd the canopy and glide low over the James. A couple minutes later a second eagle, startled by my approach across silky water, lifts off and flaps downriver. Then a third, head and tail bright against the dark trees. Then a fourth.

Kennon Marsh is midway through one of the last stretches of the James where the river feels like a river. On an S-curve beginning at Windmill Point, back at Flowerdew Hundred, and ending a dozen miles downstream at Sloop Point, near Claremont, the James is rarely more than a mile wide, and from the south bank the details of houses and piers on the north are plain, the river's linear course apparent. I paddle with the tide along this narrows throughout the morning, rounding the marsh's far side and swooping down a long, gentle arc to the southeast, pulled by the current and pushed by the wind. Brandon slides by on my right, obscured by riverbank trees. Claremont swings into view dead ahead, high above the river's confluence with wide Upper Chippokes Creek.

But below it the river jogs left and suddenly balloons to miles across. Its meanders aren't the little cuts and slow bends of the upper James, but giant swings across flat landscape. The little necks left by upstream oxbows have grown to peninsulas miles long. On some straightaways you can look ahead and see nothing but water, ten miles of it. The James has turned oceanic, and as I paddle my little boat into this big water I realize that in the Darwinian scheme, I'm suddenly at a disadvantage, a part of the food chain, prey to forces far stronger and grander than those I've experienced on the river's first 350 miles.

At Sloop Point I spot flashes on the shore, and paddle to a sandy beach backed by a picket line of small cabins, where Ian waits with a couple of cold Gatorades. On the way in I pass a fat, shirtless guy at the helm of an outbound sailboat, a sight that would have been unthinkable a few days ago. We exchange hellos as I watch him glide toward the river's middle, then race to the bank. I don't even step out of the canoe; once I have the drinks stowed in my cooler and hand my empties off to Ian, I back away from the beach and push downstream. Time's short. I'll soon lose the tide.

Before long, waves spring up in the growing river, a foot high and steep-sided, spinning the canoe's nose in circles, so I hug the sparsely populated south bank along mile after mile of cypress growing from beaches of white sand. The combination has such an exotic, almost tropical allure that at one point I beach the canoe and get out to stretch my legs. I'm walking the water's edge, stooping to examine the shards of scallop shells bigger than my hands, when I sense a movement on the water. It takes me a moment to recognize the white, blocky shape as the *Pocahontas*. Twenty minutes later I round sharp Swann's Point, where the river narrows for just an instant to a mile across, and can make out the monuments of Jamestown Island gleaming in the midday sunshine. A statue of John Smith, book in hand, at the water's edge. A spire erected by the federal government at the twentieth century's turn to commemorate the colony's three hundredth anniversary. And a bright white tent that shelters an archeological dig into the nation's foundation.

I wonder, as I paddle down the point's curving edge toward the ferry terminal, how many tourists stand among the island's cedar, magnolia, and mulberry, beholding these monuments while sanitized, upright visions of colonial life, filled with red-brick homes and knee britches and talk of God and the king, turn in their minds. How many understand, as they saunter past a bronze statue of Pocahontas, outstretched hands rubbed shiny by tourists' touch, just how mean life was here?

It's such a languid, hushed place these days that it seems the war and starvation that reigned in the days before John Rolfe's marriage to Pocahontas must have happened elsewhere. Here they were, though. And there was more ugliness to come. The peace that came with the wedding was soured over the following eight years by three developments. First, Pocahontas died thousands of miles from home. Then, two years later, Powhatan died, and the successor to the throne of his confederacy was the wily Opechancanough. Third, and most importantly, the English and coastal Indians viewed the peace in starkly different ways: the confederacy's leadership figured the marriage had sated the English, and that the foreigners would keep their place; the newcomers saw war's end as a license to expand their holdings.

By 1621, Englishmen had settled all along the lower James, all the way up to the falls. The beginnings of what would become vast plantations had taken root along the river's banks. And by that spring, the region's first landholders had been pushed beyond patience. Opechancanough was said to be traveling to his various tribes, assessing their fitness for battle. Friendly chiefs warned the English to keep watch on the situation. The colonists confronted Opechancanough with the rumors. Not true, he told them. Forget about it.

The settlers found out differently in March 1622. Early on a Friday morning, Indians paid seemingly friendly visits to English outposts all along the James, and in a sudden coordinated assault along a 140-mile front, turned on their hosts. Settlers were so taken by surprise that a good many were killed with their own weapons and tools. By noon, a quarter of the colony was wiped out. Henricus ceased to exist, as did an iron foundry just above Drewry's Bluff, and John Rolfe's Varina plantation, and a host of homesteads and settlements along the south bank. The jubilant Indians took gunpowder they'd captured and sowed it in their fields, expecting a large crop of ordnance later in the year.

But Opechancanough fell short of his goal to do away with every last Englishman, to purge his kingdom of the growing foreign menace with a single, hard blow. The night before the attack, an Indian boy living with a colonist on the river's south side, not far from Scotland Wharf, was told of the plan and spilled the details to his white master. At first light that Friday, the Englishman rowed to Jamestown and sounded the alarm. When Opechancanough's warriors showed up, the settlement was armed and ready for a fight. The Indians opted not to give one.

So slipped away a last chance to check England's embryonic might in Virginia. With Jamestown spared, the colony retained enough of a presence to plan a payback. The Virginia Company wrote the council in October 1622 that it expected "a sharp revenge uppon the bloody miscreantes" responsible for the massacre, "even to the measure that they intended against us, the rooting them out from being longer a people uppon the face of the Earth." When Opechancanough sought peace the following year, the English promised it—then killed hundreds of tribesmen with poisoned wine, and ambushed and killed scores more during supposedly friendly visits to their villages. The Indians sought revenge for the revenge, which precipitated a showdown: an open-field, two-day battle between sixty colonists and more than eight hundred bowmen. The well-armed and heavily armored settlers whipped their foe.

Fighting continued as the colony grew to better than three thousand strong, until Opechancanough and the English forged a treaty in 1632. The chief had not yet abandoned his aim of stemming the European tide, however: in April 1644, nearly a hundred years old and so frail he could be moved only on a litter, Opechancanough took a last swipe at the invaders, masterminding another massacre that claimed hundreds of English. The old werowance was captured and imprisoned at Jamestown. A guard shot him in the back.

At Scotland Wharf I paddle beneath the low ferry pier under the eye of queued motorists, land the canoe on an adjacent beach, and trudge across the sand to meet Ian. We wolf down PBJs on the porch of a weather-thrashed restaurant-store at the roadside, sweating and sapped by the heat, swatting at flies that buzz around our heads, the odd yellow jacket that strays into the shade.

There's no sense in hurrying. The tide has turned, guaranteeing that the afternoon will be slow and wickedly hot. Most of the day's traveling is done. We pull out our maps, spread them on the porch's gray-plank floor. Downstream, below Jamestown Island, the river makes a horseshoe bend around a gargantuan peninsula, Gravel Neck. On the near side of its base is a state park, Chippokes Plantation, that offers beach access, campsites, and a huge outdoor swimming pool. "If we camp there," I tell Ian, "we'll save a little time in the morning. What time's high tide gonna be, anyway?" Ian has a tide table with him. He does the math, his lips moving, counting fingertips. "About 5:45 A.M.," he groans. "You're right, though. If we camp at Chippokes, that'll buy us another half-hour of sleep."

"We could take out there," I suggest, "and pick out a campsite, leave the canoe there, run back to Jamestown, strike the tents and haul our stuff over."

"OK. Let's do it."

"OK." I shuffle back to the canoe stiff-legged and sore, my T-shirt clinging, no less exhausted for my lunch break. I don't have much farther to go, I remind myself. Chippokes is three miles away, at most. A few cars honk from the ferry pier as I ease the canoe back into the river and paddle away from the bank.

The three miles soon seems three times as far. I crawl downstream, fighting the tide and a strengthening chop, the scenery around me seemingly stationary. A mile below the pier I see two towers rising from the water—big, beacon-topped channel markers—and strike a course for them. They seem to move away from me as I paddle. Eventually the south bank drops away to form a shallow bay in the crook of the looming peninsula, and across it I can make out a high, bare bluff, a building at its lip.

I have in my mind's the map depiction of the bank here, and imagine the state park to be farther downstream. When you're traveling a sinewy river, though, so much of your judgment as to where you are and where you're headed depends on the shape of the bank you're following. Even subtle changes in the river's edge can spin you around, muddle your sense of direction. Truth be told, I don't know where I am. I'm far offshore, obliviously making a beeline for ground well beyond the state park when, luckily, Ian starts firing his flash gun. The building I saw on the blufftop is the park's visitors' center, it turns out; Ian is three hundred yards below it, standing on a forest-fringed ribbon of sand, waving.

I groan my way out of the canoe, and he pulls it onto the beach. Our canoe cart—a folding aluminum cradle attached to two fat yellow balloon tires—is lying in the sand behind him. "We have to walk the boat to the car," he says. "I couldn't get closer than the parking lot at the visitors center." We lift the boat onto the cart, try to center it on the cradle, cinch down its straps, and tow it across the sand and through a thin stand of trees to a one-lane asphalt road that climbs steadily through gloomy shade to the blufftop. Beyond it, cypress swamp glistens. Mosquitoes swirl. The road crests at the parking lot. We cross it, the cart's soft tires humming, and load the boat onto the Volvo's roof. While tying down the load I cop a nosebleed, a gusher that after a full minute hasn't slowed. Ian walks over to the visitors' center to reserve a campsite while I sit in the car, head thrown back, a T-shirt pressed to my face. When he returns the bleeding's subsided, but it hasn't stopped. "We're all set," he announces.

"Great," I mumble through the T-shirt.

"There's one thing: the swimming pool's closed."

At this, a hiss begins to emanate from the wayback, and the car fills with the strong smell of gas. "Man," Ian cries, "what the hell is *that*?" He pops the hatch and rummages through our footlockers, and finds that one of the stove's isobutane tanks has inexplicably sprung a leak. While he's making this discovery, the prospect of nursing my nosebleed through all the work it'll take to break camp at Jamestown and return here begins to weigh on me. Besides, I deeply need to go for a swim. "Ian," I mumble, "I hate to do this to you, but I'm thinking we ought to bag this place and head back to Jamestown, and just spend the night there."

Ian's chipper about the suggestion. "OK," he says. "I'll cancel the reservation. How's your nose?"

"Just about stopped," I say, pulling the T-shirt away for a moment. "I'll be fine, once we get the smell of gas out of the car."

He jogs back to the visitors' center and returns a couple of minutes later. We lower all the wagon's windows and, on the way out of the lot, dump my bloody T-shirt in a trash can. State Route 10 takes us beneath drooping roadside oaks and past lonely, wind-scraped farmhouses to Surry Courthouse, the county seat of Surry County. It's a quiet crossroads burg of bed-and-breakfasts, lawyer's offices, and gas stations nestled around the courthouse building, its lawn decorated, as most Virginia courthouse lawns are, with a monument to Confederate dead—a high-pedestaled statue of a Reb soldier facing north, toward the ferry terminal three miles away.

A few generations after Jamestown, Surry wasn't so quiet. In 1676, the territory around us was the setting for an outbreak of craziness that remains difficult to explain more than three hundred years later. Bacon's Rebellion is usually remembered as the first demonstration in the New World of an American resistance to British authoritarianism. The guy who led it, a young, well-educated newcomer to the colony named Nathaniel Bacon Jr., is often portrayed as a democratic hero, a warrior against tyranny whose ideals presaged those of the Founding Fathers a century later. Millions of schoolkids have been taught that Bacon's only mistake was being born too early.

It's at least partly a myth.

The traditional account goes like this: In 1675, Indian trouble had again erupted along the Virginia coast, prompting settlers to petition the royal governor, William Berkeley, to mount an offensive against the tribes. Berkeley failed to respond. Meanwhile, Nathaniel Bacon, settled recently on Curle's Neck, below Richmond, lost a servant to one of these Indian attacks and vowed revenge. When frustrated settlers gathered at Jordan Point to discuss the situation, they elected this rather soft blueblood their leader, and in April 1676 Bacon led an unauthorized army into battle. His men thrashed the Indians.

Berkeley, enraged at Bacon's impudence, vowed to arrest the upstarts. He made good on the promise later that spring, when Bacon won election to the House of Burgesses—the colony's governing body at the time—and traveled to Jamestown to claim his seat. Bacon won his freedom by agreeing to confess publicly that maybe leading an army in defiance of the governor, no matter how successfully, hadn't been such a good idea. In exchange, Berkeley forgave him his transgressions and promised him a general's commission.

The new House of Burgesses began its work. "Bacon's Assembly," as it became known, installed term limits on elected officials, erased tax exemptions for councilors and ministers, and extended voting rights to all free men. The governor never got around to granting Bacon the commission, however; on the contrary, Bacon left town just ahead of militiamen ordered to arrest this darling of the people. A few days later he was marching back toward Jamestown at the head of four hundred men. Berkeley met him as he strode into town, supposedly opening his shirt and daring the invaders to shoot him. "No, may it please your honor, we will not hurt a hair of your head, nor of any man's," Bacon reportedly replied. "We are come for a commission to save our lives from the Indians which you have so often promised and now we will have it, before we go."

And so he did. Leading a thousand men, Bacon marched for the Falls of the James. The evil, double-crossing Berkeley ordered the militia to follow and to suppress the mutiny. The militia responded with such lack of enthusiasm that Berkeley fled across the Chesapeake to the Eastern Shore. Word reached Bacon shortly thereafter that as soon as he'd left Jamestown, the governor had denounced him as a rebel. Furious, Bacon called a conference at modern-day Williamsburg in August, where his men swore an oath of allegiance to him and against the governor—and, if need be, against the Crown's troops—until the King was filled in on the situation in the colony. Bacon then issued a Declaration of the People, in which the grievances against Berkeley were spelled out.

Bacon resumed his search for Indians; Berkeley returned from the Eastern Shore with fresh troops and retook Jamestown. Bacon heard about it and turned toward Jamestown with three hundred men, who built a string of gun emplacements across the neck of the Jamestown peninsula and settled in to wait for a fight. Within days, Berkeley and his men again abandoned Jamestown and fled down the river. This time, Bacon's men burned the capital to the ground. Then, while Bacon was up on the banks of the York River, planning another campaign against the Indians, he died of the dreaded "bloody flux." Minus his charismatic leadership, his army fell apart. Berkeley swooped in and executed his lieutenants.

That's the traditional story. But it didn't gain favor until after the Revolution, when Americans reassessed their young country's early years and came to view any past settler who'd opposed the British, for practically any reason, as an ancestor in the fight for liberty. The stuff written about Bacon in the first century after the rebellion wasn't nearly so kind: most commentators branded him a hell-raiser, a malcontent who preyed on the frustrations and fears of neighboring colonists and helped whip up a fight that needn't have happened. Berkeley wasn't a wicked exponent of oppression, in the eyes of the rebellion's early chroniclers, but a dedicated, hard-working public servant. The Indian menace that supposedly sparked the rebellion was pretty much started by the colonists themselves, despite Berkeley's efforts to keep the peace. And it's not clear that the Indians represented a major threat, anyway, with over forty thousand settlers crowded onto Virginia's coastal plain by the time the fighting started.

Still, the rebellion threw everything into confusion for a while, and it's true that the governor executed a good many of Bacon's allies. Among them was William Drummond, the former governor of North Carolina, captured a few days after Bacon's death and dragged before Berkeley, who gave him a low bow. "Mr. Drummond, you are very welcome," the governor told his one-time colleague. "I am more glad to see you than any man in Virginia. Mr. Drummond, you shall be hanged in half an hour." It was more like two hours, but hang he did.

A remnant of Bacon's Rebellion still exists at Jamestown. In a dense grove of trees stands the ruins of a tower, all that remains from the old Jamestown Church burned by the rebels during the capital's destruction. It is a hollow square of brick, its top broken unevenly, its bottom interrupted by two arches, its interior reinforced with concrete and braces. Attached to it is a reconstruction of the church itself, decorated with plaques paying homage to the colony's first settlers and their leaders. When this new addition was built at the turn of the twentieth century, Jamestown had been abandoned for decades, and what little of it hadn't fallen off of eroding banks into the James had fallen into decay. The reconstruction was an attempt by the National Society of the Colonial Dames of America to preserve the vanished church's old footings, which you can now observe along the bottom of the new walls. But the tower and church make for an odd pairing of real and imagined history, one that Frank and Cortelle Hutchins witnessed while construction of the new church was under way. In a 1910 travelogue the couple described an ambivalent visit to the site:

> To the unimaginative visitor, the plan that has been adopted
> will appeal. To him the ancient broken tower, standing alone,
> would have little charm in comparison with this faithful restoration

of the old church, that enables him to see what he never could have seen but for its being shown to him in brick and mortar. But to the pilgrim of the other sort—day-dreamer, if you will—there must come a sense not of gain but of loss. He will feel that, for a questionable combination of a restoration with a ruin, there has been sacrificed the most impressive spectacle on the island—the ancient church tower of vanished James Towne, standing in the shadow of the little grove by the river, broken desolate, alone.

As for the tribes hereabouts—well, they weathered the years after Bacon's Rebellion far less successfully than the church tower. In his *Notes on the State of Virginia,* Thomas Jefferson delivered a tragic epitaph for the once-proud Powhatan confederacy:

> The *Chickahominies* removed, about the year 1661, to Mattapony river. Their chief, with one from each of the tribes of the Pamunkies and Mattaponies, attended the treaty of Albany in 1685. This seems to have been the last chapter in their history. They retained however their separate name so late as 1705, and were at length blended with the Pamunkies and Mattaponies, and exist at present only under their names. There remain of the *Mattaponies* three or four men only, and they have more negro than Indian blood in them. They have lost their language, have reduced themselves, by voluntary sales, to about fifty acres of land, which lie on the river of their own name, and have, from time to time, been joining the Pamunkies, from whom they are distant but 10 miles. The *Pamunkies* are reduced to about 10 or 12 men, tolerably pure from mixture with other colours. The older ones among them preserve their language in a small degree, which are the last vestiges on earth, as far as we know, of the Powhatan language.

Mementos of this destruction are on display in a state park adjacent to Jamestown, and we can see them from the ferry's bow—the masts and upper decks of three brightly trimmed wooden ships, replicas of the vessels that Christopher Newport, John Smith, and their band of adventurers sailed up the James to establish the Virginia colony. They're shockingly puny.

We're too beat to examine them more closely. We drive back to our campsite and slump at the picnic table over our laptop computers, writing and cropping, and by the time we've finished we're too spent even to cross the grounds to the swimming pool. Nor do I have the energy to cook, so when Ian offers to drive into Williamsburg for fast food, I gratefully take him up on it. He returns with twenty-one dollars' worth—such an obscenely high pile that when we're finished, we both feel a bit disgusted with ourselves.

But he also brings beer, which helps us get over it.

DAY TWENTY-ONE

On which the expedition
suffers one last blow

Sailors know that the longest hours of any voyage are its last. Minutes and miles stretch in inverse proportion to the distance from journey's end, until, as a ship makes its final approach to port, it seems it might never get there. The navy calls this torturous blend of excitement and frustration "channel fever," and I feel its twinge an hour before dawn.

Ian and I are up early, eager to ride the tide around the river's last great bend and into its final long straightaway to Hampton Roads. We've come more than four hundred miles from the James's Highland County wellspring. Now just thirty miles separate us from the river's mouth. We strike our Jamestown campsite, cinch the canoe to the Volvo's roof and board the *Pocahontas,* the James a formless black ocean beyond the yellow sodium lights of the long ferry pier. It's not a busy run to the south bank at this hour; we're among only a dozen cars and pickups that rumble across the ferry's steel deck plates and stop before its open bow, which is guarded with a chain and a net of nylon webbing. We step out of the car as the boat pulls away from its dock, walk to the webbing, stare into the dark as wind-whipped waves hiss against the hull.

Halfway across, as we're standing there wordlessly, jackets zipped to the throat against the chilly breeze, trying to make out the low-lying shore downstream, I think, "We are so close." And at almost the same moment I remember that we're starting the day's paddle at Chippokes Plantation State Park, a solid hour's drive from Hampton Roads. "God," I think, "we have so far to go."

It's 6:15 A.M., just minutes before high tide, when we pull into the empty parking lot at the state park's visitors' center. Ian stops the car at the top of the steep asphalt path to the water's edge. A post in the path's center blocks access to vehicles. "I don't know about you," Ian says, staring at the post, "but I don't feel like lugging the canoe all the way back down there." I sigh my agreement. "Unfortunately," I mutter, "I don't see as to how we have much of a choice."

With that, Ian steps out of the car, walks to the post, and with little effort yanks it from a hole carved in the asphalt. He lays it off to the side, runs back to the Volvo, kills the headlights and steers the wagon down the slope. "Well, that was pretty handy," I tell him.

"Yeah," he nods. "Now let's get you in the water so I can get back up to the lot before the rangers show up."

At the bottom of the hill we trot the canoe onto the park's shallow beach, head back for the gear. Ian doesn't stick around to see me off; as soon as we've carried the last of the load to the riverbank, he jogs back to the car and heads back up the hill in reverse, engine whining through the trees. I climb aboard the loaded boat with my headlamp strapped to my forehead. The sunrise is still thirty minutes away, and while I can vaguely make out pieces of driftwood and dark seashells lying in the sand, once away from the beach I'm enveloped in a blackness so dense it seems to have texture, like rough wool. With the sterile beam playing on the river a dozen feet ahead, I start up the shoreline of Gravel Neck.

It is a big peninsula. The neck's upstream side is roughly two miles long, its downstream side nearly three times that length; at its crown lies a marshy doily of lowland and pool called Hog Island. The miles-wide James makes a tight hairpin turn around this jutting thumb, the river's last such twist before it ploughs southeast. I paddle up the neck's west side, its low shore off to my right, as the sky lightens to dark gray, then pale yellow, then a deep orange. I'm making good time, I think happily; the tide's barely turned, hasn't flexed the muscle that a couple hours from now promises to whisk me downstream far faster than I can paddle alone, and already I'm slicing easily through the blackness.

The cypress groves that lined the south bank yesterday have given way to sandy shoreline clumped with tall grasses. From them I can see two rock jetties jutting into the water up ahead. I figure they're protection for the mouth of a small harbor, but when I've paddled around the nearer jetty, I realize that water is streaming from between them, forcing its way into the river. Where the water meets the James is a roiling wedge of foot-tall, noisy waves. I paddle through it, the canoe rocking, its rear end fishtailing, and glance over my shoulder for the source of the outflow. What I see, framed by water ablaze with reflection of the rising sun, is a postcard view of Virginia Power's Surry Nuclear Power Station—the two squat concrete domes of its containment buildings, the pale blue-green metal shell around its turbines.

The James has played a vital role in generating power throughout its length, from Bath County to the dams above Lynchburg to the power plants at Bremo Bluff and Dutch Gap, and so it does here, at one of the nation's oldest nuke plants. Surry's two units each generate enough electricity to power the lights, appliances, and machinery of more than 400,000 customers. In some years, nearly half of Virginia Power's juice, utility-wide, has come courtesy of Surry and the state's other nuke plant, the two-unit North Anna Power Station north of Richmond.

Surry wouldn't work without the river, because when you strip away all the complex lingo that surrounds its operation, a nuclear power plant is a giant steam engine—and any steam engine relies on water. In the plant's cores a nuclear reaction occurs that cranks out a spectacular amount of heat. "Cooling water," circulating through the core under pressure, steals away this heat in much the same way that a car's water jacket lowers its engine temperature. The cooling water is pumped to a steam generator, where the heat it has picked up from the core is, in turn, stolen away by another system of circulating water, called "feed water." The cooling water is so hot when this happens, and the steam generator so efficient, that the feed water is instantly transformed to superheated steam, which is then used to turn turbines and generate electricity. The cooling water, its temperature lowered by its hand-off to the feed water, returns to the core to start the process over. Thanks to the James, a supply of fresh feed water is always on hand. Besides new fuel for its core, which it needs only occasionally, the plant needs only this flow from the river to generate clean, cheap, bountiful power.

So goes the theory, anyway. In practice, Surry's had a troubled history. In 1972, the year the plant went fully online, two workers died here when they were sprayed with steam from a malfunctioning vent. Eleven years later, another worker died when a steam joint ruptured, and a year after that, two others were electrocuted when they drilled into a live cable. Then, on December 9, 1986, an eighteen-inch pipe in Surry Unit No. 2 ruptured, scalding eight workers with steam and 370-degree water. Four of them died. It was the deadliest nuclear-plant accident in American history.

The plant was plagued, besides, with management and design problems that saw it slapped with $800,000 in fines in the late 1980s. In one incident, 26,000 gallons of radioactive water spilled on the floor of a refueling chamber. The Nuclear Regulatory Commission put Surry on its list of problem plants, and the station shut down for ten months to get its act together. I stop paddling for a minute and turn the canoe around to get a better look at the plant, to stare at the twin containment buildings, their round tops sprouting antennae. The light's coming up. For most of the river's watershed, the day's just starting. In there, however, night and day meld; the uranium deep inside those concrete bunkers works all hours, cooks along without pause. God willing.

In June 1990, the NRC removed Surry from its problem list, and Virginia Power officials announced that the plant had put its problems behind it. But trouble stuck around, and a couple of the new vexations were directly linked to Surry's reliance on the James. In 1991, the NRC again fined Virginia Power when microscopic marine organisms from the river, called hydroids, clogged water pipes into the plant. The animals are cousins to jellyfish and coral, and multiply like mad in the river and the Chesapeake Bay during the summer. In Surry's pipes they formed "long, stringy mats of what resembled spinach casserole," as one newspaper report put it. This was more than an inconvenience: the plant depended on the pipes, and a steady flow of water, to cool things down in emergencies. The utility installed new screens on the station's intakes in the river, and sent crews into the pipes to tear the collected hydroids off the walls. Some days they filled a dozen large trash bags with the mess.

An even tougher problem arose in October 1991, when the NRC worried publicly about a design quirk at the Surry plant that, on first glance, seemed a piece of clever engineering. Most nuke plants pump feed water into their guts. The reliability of this flow is only as good as the pumps they use—and pumps are balky things, prone to wear and malfunction. Gravel Neck sits so low, however, that Virginia Power was able to build gravity-feed pipes into the station. They're mammoth things, eight feet across, through which the river simply rolls into the powerhouse. No pumps.

Pretty smart. Except that now the NRC was spooked by a long-shot possibility: what would happen if such a huge pipe burst? At most plants, workers would turn off the pumps feeding the pipes, thereby limiting the damage. But Surry wouldn't be able to stop the flood—the James would pour into the station unchecked. And once it did that, it might short out all the plant's electrical systems, including those that powered the pumps that kept cooling water flowing through the cores, and those to the station's control consoles—the boards of gauges and dials with which the plant controlled the nuclear reaction cooking away at its heart. With its cooling system down, the core would heat up until, within a few hours, it melted down, and the plant's control room crews might be powerless to stop it.

All this hand-wringing started when Virginia Power submitted a report to the feds indicating that the odds of such a disaster were 1 in 1,000 in any given year—odds way too high for the NRC's comfort. The plant eventually made changes to its systems and lowered the odds to 1 in 10,000 to 100,000. That satisfied the NRC. Still, were the James to beat those odds, and gush into the plant's controls . . . well, nobody would talk much about Kepone any more.

There have been other problems at Surry—the sixty-one sirens that warn the surrounding populace of an emergency didn't work in one 1995 test, and the following year managers learned that some important switches had been flipped to the wrong settings for perhaps as long as ten years. But you'll be happy to know that in April 1998, the station earned high marks from the NRC.

Just to the north Gravel Neck's woods fade to the marsh of Hog Island, settled in the Jamestown colony's first few years and named, reputedly, for the animals the colonists raised here. It's a wildlife management area now, soggy and mosquito-infested and empty but for a Virginia Department of Game and Inland Fisheries trailer and a couple of houses at its northern tip. And animals: the island's managers flood and drain its ponds with the seasons, attracting a slew of ducks, geese, swans, and bald eagles. Some springs, the wardens on the island have seen as many as fifty-five eagles congregating around one pond, feeding on the carp stranded by its draining. They've seen thirty around another.

The island's home, too, to a holly tree, gnarled and hollowed by centuries, that rises from long grass about two hundred yards from the western shore. Several years ago, the wardens say, researchers bored the tree's trunk and found that it was about four hundred years old—meaning that the tree likely was standing here when the first colonists' hogs rooted around the place. Tradition holds that it was used as a Confederate lookout during the Civil War, as well. You'd not guess it now: its trunk, once four feet across, is today a crescent just inches thick, from which a few living branches weakly sprout.

I paddle around the island's northern tip, eyeing a chain of blond bluffs far across the river, taking the bend wide to avoid the stumps of old piers and a cloud of mosquitoes swarming on the beach. And as I do, I realize I'm in trouble. For three weeks, Ian and I have been blessed with a remarkable run of good weather. We've been rained on three times at night and just twice on the river, and never have had to flee lightning. The canoe's been gently pushed along all but short, curving stretches of the James by a steady southwest breeze. But as I round Hog Point, the canoe is suddenly buffeted by a gusty wind from the southwest. The boat's nose slaps loudly in the troughs between two-foot waves. It yaws and rolls crazily. Sheets of water slide over the gunwales. White-caps explode against the bow. I keep paddling, but my course becomes a zigzag. My speed, lavish just minutes ago, slows to a near-standstill. Landmarks on shore begin to crawl by. The wind shows no sign of abating, and I realize with alarm that the river ahead runs directly into it. Worse, just downstream it grows to five miles wide between low banks. There's no cover from the wind or the waves it creates.

I claw at the water with my paddle, trying to get the canoe up to normal cruising speed, but no matter how much force I put between my strokes, the boat wallows, slurps, and sloshes drunkenly in the chop. My cursing becomes extravagant. Lurking at the back of my brain is a thought that pushes its way to the front as I paddle: This is beyond uncomfortable. It's dangerous. Uncomfortable is dumping the canoe on a stretch of shallow whitewater. But out here, where my little boat is slave to the tide, turning turtle could mean big trouble. I'd be in water over my head. I'd have a hell of a time climbing back in, assuming I could do it at all. Swimming to shore likely would mean abandoning the canoe, and ending the trip. Staying with the boat might see me sucked downriver by the tide and into the ship traffic in Hampton Roads. I steer the canoe a little closer to shore, but find the water is more riled there than farther out. What do I do? Hug the shore, just in case, and battle water that makes it more likely I'll dump? Or stay well off the bank, where the paddling is marginally easier, the canoe's rocking a little less terrifying, but capsizing is disastrous? As I mull this choice and flail with the paddle, a thick fog descends on the water, swallowing the river's far side. For all appearances, the James has become an endless ocean. I have dwindled to a meaningless speck.

Ian and I meet on Gravel Neck's eastern side, on a thin patch of shell-littered sand at the foot of a crumbling, pine-forested bluff. By the time I reach it, I've been on the water for nearly four hours, three of them battling the wind beyond the peninsula's protected lee. The day is half-finished, and I've made very little progress. Waves crash onto the sand as I crawl from the canoe, muscles sore, my mood foul. "Feel this wind?" I ask him.

He nods. "Pretty strong."

"Real strong," I wheeze. I point out seven or eight inches of water that's washed over the gunwales to make a lake of the canoe's floor. "Real strong. I gotta tell you, if this stuff continues, we won't be home tomorrow. Or the next day. Or maybe at all. It was hairy out there."

Ian scans the water. From here, I realize, the chop doesn't seem particularly daunting. The waves that slide ashore hiss loudly, and those a few yards off the beach collide with deep thumps and sharp slaps. None of them, however, adequately reflects the butt-kicking I've suffered in the boat. The illusion of calm is sharpened by the backdrop to our meeting. A few hundred yards offshore, the ships of the Maritime Administration's James River Reserve Fleet, a flotilla of warships and freighters, tankers and troop ships, are lying at anchor. They're rock-steady in the fog, heavy and rusted and motionless in water and wind that have tossed the canoe like a toy.

Nearly a hundred ships are parked here, awaiting the day when some national emergency might require their service. They're rafted up side by side, the bow of one beside the stern of the next. Bristling with masts and spires, the groups of ships seem steep-sided islands covered with the gray trunks of lifeless trees. Some are mothballed, their hatches and portholes sealed, their guts dehumidified. Some are maintained as ready reserve ships, and could be prepared for use with only a few weeks in the shipyard. Some, if not most, have been laid up so long that they'll never again go to sea under their own power. The "idle fleet," as it's nicknamed, includes Liberty ships, which were churned out by the score during World War II and helped win the Battle of the Atlantic against Hitler's U-boats. Decrepit now, they're anchored alongside troop-carriers that look like ancient passenger liners, and square-housed, skinny-flanked destroyers long eclipsed by changes in the navy's style of combat. "Seriously," I tell Ian, who's still eyeing the water. "I know it doesn't look like the end of the world from here, but in the canoe, it's another story. I'm getting nowhere, and we've already lost all but a couple hours of good tide."

Ian nods, says nothing for a minute. "Would it help to cross to the other side of the river?" he eventually asks. I look at the map, peer across the water, past the anchored ghost ships to the giant cranes of Newport News Shipbuilding, a dozen straight-line miles off and silhouetted against a pale gray sky. The fog is lifting. Just a couple of miles beyond those cranes is Newport News Point, the river's mouth. So close. But the north bank offers no better protection from the wind, which blows harder than ever. I shake my head. "Just getting across would be rough," I say.

"Maybe it'll die down," Ian offers. "Maybe we can kick back for part of the afternoon, and make a run for it once the wind drops."

"What's the forecast?"

"I don't know."

"Well, let's get a forecast," I say. We use Ian's cellular phone to call the *Pilot* newsroom. An editor comes on the line. He calls up the National Weather Service's marine forecast for Hampton Roads on his computer, and reads it to me. It's not good news. The wind's cranking at twenty knots at Cape Henry, out at the Chesapeake's junction with the Atlantic. It's expected to stay that way for a day or more. I hang up. "Twenty knots," I moan. *"Twenty* knots!"

Ian swears. I swear. We shake our heads. "I can't believe this," Ian says, and swears some more. We pace the beach for a few minutes, pausing to scream obscenities and to glare out over the water, to wonder aloud at the cruel joke the heavens have tossed our way after three weeks of luck-filled travel down the James. It's not fair, we conclude. Just isn't.

As we talk, I realize there is one possible solution to our predicament, but dismiss it—it'd take too long. But the wind keeps blowing as Ian and I pace the water's edge, over the tracks of giant three-toed birds and the almost human footprints of raccoon, and I keep thinking: Twenty knots. "There's always the kayak," I finally say. Hanging in my garage in Norfolk is a fiberglass sea kayak, eighteen feet long and knife-thin, in which I've paddled in far rougher water in the Chesapeake. Its deck is fully enclosed. Waves washing over its top simply run off the other side. And if I capsize, I could—in theory, anyway—pull an Eskimo roll, in which you snap your hips while dangling upside down, underwater, and pull yourself upright with your paddle. True, I've only successfully rolled the thing in dead-calm water. But still.

Ian seizes on the thought. "You think it would work better than the canoe?"

"Way better. And way faster," I say. "But it's not the canoe. It's not finishing the trip the way we started it."

"That's true," he says. A pause. "But at least we finish it."

We can't take the canoe out of the water immediately: the bluff rising behind the beach can be climbed only hand-over-hand, using bushes and weeds sprouting from its face as toeholds. Our maps—we have two that depict this stretch of shoreline—show the nearest point accessible to both the Volvo and the boat as a settlement farther down Gravel Neck, though one calls it Rushmere Shores, and the other Tyler's Beach. So we set out our separate ways to reach it, pausing before we do to eye the idle fleet, which in any other circumstance would have dominated our attention until now. One ship gleams bright white against the haze gray of its sisters. Its silhouette is lower, sexier, yachtlike, its hull fine and flared. The *Savannah*.

It looks far too new, and fast, to be tied up here in this lonely flotilla, admired only by boaters and intrepid motorists who happen onto the narrow dirt lane that Ian has taken to reach the beach. The world's first and only nuclear-powered merchant ship, the 595-foot *Savannah* entered service as a combination freighter and passenger vessel in 1962, and lingers now as a monument to a time when it seemed that nuclear power might someday drive all of American shipping. Needless to say, it didn't happen. As efficient as nuclear power is for long-distance travel, and as safe—the navy boasts it's never suffered a reactor-related accident in forty years of steaming, during which its nuclear ships have traveled a distance beyond that to the sun—a nuke is wildly expensive to build and to refuel after it's cruised a dozen or so years on its first fill-up.

The *Savannah* was small, too small to carry the sort of cargo that might justify that expense. Even the navy backed away from nukes shortly after the *Savannah* hit the water. Today, the only active American warships using reactors to build steam are aircraft carriers and submarines. Save for a few aging oil-burners, the bulk of the modern navy is driven by diesels and gas-turbine engines. The U.S. Atomic Energy Commission and the Maritime Administration backed the project more as a test than as a moneymaker, but even so, it didn't stay on the water long. It was laid up for years as a museum ship in its namesake city, then wound up here. And it'll stay for a good while: the government can't economically scrap the thing, because its reactors still cook with radiation.

I push off, paddle through the chop, and after a hard forty-five minutes pull up to a forlorn stretch of honey-colored sand between the shattered concrete foundation of a long-ruined building and a burning trash pile. Its white smoke, held close to the ground by the wind, blows over a tiny marina filled with working crab boats. A couple of others rest on blocks in an unpaved parking lot just off the beach, their paint flaking and wood spongy with rot.

Tyler's Beach is the marina, it turns out. Rushmere Shores is the nearest settlement, a cluster of small houses built among loblolly pines on the water's edge. We haul the canoe across the sand to the car, and with heavy hearts lash it to the rack.

The drive into Norfolk is weird, busy with traffic, the relative absence of trees making the interstates seem overly bright. At my apartment we lower the kayak from the garage's rafters and slide the canoe onto the concrete floor, then adjust the roof rack to accommodate the longer, narrower boat. It is a radically different craft from the plastic canoe—daggerlike, slippery-looking. On the drive back we seek out a municipal campground we've found on the map in Suffolk, a farming community-turned-suburb that meets the James at the river's mouth. We set up the tents under a stand of loblollies, through which we can make out our fellow campers, most of whom seem to be permanent residents. At one elaborate campsite we see a woman using yarn to string a giant dream-catcher in the trees. We see a kid coming home to another site from her day at school.

An hour later we are back on the beach, where the wind's still blowing, waves still crashing. I'm feeling glum as I pull the kayak's spray skirt over my head, then zip up my life vest. The new boat makes much more sense in this wind-tossed water, in waves that now roll three feet high onto Gravel Neck. But it doesn't bear a scar for each of the thousands of rocks I've slammed into upriver. Isn't stained brown by the river's water. Doesn't stink. "I really hate this," I mumble to Ian as I straddle the kayak and lower myself straight-legged into its snug cockpit. "I miss the canoe." Ian nods somberly. "I know," he says. "I really feel kinda emotional about it."

Our trip into Norfolk has chewed up a lot of time. We have just a couple of hours before darkness falls, and the tide will be foul throughout the rest of the day's paddle. Ian studies the map as I seal myself into the cockpit with the elastic hem of my spray skirt—you wear a kayak, rather than ride it—and suggests we meet at Mogarts Beach, a dot on our maps perhaps four miles downstream, as the crow flies. It's a conservative target, but we don't yet know what kind of speed I'll make. "Mogarts Beach it is," I agree. "If I'm making good time, though, and you see me staying offshore, don't call me in. Just head downstream to the next place that seems logical, and signal me from there."

"Good enough," Ian says. He grabs the stern and gives me a sharp push, and the kayak glides through the surf.

It's a strange first few minutes in the boat. The canoe was flat-bottomed, three feet wide in its middle, and short; the kayak seems to taper to a point a ridiculous distance ahead of me as I paddle away from the shore, and it's tippy—it's only twenty-two inches wide, round-bottomed, a much twitchier craft than I've grown accustomed to the past three weeks. My surroundings, too, seem odd. The south shore below Gravel Neck forms a semicircular bay five miles wide at its mouth and almost two miles deep. Burwell Bay, or Burwell's Bay, spreads vast before me, its far shore faint and low. From the kayak I can barely make out Mulberry Island on the James's north bank, where the army runs a vast transportation base. It is big water. From the rear of Burwell Bay to Mulberry Island's marshy bank, the James is every bit of five miles wide. As a matter of fact, "bank" is the wrong word to use. The river now has coasts.

Unsteadily at first, I paddle toward the bay's middle. I've kayaked a lot over the past five years, but I'm now disoriented, thrown off by the craft's responses to my paddling. I'm also undone by the body language it requires. A kayak isn't necessarily more difficult to drive than a canoe, but you do it differently, using your hips and legs for balance and control. After a while it becomes intuitive, but I seem to have lost my intuition. I try to offset my shakiness with the hardware at my disposal. The boat's fitted with a rudder, which helps not so much with steering as with tracking in a straight line in the sort of waves and wind now raking Burwell Bay. You flip it down into the water via a cable rigged to the deck. I do that, feeling around with my feet for the pedals that control it. They're jammed. The cables linking rudder and pedals have snagged on something. Great, I think. This is why pilots do a preflight checklist. I unhitch my spray skirt and find the cables running inside the hull, give each a twang with my fingers, and try the pedals again. Still stuck. The hang-up is evidently back at the stern, too far to reach, so I pull the spray skirt back over the cockpit and paddle on. I'll try to cut straight across the bay, I figure, and if it gets too hairy, I'll turn toward the beach and hug the curving shoreline.

Gravel Neck is where the James turns from freshwater to brackish. The waters off to my left, out in the river's main channel, have through history washed over some of the most productive oyster beds in the world. Until just a few years ago, I might have shared the James with a fleet of low-riding work boats, their crews pulling the shellfish aboard with ungainly, rake-ended tongs. But disease has decimated the oyster since, and although the beds show signs of new life, they're nowhere near what they used to be. Whether the disease would have come without centuries of industrial waste, sewage, and farm runoff fouling the water here is beyond me, but you have to wonder.

A beacon slides by on my left, the descendant of a screwpile lighthouse that once stood sentry over the shoals. Beyond it is nothing but river; I'm soon two miles from the nearest land. I don't know this waterway, I think to myself. This isn't the James I've come to understand, to view as mine. Its vastness turns it impersonal.

But I gain confidence in the kayak as I paddle, feel steadier with each passing minute, and press on in a straight line across the bay. Houses appear on high bluffs along the south shore, and I swoop toward land just above Mogarts Beach. The bluffs rise thirty feet beyond a shallow beach flecked with broken shell, luminous mother-of-pearl, and pebbles of quartz, and along the clifftops rise hollies and oaks, loblolly pines and cedar. Just beyond them, invisible on the high ground, is an old earthworks with the distinction of having seen use in four wars, and a pretty miserable end.

The Warrascoyack Indians once lived along Burwell Bay. They were a seemingly friendly bunch; in 1608, with Jamestown starving, John Smith came begging from across the river, and the Warrascoyacks gave him fourteen bushels of corn to take back. Their charity saved lives. But after fifty-three Burwell Bay residents died in the 1622 massacre, the colonists found that the Warrascoyacks were among the conspirators. The English destroyed the tribe's village, and in 1623 erected a fort nearby, on this bluff just west of Mogarts Beach. They found a network of deep ditches that mimicked trenches, and built their redoubt within them. They called the place "The Castle."

With peace and the colony's firmer footing, the fort lay idle. More than a century passed before it was garrisoned again, during the Revolution. It didn't see action, but was put to use again in the War of 1812, when it was redug and enlarged into a complex of tall earthen bulwarks that formed a seven-pointed star. That time, its guns apparently fired on British warships. It was known, by then, as Fort Boykin, after a local landowner and Revolutionary soldier. When the Civil War came, the fort was rebuilt and enlarged again, and fitted with guns and underground magazines and reinforced "bombproofs." Ten months it took the Confederates to dig it out, all for naught. On May 8, 1862, a week before its sister fort's much better showing at Drewry Bluff, Fort Boykin's gunners spotted a trio of Yankee gunboats leaving Hampton Roads and heading up the James. They opened fire.

This wasn't a good idea. The Rebel guns were puny, and their shots fell way short of their targets. The guns aboard the *Galena,* the *Minnesota,* and the *Susquehanna,* on the other hand, had no trouble firing back. They immediately began lobbing shells into the fort, which became such an unpleasant place to be that the Rebs spiked their cannons, tossed a pile of ordnance down a well, and ran away.

Today, wooden stairs traverse battlements cloaked in pine needles, ivy, and tiny saplings. A forest of holly, gingko, oak, and maple has grown up in the ditches outside the walls, and the old parade field is shaded by an enormous black walnut. The place is remarkably well-preserved, its earthworks still tall and intact. That's a surprise, seeing as how the Yankees came ashore just after the Confederates left and did their best to make a mess of the place. They paid special attention to Fort Boykin's two magazines, using 120 pounds of captured Reb powder and 600 pounds of their own to blow them to bits.

Just the same, the fort didn't witness its last shooting until fifty-six years later. In 1918, the army was practice-firing its guns across the James, and two shells failed to splash down as expected. Instead, they skipped along the river's surface like a flung pebble. The shells whistled into Fort Boykin and came mighty close to hitting its owner as she tended her roses.

The evening grows dusky. I paddle past Mogarts Beach, where fine houses sit atop more high bluffs, and the water laps at their feet around the black-stump bones of old forest swallowed by river. Fossils abound along this shore, shark's teeth with serrated edges still sharp. I don't have time to look for any. Big houses give way to small cabins and trailers. The hardwoods slip away, then the pines, then the land itself. A marsh blooms to my right. Finally, there's only water. The Pagan River.

A flash of light appears across its mile-wide mouth. I paddle hard through big waves and twenty minutes later beach the kayak at the foot of a steep bank crowned with a half-built house, and Ian packing up his flash gear. Construction equipment surrounds the place. The Volvo's parked next to a portable outhouse. By the time we've strapped the boat to the roof, the light is failing fast, but in the twilight we can see the lights of the James River Bridge, three miles downstream. We drive to camp, pull into our site in night as black as pitch, get the candle lanterns going. The temptation to get fast food along the way was nearly overpowering, but we resisted it; as good and easy as a mountain of burritos would be, we're resolved to cook dinner on our last night in camp. The choices: freeze-dried Santa Fe chicken; freeze-dried tetrazzini; Mac and Gack. "Mac and Gack," Ian votes. I boil water, the gas stove whooshing. "One more day," I say. "Hard to believe."

"It is." Ian opens a Sam Adams. "I'm going to miss it."

"Me, too. Big time."

The water boils. I take it off the stove, kill the flame, and pour the water into a pot with the macaroni. We drink our beers, the woods around us flickering in the candlelight. I take out the cheese packets, squirt the yellow goo over the cooked macaroni, stir in the tuna, slop a mound of the mix into a pot for Ian. He snorts with pleasure as he ploughs in, and after a minute I realize he's humming. I recognize the tune. I groan. He keeps it up. "Go ahead and sing it," I finally tell him. "Get it over with."

He does.

DAY TWENTY-TWO
At the James River's mouth

Drizzle is tapping a tattoo on my tent's nylon roof when I wake before daybreak, and I lie in the dark for a few minutes, listening to its rhythm, thinking: This is the day.

Three hours left. After three weeks on and beside the water, after 425 miles of hard, hot hiking and paddling, I have just three hours left. I kick off my sleeping bag, unzip my tent, crawl outside. The drizzle is intensifying into a cool, steady rain, so I hunt by flashlight through the back of the car for my dry bag, and from its bottom pull my rain jacket. The coat has been stuffed in the bag since the trip's first day, when I pulled it on at Jacob Hevener's farm house to armor myself against the cold wind raking Lantz Mountain. It's wrinkled and smells of hot plastic as I pull it on. I close up the car and walk the campground's curving road toward the bathrooms, passing campers still sleeping in their tents, fire rings blackened and wet and exhausted. I pass the dream-catcher, which has collected raindrops like a spider's web.

The bathroom is empty. I splash hot water on my face, study my beard in the mirror. It's turned bushy on the river, and has been bleached blond by the sun. My nose, cheekbones, arms, and legs have tanned deep brown. I pull on a fresh T-shirt, slip my jacket on over it, and head back to camp. And as I start to zip the coat against the steady shower falling outside, I feel a lump in its left pocket. I fish for the object, come up with a fuzzy, egg-shaped thing, and stand there in the rain, in the predawn darkness, turning it over in my hand and trying to place it.

I realize what it is with a flashback to my odyssey's beginning, and Hightown. Ian and I hiked up the ridge that early September morning, wandered half-lost through the trees to the barn above Hevener's farmhouse, then to the

(IAN MARTIN PHOTO. USED BY PERMISSION.)

AT GOODWIN POINT, THREE HOURS
FROM THE RIVER'S MOUTH.

rockpile at the base of a gnarled tree, and in that rock found the river's birth-place. We crouched at the foot of the tree, watching icy-clear water trickle meekly from the earth. Above, I spied walnuts dangling from the tree's limbs, fuzzy and green and sticky, and reached up, plucked one, shoved it in my pocket.

The walnut has lost its stickiness, has turned a velvety brown. And the tiny, centimeter-wide stream on Jacob Hevener's farm has grown to a behemoth five miles across.

At Goodwin Point, just outside of Smithfield, we slide the kayak into the James, and I push off in the blue-gray light of a new day, headed downstream. The river is placid this morning, settled from yesterday's windy chop, but a spearhead of dark clouds, low-hanging and full of rain, is sliding overhead from the southwest, and the breeze is rising. I paddle briskly, hugging the right bank.

A marshy wildlife preserve, Ragged Island, stretches off to my right. I pull into a leeward notch in the bank and watch fiddler crabs slide nervously into their burrows, which are stacked like ancient cliff dwellings into a waist-high scarp of mud. I float a yard offshore, waiting for them to reappear. They edge cautiously to the mouths of their holes, only to dart back into their depths if I make even the slightest move. After four or five minutes I decide I've pestered them enough. As I rejoin the river I try to catalog all the wildlife we've witnessed on the trip. Deer. Turtles. Beaver, one dead, one alive. Torpedo-shaped trout darting beneath the canoe on the upper Jackson. More spiders than I ever hoped to see in one place, let alone crawling on me. A groundhog in Bath County. A muskrat in Alleghany. Blue heron, Canada geese, osprey. The snapping turtle near Norwood. Bald eagles. Early colonist George Percy crowed that the James and its tributaries "runne flowing through the Woods with great plentie of Fish of all kindes," and so it has been on this journey, nearly four hundred years later: silvery flashes of leaping fish have punctuated most of my days on the river, and I've often caught glimpses of smallmouth bass and long-snouted gar cruising below the boat.

I've beached the canoe in the tracks of raccoon, possum, and bobcat, had brushes with other animals that remain mysteries. At Natural Bridge, Ian and I were unnerved by a wailing creature that circled our campsite time and again, its cries almost human. It always stayed beyond the reach of the two candle lanterns we burned on the picnic table, dodged our flashlight beams when we threw them toward the sound. Kept circling, circling and moaning. Finally, when I felt I'd become the unwilling protagonist of an Edgar Allan Poe story, I insisted we track the thing down. We waited until it reached the point in its loop between our campsite and the camp's main building, hemmed by light on two sides, then flicked on our headlamps and sprang from the picnic table, charging straight for where we thought it would be. Our jerking lights caught nothing; then we heard the wail again, in the dark down by the river, and chased it onto the flat beach below the bridge linking Natural Bridge Station and the Arnold Valley. By the time we stopped we were in inky blackness, and the cries were somehow coming from behind us, back up the hill.

Later that night, a lightning storm moved in—not a thunderstorm, just a steady, at times heavy, rain, accompanied by silent flashes. The sound of the drops woke me, and I opened my eyes to see a creature silhouetted by lightning against my tent's green nylon wall. Four-legged, bow-backed, creeping with exaggerated strides. The next morning, I couldn't find my Lexan coffee cup, which I'd left turned upside-down on the picnic table. "I saw something last night," I told Ian. "And I'll bet it took off with my cup."

He asked what it looked like, and I tried to describe it. "Like a three-toed sloth," I said. "Or a baboon. Yeah. A baboon."

"A baboon." Ian was making coffee, but he paused long enough to fix me with an intent stare. Whatever. I haven't seen the cup since.

Before long I reach the James River Bridge, the first span I've seen since Jordan Point, more than two days back. It seems a gargantuan centipede stretched across the water on thick concrete legs, and as I approach its belly, several cars speeding along its back slow sharply, their drivers apparently unaccustomed to seeing such a tiny boat below them here. When completed in 1928, the four-and-one-half-mile span was the longest highway bridge in America, "a veritable pavilion from which may be viewed the setting of the drama picturing the birth of American Statehood." So said the program for opening day. It was part of a project that cost $7 million, a lot of scratch back then. The original bridge crossed most of the river on concrete pilings "of record-breaking proportions," but bowed upward near its northern end to 52 feet above the water, meeting a 300-foot section that could be vertically lifted 147 feet above the shipping channel below. The program called it the "longest direct-drive vertical-lift bridge in existence."

A trucker blasts his horn as his rig rumbles above me, three hundred yards from shore. I wave. It takes me back to a half-dozen afternoon meetings with CSX trains on the upper James, and their engineers' waves and whistle blasts as they piloted their loads along the river's north bank. In particular, it takes me back to the amphitheater of rock near Alpine, to the din of the two passing trains and the herd of wailing cows. The hiss of tires on the bridge deck above me is magnified to deep growls in the bridge's cavelike underside. The original crossing, just twenty-two feet wide, was eventually replaced with the current four-lane span. Even this wider trestle, which took seven years to build, looks skinny and fragile bridging such a big piece of water.

I paddle back into the light, now with an uninterrupted view of the James's last few miles. The Monitor-Merrimac Bridge-Tunnel is a creamy line on the horizon, perhaps five miles ahead. Just this side of it, at the lower end of Ragged Island, a wide gap in the right bank appears: the mouths of Chuckatuck Creek and the Nansemond River. Across the James, the staple-shaped cranes of Newport News Shipbuilding hover sky-blue and massive over a waterfront bristling with docks and piers, machine shops, design studios, offices, and railroad spurs. I can see a Nimitz-class aircraft carrier, more than a thousand feet long, parked in the yard among smaller ships under repair. Its squarish "island" rises higher than all but the tallest buildings in downtown Newport News.

At the close of the Civil War, the stretch of riverbank now consumed by the yard was empty marsh and sand, and the land beyond it was open field dimpled with the ruins of Confederate earthworks. One man pretty much turned them into what they are today: America's largest private shipyard surrounded by a sprawling city of heavy industry and cul-de-sac suburbs, shopping malls, and railroad tracks.

Collis P. Huntington was a Connecticut native who made a fortune, and a name for himself, long before he showed up alongside the James. He'd scored big selling groceries and equipment in California during the gold rush, and had gone on to help create the first transcontinental railroad line. A few years after Appomattox, Huntington became interested in Virginia railroading, and in 1881 he bought the newly organized Chesapeake and Ohio. Among his first acts with the company was to build a rail line from Richmond to the James's mouth, where he constructed a terminal that enabled travelers to transfer from ship to train, and vice versa. A city sprung up around the complex. That'd be Newport News.

Soon it became obvious that the ships serving the terminal could use a repair yard, so Huntington started that, too. He called it the Chesapeake Dry Dock and Construction Company. Before long the yard got a major rebuilding job, and had to hire on a whole mess of shipbuilding specialists, so the company was renamed the Newport News Shipbuilding and Drydock Company. It grew into a giant, a major supplier of U.S. warships and builder of perhaps the most renowned merchant ships in American history. Every nuclear-powered carrier—floating factories that are big enough to put up six thousand sailors and eighty aircraft, and that can move at highway speed— has been built at Newport News, along with scores of nuke submarines. The S.S. *United States,* arguably the greatest ship ever built by anyone, anywhere, for any reason, was a product of the yards here, a sleek fusion of elegance and power that smashed the transatlantic speed record on its maiden voyage in 1952. The ship's older, smaller sister, the *America,* the largest prewar U.S. passenger ship and the biggest American troop carrier of World War II, was built here, as well. On one trip, it carried the entire Ninth Infantry Division.

Huntington died in 1900, before seeing the shipyard blossom. Before he did, though, he delivered one of the most memorable mission statements in American corporate history: "We shall build good ships here: at a profit if we can, at a loss if we must, but always good ships."

It takes me an hour to cross the mouth of the Nansemond, a broad tidal estuary that snakes southward to water the peanut and cotton fields of Suffolk and Isle of Wight County. From the lower end of Ragged Island I aim straight across it for a water tower that sprouts from the James's south shore. I put some muscle behind my strokes, and the kayak slides smoothly through the river's uneven surface until I'm chopping through swaying seaweed and grinding onto an eroded beach of sand and shell and broken brick.

The Frederick campus of Tidewater Community College spreads beyond a riprap pile lining the bank. Students hurry between classes on its lawns. I'm struck by how clean and well-groomed they look. Ian is waiting atop the riprap. He waves.

"Dude." I yank my spray skirt's rip cord, clamber out of the boat.

"I've found a place to pull out," he announces. He hands me a Gatorade as I scale the riprap and find a seat on a flat rock. "Yeah? How far?"

"Not far at all." He tilts his map my way. Where the James ends and Hampton Roads begins is actually right here, at Pig Point, along an imaginary line from this shoulder of low, scrubby land to Newport News Point, about four miles away. But since starting the trip we've operated under a tacit agreement that the river's mouth really lies a couple miles east of here. At the least, it seems to me, the true mouth, the poetic mouth, lies below the Monitor-Merrimac Bridge-Tunnel, which sprouts from Newport News Point, dives into a forty-eight-hundred-foot tunnel below the floor of the shipping channel, and emerges to ride a three-and-a-half-mile trestle to the south shore just a mile from where we stand. An even more fitting end to the James is Newport News Middle Ground, a treacherous shoal of sand and clay marked by a rust-colored, cast-iron lighthouse just below the bridge-tunnel. The light, visible for nine miles, has guarded the river since 1891. It was built to last: its base is planted thirty-four feet deep in the shoal, packed with tons of cement and ringed with a thousand tons of riprap. *Try* to move it.

"Here," Ian says, pointing to the map. His finger lies beside a small notch in the southern shore. "There's a boat ramp there, just inside the mouth of this creek." The inlet is maybe a mile beyond the bridge-tunnel. We'll end the trip in two miles. A half-hour.

Suddenly the prospect of being finished with our voyage hits me, and for a moment I'm almost winded. I take a deep breath. "Wow," I say.

"We're there," Ian says, smiling. "Just past the bridge-tunnel you'll come to a creek. Skip that one. The second one's the one."

"Not far," I hoarsely offer.

"Not far at all."

"So we're pretty much done."

"Yeah," Ian says. He holds up a hand. I weakly high-five him.

We linger on the riprap for more than half an hour, leaning back on our elbows to bask in the midmorning sunshine. "Almost lunchtime," Ian observes.

"Yes."

"And I'm thinking: You know, some Taco Bell might be good."

"Ten-four," I say.

"So, do you want to get going?"

I sit up slowly. "I suppose."

Ian climbs to his feet. "I'll be waiting for you," he says. We high-five again, and nudge our way down the riprap to the beach. I bungee myself into the kayak, and Ian gives me a shove off the shore. "See you there," I tell him.

I paddle shoreline littered with brick and chunks of concrete to the bridge-tunnel and float for a few minutes between its twin spans, marveling at the one-point perspective they offer as they shoot parallel across the water. Listening to the echoes of trucks rumbling up there. How many bridges have I traveled over and under on this trip? I can't even begin to estimate. Narrow culverts under two-lane back roads in Highland County. Remote McClintic Bridge at the head of Lake Moomaw. Abandoned crossings at Eagle Rock and the washed-out remnant of a wooden truss bridge at Springwood, pieces of which lie mangled downstream. The world's widest railroad bridge at Clifton Forge, and the bleak shelf of mud, weeds, and litter beneath the Route 60 crossing at Covington, spanning a river pummeled by its first encounter with industry.

As I paddle, the James is leaving behind the last of that industry. Since Covington it's passed factories of all stripe, and in most of those meetings, it's come out the worse. The river here is pumped full of fertilizers and sewage, laden with the outflow of chemical plants and paper mills, stained and sick. Virginians pay a high price for the jobs and the tax revenue that industry provides in the James River basin. I have little urge to take a dip.

The lighthouse appears to my left, spark plug–shaped—tiny from here, though it rises better than five stories. Its iron hull is girded in two places by roofed catwalks, and a ladder dangles near the water, offering the adventure-some a romantic, if melancholy, haven. It's been empty since 1954, when the

Coast Guard automated the light and stripped the tower's three rooms of living space. With time, the service even moved its white beacon from the lantern cupola to the tip of a mast outside.

A short stretch of marshy shore, and the mouth of a creek appears. A few hundred yards farther, and houses crop up, smallish, not far off the water. A sign on a riverside tree: Respass Beach. Then, the second inlet.

I paddle in. Ian swings into view on my right, on an asphalt boat ramp just inside the creek's mouth. Smiling. "Hello, Earl," he says. A few more strokes, and I'm scraping against the slope. As I struggle out of the cockpit, a silver-haired fellow in shorts, a plaid polo shirt, and a ball cap pulls up in a golf cart. "How're you doing?" he asks.

"Good," I answer. "Real good." Ian helps me tote the boat to the sandy high ground near the car.

"You aren't the fella who's been going down the James River, are you?" Bob Aycock hollers. We set the kayak down, and stroll over to the cart. "Yes, sir, I am," I tell him. Ian beams.

"Where you gonna end this trip?" Aycock asks.

Ian and I shake hands, start to laugh. "Well, sir," I reply, "we just did."

Unloading the kayak, I pull my jacket from the rear hatch, and feel for the walnut in its pocket.

So ends our twenty-two days on the James River.

We have followed America's most historic stream from its highland well-spring to its mouth, have traveled 430-odd miles from mountain to piedmont to coast to shore. Ian's Volvo has acquired 3,251 new miles.

We've followed water sparkling clear and cold and clean among the ridges of western Virginia, accompanied by the whispers of a frontier past. We've thrilled in its rapids and falls, marveled at the cave-laced bluffs on its banks.

We have seen its water spoiled, only to see the James somehow rebound— visibly, at least—from the damage. We have seen it worm inches-wide through tussocky uplands and swell at its meetings with springs and tributaries until its far bank was a distant line on the horizon. We have come to feel a part of its long course to the sea, and to feel it a part of us.

Like most Americans, I've always lived within a shout of a stream, a creek, or a great inland waterway. I've depended on them, as we all do, for food and drink, for the energy to power my home, as dumps for my waste, as weekend playgrounds. Now I understand something about them that I didn't before: that a river has no single character, no one personality. The James has been a constantly evolving, living organism, by turns trusted friend and impassive stranger, its mood shifting with each mile. And with each day, as well, for the whims of weather can swell it into a foaming terror, or bake it almost dry.

We think of our rivers as specific places, as fixed lines on our maps. The truth is that there is nothing fixed about them. The ounce of water bubbling from a stream's fountainhead one moment is a foot downstream by the next, has been replaced by new water seeping from the rock, and that constant turnover never flags.

Our maps depict a river's typical banks, but—as an obituary can only trace the boundaries of a life just ended—they cannot depict the river itself.

NOTES

Journey on the James is based on a twenty-two-part series of the same name published in the *Virginian-Pilot* of Norfolk, Virginia, from Sunday, September 13 to Sunday, October 5, 1998. The series was "live," meaning that it appeared in the paper as I wrote it and Ian photographed it. This approach made for a rather breakneck pace on the water and long evenings spent, exhausted, in front of our laptop computers, often at picnic tables in camp. It also translated into a series that bears little resemblance, beyond basic organization, to this book: the physical confines of the newspaper and the scarcity of free time we had for research restricted us to shorthand references to the history, geology, and wildlife around us. What follows, then, are references to the sources that contribute to the parts of the book not contained in the series, as well as notes on features of our journey that I think deserve further explanation.

ABBREVIATIONS

HCV	Henry Howe, *Historical Collections of Virginia*
HV	Robert R. Howison, *A History of Virginia, from its Discovery and Settlement to the Present Time*
LS	Norfolk *Ledger-Star*
VMHB	*Virginia Magazine of History and Biography*
VP	Norfolk *Virginian-Pilot*
VPLS	Norfolk *Virginian-Pilot & Ledger-Star*

DAY ONE (AT THE HEVENER FARM)

The bulk of this chapter was gleaned from Ian's and my visit to Jacob Hevener's Dividing Waters Farm in Hightown on Wednesday, September 9, 1998. We decided to follow the Jackson, rather than the James's other source streams—most notably, the Cowpasture—on the basis of a reconnaissance trip I made to the area on June 24–26, 1998, during which I concluded that if one likens the James's headwaters to a tree, the Jackson is its trunk, the other streams mere branches. I located the barn on this earlier trip, using the U.S. Geological Survey's 7.5–minute Hightown quadrangle map. It clearly depicts the building flanked by both the Jackson and Potomac. During the recon I also visited the Highland County Library in Monterey, where librarian Pat Shields suggested I contact a local canoeist, John Sweet, for advice on how best to travel the Jackson's upper reaches. I was able to reach him via E-mail; he gave me Hevener's name and phone number, and I arranged the journey's start with the farmer by phone.

General background on the farm's environs can be found in Oren F. Morton, *A History of Highland County, Virginia* (1911; reprint, Baltimore: Regional Publishing Co., 1969); and Raymond S. Edmundson, "The Valley and Ridge Province," *The James River Basin, Past, Present and Future* (Richmond: Virginia Academy of Science, 1950). I also relied, as I did throughout the journey, on Henry Howe's wonderful *Historical Collections of Virginia* (Charleston, SC: Babcock & Co., 1845; abbreviated *HCV*), a county-by-county snapshot of Virginia in the mid-nineteenth century; and on *Virginia: A Guide to the Old Dominion* (New York: Oxford University Press, 1940), compiled almost a century later by writers employed by the Work Projects Administration.

DAY 2 (THE HEVENER FARM TO THE U.S. ROUTE 220 BRIDGE)

Most of this chapter is based on our explorations in Highland and Bath counties on September 9 and 10, 1998. Otherwise:

9–10. My description of the Valley and Ridge district relies in part on articles by Charles F. Lane and Edgar Bingham in *The Virginia Geographer,* the journal of the Virginia Geographic Society. Lane's, titled "Physiographic Provinces of Virginia," appeared in Volume 15, Number 2 (fall-winter 1983); Bingham's, titled almost identically "The Physiographic Provinces of Virginia," was published in Volume 23, Number 2 (fall-winter 1991). I also relied on Raymond S. Edmundson's "The Valley and Ridge Province" and Marcellus H. Stow's "Geology" in *The James River Basin.*

12. The reference to John Vanderpool comes from Morton, *History of Highland County.*

13. The turnpike reference is from Morton. Ian and I learned of the presence of Mackey Spring and the Blue Hole in a piece of small-world serendipity. I was striding south on 220 when a station wagon headed the same way slowed and a thin, middle-aged guy stuck his head out of the window. "Do you need a hand?" he asked. I assured him I was fine, and he sped off. A half hour later I passed him on the roadside, where he had been fixing a flat on his wife's car. He again asked whether I needed help; I again told him I did't. We got to talking, and he introduced himself: it was John Sweet, the Highland County canoeist who gave me Jacob Hevener's name and advised me, quite accurately, that the upper Jackson is nearly empty of water in the early fall. John then consulted our maps, and showed us where we could find the springs.

15. The description of the Bolar spring is from Morton.

16. Material on Bath County's resort past draws from *HCV;* E. Lee Shepard, ed., "Trip to the Virginia Springs: An Extract from the Diary of Blair Bolling, 1838," *VMHB* 96, no. 2 (April 1981); Perceval Reniers, *The Springs of Virginia* (Chapel Hill: University of North Carolina Press, 1941); and Fay Ingalls, *The Valley Road* (Cleveland: World Publishing Co., 1949). The bathhouse's age is from Calder Loth, ed., *The Virginia Landmarks Register* (Charlottesville: Virginia Department of Historic Resources/University Press of Virginia, 1999). Jefferson's remarks are from his *Notes on the State of Virginia* (Chapel Hill: North Carolina Press, 1955).

18. The history of Warwickton and Hidden Valley relies on *The Virginia Landmarks Register;* interviews with the Stidhams; materials supplied on-site by the U.S. Forest Service; and W. Roy Wheeler, ed., *Historic Virginia* (Charlottesville: Roy Wheeler Co., n.d.).

DAY 3 (U.S. ROUTE 220 TO STATE ROUTE 39)

Most of the chapter is based on our hike through Little Mountain Gorge and my disastrous inner tube voyage, both on September 11, 1998. Otherwise:

22. Information on Forts Dinwiddie and Young draws on Louis K. Koontz, *The Virginia Frontier, 1754–1763* (Baltimore: Johns Hopkins Press, 1925); on interviews with Harry Jaeger, president of the Archeological Society of Virginia, and Howard A. MacCord, the retired state archaeologist, in early June 1999; and on MacCord's "Fort Dinwiddie Site," *Quarterly Bulletin of the Archeological Society of Virginia* 27, no. 3 (March 1973).

The Indians' use of the neighborhood as hunting grounds is related in Morton, *History of Highland County,* and Oren F. Morton, *Annals of Bath County, Virginia* (Staunton, VA: McClure Co., 1917). The quotation is from Robert R. Howison, *A History of Virginia, from its Discovery and Settlement to the Present Time,* vol. 1 (Philadelphia: Carey & Hart, 1846; abbreviated *HV*).

22–23. The war's beginnings are detailed in Louis Knott Koontz, "Washington on the Frontier," *VMHB* 36, no. 4 (October 1928); and Koontz, *Virginia Frontier.* Details on the French situation and the Indians' ferocity can be found in Matthew C. Ward, "Fighting the 'Old Women': Indian Strategy on the Virginia and Pennsylvania Frontier, 1754–1758," *VMHB* 103, no. 3 (July 1995).

23. The firsthand description is from Nicholas Cresswell, who met four Shawnee chiefs in December 1774. He's quoted by Joseph C. Jefferds in *Captain Matthew Arbuckle* (Charleston, WV: Education Foundation Inc., 1981).

Material on Braddock's defeat can be found in *HCV* and *HV;* Washington's quote is from *HCV,* as is the reference to Thomas Fausett.

24. Description of the dig is from my interview with MacCord, and from his "Fort Dinwiddie Site."

25. The quote is from John A. Stuart's *Memoir of Indian Wars, and Other Occurrences* (New York: The New York Times & Arno Press, 1971). Stuart was a Greenbrier settler who rose to colonel in the colonial militia and fought at Point Pleasant. The slim volume contains his firsthand, fast-moving account of violence between whites and natives in Virginia's western counties.

The description of the three types of fort is from Koontz, *Virginia Frontier.* The garrisons' lack of fortitude is ibid., and from Koontz, "Washington on the Frontier."

DAY 4 (ROUTE 39 TO THE GATHRIGHT DAM)

Most of the observations in this chapter were made by Ian and me during our trip through Richardson Gorge and across Lake Moomaw on September 12, 1998. Otherwise:

28. Wilson's description of Cornstalk is from Samuel G. Drake's *Indians of North America,* as quoted in Robert Douthat Stoner's history of Botetourt County, *A Seed-Bed of the Republic* (Roanoke: Roanoke Historical Society, 1962). Col. Wilson heard the chief speak at Camp Charlotte, where the Indians made peace with Dunmore following the Battle of Point Pleasant.

28–30. The quotes detailing the Muddy Creek and Clendenin homestead massacres are from Stuart's *Memoir of Indian Wars.* Numerous other sources, among them Morton's *Annals of Bath County,* detail the Kerr's Creek killings. While pretty much all of them agree on the details, they vary in the dates of the attacks: I've seen them given as 1759 and 1763, 1761 and 1763, 1761 and 1765, etc. Further confusing things, a bronze marker mounted on a boulder at the shoulder of U.S. Route 60 at Big Spring insists the second attack occurred on October 10, 1764, ten years to the day before the Battle of Point Pleasant.

31–32. The origins of the Gathright project are detailed in the files maintained by the U.S. Army Corps of Engineers' Norfolk District in Norfolk, Virginia; "Gathright Report March 20," *VP,* March 13, 1964; George Taylor's Associated Press report, "Controversial Dam Fiscally Feasible," *VP,* March 21, 1964; John Koening Jr.'s AP report, *VP,* February 7, 1965; Koening, "Gathright Dam Need 'Urgent,'" *VP,* April 28, 1966; Koening, "Gathright Dam Talk Returns to House" *VP,* May 1, 1966; Koening, "Several James Dams Possible," *VP,* May 22, 1966; and Kenneth Bredemeier, "Gathright Dam: Boon or Boondoggle?" *Washington Post,* August 4, 1974.

32. The EPA's remarks are drawn from "Comments by EPA Region III on the Draft Environmental Impact Statement for Gathright Lake, Virginia, prepared by the U.S. Army Corps of Engineers, Norfolk District," June 1972. I found a copy of this typewritten position paper in the *Virginian-Pilot*'s library, and numerous stories describing its contents: see Greg Glassner, "EPA Requests New Construction Stop on Gathright Dam Project," *LS,* December 4, 1972; Gene Owens, "Ecologist Urges End to Gathright Project," *LS,* December 29, 1972; "U.S. Urges Study of Halt in Dam Work," *Washington Post,* December 30, 1972; and "Halt Gathright Dam, EPA Says," *VP,* December 30, 1972.

34. Material on the dam's purpose and construction can be found in Gene Owens, "Time Runs Out along Scenic Jackson River," *LS,* October 23, 1972; "$18.8-Million Low Bid for Gathright Dam," *VP,* December 15, 1972; and "Gathright Dam Workers, Bosses Celebrate Finish," an Associated Press report in the May 26, 1978, *LS.* My characterization of Covington's stance is from "Tide of Industries Foreseen for Dam," an Associated Press report in the March 31, 1962, *VP;* Owens's story of October 23, 1972; Bill Lumpkin's AP report, "Covington Man Says Disputed Dam to Aid Environment," *VP,* December 10, 1972; and Bredemeier's *Washington Post* story of August 4, 1974.

A lengthy denunciation of multipurpose dams can be found in Elmer T. Peterson, *Big Dam Foolishness* (New York: Devin-Adair Co., 1954). The downstream confluences of Dunlap Creek and other streams is mentioned in Owens's *LS* story of October 23, 1972, and Bredemeier's August 4, 1974, *Washington Post* story.

34. Flow augmentation is discussed in "A $20-Million Business," *VP,* February 6, 1972; Owens, *LS,* October 23, 1972; Marvin Lake, "Court Agreement Made on Gathright Dam Job," *VP,* December 6, 1972; Linda Schamber, "This Dam's Flooded With Controversy," *VP,* June 29, 1975; and Associated Press reports in the March 13, 1973, *VP* and *LS,* and the March 14 and 16, 1973, *LS.* The EPA quote is from the June 1972 "Comments by EPA Region III."

The court fight was faithfully reported by the *Virginian-Pilot* (see "Suit Filed to Block Va. Dam," November 30, 1972; "U.S. Files Brief in Gathright Suit," December 3, 1972; "Washington Asks Va. Probe of Gathright Plan," December 5, 1972; Lake, "Court Agreement Made on Gathright Dam Job," December 6, 1972; Clifford Hubbard, "Price Tag on Dam 'Too Low,'" December 16, 1972; "Council to Join Gathright Suit," January 28, 1973; and "More Groups May Join Suit against Gathright," February 27, 1973); by *The Washington Post* (see "Gathright Dam Plans Ruled Legal by U.S. Judge Dalton," April 4, 1973); and by *Engineering News-Record* (see "Corps Wins a Bout," April 12, 1973). The dam's dimensions are from *Virginia Hydro Dam Inventory,* vol. 2, prepared by the U.S. Department of Energy, Region III, and the Virginia State Office of Emergency and Energy Services (Afton, VA: Rockfish Corp., 1981).

35–36. The details of earthen dam construction can be found in Nicholas J. Schnitter, *A History of Dams, The Useful Pyramids* (Brookfield: A. A. Balkema, 1994); and in Bredemeier's August 4, 1974, *Washington Post* story and accompanying graphics.

The passages on the relative risks of earthen versus concrete dams, the number of large dams, and statistics relating to dam failures rely on Schnitter, *History of Dams*.

36–37. The description of the Coles Mountain caverns and Gathright's concrete curtain draw from Clifford Hubbard, "Limestone Holes Found in Gathright Dam Cost Estimate," *VP*, June 8, 1974; "Tunnels Pose Big Problem at Gathright," *VP*, June 28, 1974; "More 'Time and Money' Urged for Gathright Dam," *VP*, July 4, 1973; "Caverns Hike Dam's Cost," *LS*, July 4, 1974; Bredemeier's August 4, 1974, story; Wayne Woodlief, "Gathright Dam Cost Goes Up," *VP*, February 28, 1975; and Schamber's June 29, 1975, story in the *VP*. The contractor's warnings are from the July 4, 1973 *VP* and *LS* stories; Jack Betts, "Dam's Cost May Rise by $28.5 Million," *VP*, December 1, 1974; the *Engineering News Record* quote is from an editorial, "Folly in Virginia?" excerpted by Clifford Hubbard's *VP* story of June 8, 1974. The *Washington Post* story mentioned is Bredemeier's of August 4, 1974.

37. The passages regarding the Bath County project draw from an interview with Virginia Power's Ken Baker in late April 1999, and from Sara Layman, "The Virginia Power Project: Powerhouse for Bath County's Economy," in *The Bicentennial History of Bath County, Virginia* (Marceline, MO: Heritage House Publishing, 1991). Among the host of general sources on dams that I consulted are Sasha Nemecek, "Frankly, My Dear, I Don't Want a Dam," *Scientific American,* August 1997; Joe Skorupa, "The Problem With Dams," *Popular Mechanics,* December 1991; and William G. Hoyt and Walter B. Langbein, *Floods* (Princeton, NJ: Princeton University Press, 1955).

Day 5 (Gathright Dam to Covington)

The bulk of this chapter is from our observations while under way on Sunday, September 13, 1998. Along this stretch of the river, and on all the legs downstream to Lynchburg, I relied on William E. Trout's remarkable *Upper James Atlas,* at the time an unpublished manuscript that Trout was preparing as part of his series of annotated river atlases. Trout probably knows parts of the James better than any man alive, and he knows the rest pretty darn well. He was kind enough to spend an afternoon with me before the trip, to walk me through the stretches of the James he thought might prove problematic, and to allow me to photocopy his manuscript—a series of blown-up USGS 7.5–minute quad views of the river, supplemented with historical notes, quotes, and observations. Otherwise:

41. Some explanation of the riverbed ownership tussle can be found in "Gathright Fishermen Hit Snag," an AP report in the March 21, 1973, *LS;* in the March 12, 1978, *VPLS;* and in "Corps' Plan for River Opposed," an AP story in the October 7, 1979, *VPLS.*

42. The tale of the beaver is related by Charles O. Handley Jr. and Charles O. Handley Sr. in *The James River Basin.* The beaver's rebirth is also described in James W. Engle Jr., "The Beaver in Virginia," *Virginia Wildlife* 15, no. 4 (April 1954).

42. The quote is from the edition of Jefferson's *Notes* cited previously.

42–43. Mad Ann Bailey is described in *HCV;* by Oren F. Morton in *A Centennial History of Alleghany County* (Dayton, VA: J. K. Ruebush Company, 1923); by W. A. McAllister in "Pioneer Days in Alleghany County," *VMHB* 10, no. 3 (January 1903); and in WPA, *Virginia*. The death of fifteen settlers south of Fort Mann is included in Morton, *Centennial History of Alleghany County*, and in McAllister, "Pioneer Days."

The quote is from the section on Alleghany County in *HCV*. Morton has her dying in Gallia County, Ohio, on property owned by her son. McAllister places her death "in a rail shanty—the product of her own hands—on the Ohio River, just below Point Pleasant."

43. The "shooting, riding, and profanity" quote is from WPA, *Virginia*.

43. The clashes between settlers and Indians are described in *HCV*; in McAllister, "Pioneer Days in Alleghany County," *VMHB* 10, no. 2 (October 1902) and 10, no. 3 (January 1903); in Morton, *Centennial History of Alleghany County*; and in Morton, *History of Highland County*. The attack on Logan's family is described by Jefferson in his *Notes*.

Howison writes of the Dunmore conspiracy theory: "The evidence to prove these charges is too vague to bring conviction, yet the facts furnished are suspicious," *HV*. J. T. McAllister supplies some of the evidence in "The Battle of Point Pleasant," *VMHB* 9, no. 4 (April 1902).

45–46. Descriptions of the Battle of Point Pleasant appear in *HCV*; in *HV*; in Jefferds, *Arbuckle*; in J. T. McAllister, "The Battle of Point Pleasant," *VMHB* 9, no. 4 (April 1902) and *VMHB* 10, no. 1 (July 1902); in Morton, *History of Highland County*; and in Edward A. Pollard, *The Virginia Tourist* (Philadelphia: J. B. Lippincott & Co., 1870).

46–47. One such song about Point Pleasant is included in Pollard, *Virginia Tourist*. A better one, "The Battle Song of the Great Kanawha," is posted as an online exhibit on the website of the Blue Ridge Institute and Museum <http://www.blueridgeinstitute.org/>. The later exploits of the battle's survivors are included in McAllister, "Battle of Point Pleasant" (July 1902).

48. The FSA photo was shot by Arthur Rothstein, and reproduced in Brooks Johnson, *Mountaineers to Main Streets* (Norfolk: The Chrysler Museum, 1985).

48–49. The quote is from Shelby Coffey III, "The Tainted Haze That Hugs Covington," reprinted in *VP*, February 9, 1969.

Day 6 (Covington to Glen Wilton)

Most of the material included in this chapter was gleaned from our travels downriver on Monday, September 14, 1998. Otherwise:

52. The Peter Wright anecdote is mentioned by Howe, *HCV*, by Morton in *Centennial History of Alleghany County*, and by W. A. McAllister in "Pioneer Days in Alleghany County" (October 1902).

53. The sliced oxbow can be found on the USGS 7.5–minute Clifton Forge quad.

55–56. The article is "New Ways in the Old Dominion: The Chesapeake and Ohio Railroad," *Scribner's Monthly* 5, no. 2 (December 1872).

Day 7 (Glen Wilton to Salt Petre Cave)

Most of the information included in this chapter was gathered firsthand by Ian and me during our trip down this section of river on Tuesday, September 15, 1998. Otherwise:

61–62. My sources on the JR&K include the story in the December 1872 *Scribner's Monthly*;

Bill Trout's *Upper James River Atlas;* Trout's equally impressive *James River Batteau Festival Trail* (Richmond: Virginia Canals and Navigation Society, 1996); *HCV;* Alexander Crosby Brown, "The Canal Boat 'Governor McDowell,'" *VMHB* 74, no. 3 (July 1966); Alexander Crosby Brown, "The Tomb of a Dream," *Virginia Cavalcade* 22, no. 4 (spring 1973); Kent Druyvesteyn, "With Great Vision: The James River and Kanawha Canal," *Virginia Cavalcade* 21, no. 3 (winter 1972); Lynda Mundy-Norris Miller, *Glasgow, Virginia: One Hundred Years of Dreams* (Natural Bridge Station: Rockbridge Publishing Co., 1992); Oren F. Morton, *A History of Rockbridge County, Virginia* (Baltimore: Regional Publishing Co., 1973); Virginia Moore, *Scottsville on the James* (Charlottesville: Jarman Press, 1969); and Blair Niles, *The James, from Iron Gate to the Sea* (New York: Rinehart & Co., 1939).

Washington's involvement is detailed in several of the above sources, as well as by J. J. Forrer, Robert E. Steele III, E. Walker Turner, and Mildred Lawrence Barret in a chapter on highway transportation in *The James River Basin.* Jefferson's comments are from his *Notes.*

Day 8 (Salt Petre Cave to Alpine)

Most of this chapter was gathered by Ian and me as we traveled this stretch of the James on Wednesday, September 16, 1998. Otherwise:

66–67. An explanation of floodplains can be found in Hoyt and Langbein, *Floods.*

67. The tunnel I mention is the 192-foot John Y. Mason Tunnel. According to Brown's "The Tomb of a Dream" in *Virginia Cavalcade,* it eliminated a three-mile slog around an oxbow.

Spreading Spring Branch is clearly marked in Trout's *Upper James River Atlas.* I've perhaps understated the severity of the dumping that's occurred there; Ian recalls that a second appliance lay in the brush near the pool, along with a bunch of other trash. Springwood, by the way, was once named Jackson. This was apparently a reference to Andrew—the local post office was called "Old Hickory"—and was unrelated to the river of the same name a few miles upstream, which was named for an early settler, William Jackson, who lived near the site of Fort Dinwiddie.

68–69. The Hannah Dennis story is recounted in *HCV;* in Niles, *The James;* by Robert Douthat Stoner in *A Seed-Bed of the Republic* (Roanoke: Roanoke Historical Society, 1962); by Oren F. Morton in *History of Rockbridge County;* and by Harry Fulwiler Jr. in *Buchanan, Virginia: Gateway to the Southwest* (Radford, VA: Commonwealth Press Inc., 1980). Fulwiler, citing historian L. C. Draper, writes that Joshua Renick was raised by Tecumseh's parents, and was a playmate of the future Indian leader and his brother, The Prophet.

69–71. Cornstalk's murder is recounted in Stuart's eyewitness account, *Memoirs of Indian Wars;* Jefferds, *Arbuckle;* and Pollard, *Virginia Tourist,* where the deed is described as "one of the foulest and most pitiful assassinations that ever drew sympathy for the wrongs of the red man and reflected the fierce and cruel spirit of his conquerors."

72–73. The history of the Valley Road is detailed by Fulwiler, *Buchananan;* Forrer et al. in *The James River Basin;* Charles E. Kemper, "The Settlement of the Valley," *VMHB* 30, no. 2 (April 1922); Thomas Perkins Abernethy in *Three Virginia Frontiers* (Gloucester, MA: Peter Smith, 1962); and in the *Buchanan, Virginia Business & Newcomers' 1999 Guidebook* (Bedford, VA: Landmark Community Newspapers, 1998). See also Morton, *History of Rockbridge County.*

The bulk of this chapter was gleaned from personal observation during our travels along this stretch of river on Thursday, September 17, 1998. Otherwise:

75–77. Jefferson is quoted from his *Notes*. Caldwell's comment is from *A Tour through Part of Virginia in the Summer of 1808* (Richmond: Dietz Press, 1951). His journal, published in two nineteenth century editions, is reprinted in this version edited by William M. E. Rachal. The Porte Crayon quotes here and later in the chapter can be found in Edmund P. Tompkins and J. Lee Davis, *The Natural Bridge and Its Historical Surroundings* (Natural Bridge, VA: Natural Bridge of Virginia Inc., 1939), and in a collection of Crayon's work edited by Cecil D. Eby Jr., *The Old South Illustrated* (Chapel Hill: University of North Carolina Press, 1959).

By the way, the Natural Bridge isn't quite as natural today as it was at the time of our trip. On October 23, 1999, a Georgia tourist was killed when a shower of rocks broke away from the arch's underside and fell to the walkway below, where participants in a cross-country bus tour were strolling. The Natural Bridge's owners had a team of Canadian specialists scrape away the arch's remaining loose stone, then drilled heavy bolts through Route 11 to shore up the underside with steel plates. What is arguably the oldest traffic bridge on the continent thus sustained its first structural improvement.

77–79. Passages detailing Natural Bridge Station are drawn not only from our visit of September 1998 but my scouting trip of June 24–26, 1998, and subsequent forays I made to Nelson, Amherst, and Rockbridge counties on April 7–11 and July 15–18, 1999. Two locals I met near the old depot site in Natural Bridge Station told me of the elevator; one of them, a lifelong NBSer residing in a house next to the vanished stagecoach barn, noted that the ghost village "used to be right famous." Morton, in *History of Rockbridge County*, is more restrained: "At the railroad station the tracks of the Norfolk and Western and the Chesapeake and Ohio cross," he wrote, "and somewhat of a village has been called into existence."

The once-busy street beside the depot site is named Lloyd Tolley Road, for Charles Lloyd Tolley, whom Winifred Hadsel's *Roads of Rockbridge County* (Lexington, VA: Rockbridge Historical Society, 1993) describes as "the kind, obliging, efficient keeper" of the Chiles-Barger general store from 1955 to 1973. The store closed, Hadsel writes, after Tolley and his wife gave up the business; Lloyd died a year later.

79. The Devil's Marbleyard legend is courtesy of Tompkins and Davis, *Natural Bridge*; my description of the place is based on my own ascent of the Belfast Trail in April 1999.

81. The improbable adventures of John Peter Salling are related by Fairfax Harrison in "The Virginians on the Ohio and the Mississippi in 1742," *VMHB* 30, no. 2 (April 1922). Salling's story is paid passing attention by several other writers, at least half of whom call him Salley, rather than Salling, and a good many of whom have him captured by Indians and transported hither and yon between the Great Lakes and the Gulf of Mexico. While these tales don't jibe with Salling's own journal, on which Harrison relies, there *is* good reason to think that his name might have been Salley; I've chosen to use the spelling reflected in Glasgow's geography to avoid confusion. (By the way, the explorers who didn't escape wound up dragged off to France.)

82. Numerous sources describe John McDowell's fight with the Indians, among them Mor-

ton, *History of Rockbridge County;* Tompkins and Davis, *Natural Bridge;* and Miller, *Glasgow, Virginia.* A particularly detailed, if opinionated, account is Howison's in *HV.*

Glasgow's aborted boom is laid out in Edmund P. Tompkins, *Rockbridge County, Virginia* (Richmond: Whittet & Shepperson, 1952); Morton, *History of Rockbridge County;* and Royster Lyle Jr., "Rockbridge County's Boom Hotels," *Virginia Cavalcade* 20, no. 3 (winter 1971). Lest you write off Glasgow's investors as nuts, consider that Buena Vista's boom went as planned—a host of factories moved in, and the grand hotel built by the town's developers still stands, as the main building of Southern Virginia College. The Depression-era guidebook I cite is WPA, *Virginia.*

82–83. Details about Glasgow's layout are the product of our rendezvous with Hope Zollman, and my return trips to Nelson, Amherst, and Rockbridge counties in April, June, and July 1999. Portions of my description originally appeared in the *VP'*s "Europe in Virginia" feature of June 6, 1999.

83. A wealth of data is available on the floods of 1969, though most concern the death and damage in neighboring Nelson County. I relied here on Miller, *Glasgow, Virginia;* J. D. Camp and E. M. Miller, *Flood of August 1969 in Virginia* (Richmond: Water Resources Division, U.S. Geological Survey, Department of the Interior, 1970); and *The August 1969 Storm and Flood in the Virginias Associated with Hurricane Camille* (Norfolk District, U.S. Army Corps of Engineers, 1970).

83. The 1845 account of the stage road through the gorge is from *HCV.* A similar description is included in Pollard, *Virginia Tourist.*

84. For the lowdown on the Maury River's canal system I depended on the redoubtable Bill Trout, whose *Maury River Atlas* and unpublished *Upper James Atlas* were indispensable. In addition, I found a trove of information in Trout's "An Automobile Tour of the North River Navigation," which is included in *Proceedings of the Rockbridge Historical Society,* vol. 8 (1970–74), published in Lexington in 1979.

DAY 10 (GLASGOW TO LYNCHBURG)

The bulk of this chapter is based on Ian's and my observations and experiences on Friday, September 18, 1998. For general background I relied on Bill Trout's *Upper James Atlas* and Robert O. Bloomer's article on the Blue Ridge in *The James River, Past, Present and Future.* Otherwise:

87–92. The Frank Padget saga is described in Niles, *The James;* in Trout, *Upper James Atlas;* and in a *Lexington Herald* article that is reproduced in facsimile in Trout's manuscript.

88. Miller describes the Balcony Falls Dam's destruction in *Glasgow, Virginia;* so does "Dam at Balcony Falls Falls!" in the August 1977 issue of *Coastal Ca-News,* the newsletter of Coastal Canoeists Inc.

93–94. The section on Cushaw Dam relies on a telephone interview with Virginia Power's Ken Baker in late April 1999, and on the *Virginia Hydro Dam Inventory,* vol. 2, a listing of every hydro dam in the commonwealth prepared for the U.S. Department of Energy and the state Office of Emergency and Energy Services in 1981. Neither source revealed how the dam acquired its name, which seems to be a misspelling of "Cashaw," a creek that enters the James on the gorge's north side.

94–95. My descriptions of the chain of dams are based on data from the *Virginia Hydro Dam Inventory* and on observations made during the trip and a subsequent auto tour of the river in July 1999.

DAY 11 (LYNCHBURG TO BENT CREEK)

Most of the material for this chapter was gathered firsthand during our trip downriver on Saturday, September 19, 1998. Otherwise:

95–100. Worried that my impressions of Lynchburg had been too harsh, I drove back to the city in April 1999 for another, more leisurely look at the place, and on this trip noticed something that I either overlooked or that wasn't yet in place seven months earlier: near the blue-vinyl banners—which, by the way, were still flapping from the same chain-link fence, in the same weedy, desolate bottomland—was a building in the midst of restoration. An architectural firm was apparently setting up shop in the place. I saw it as a first, tiny step toward a new partnership with the James. With that hopeful qualification, my initial reaction to the city—or that part of it along the river, which is all I concerned myself with—survived the visit. There will be those in Lynchburg who will complain that it's not fair to judge an entire city by a sliver, that no place looks good if your assessment is focused on its worst neighborhood. But I haven't visited too many river towns that have so thoroughly damned their waterfronts.

On to the sources. The history I rattle off throughout the sections on Lynchburg relies on WPA, *Virginia;* Trout, *Batteau Festival Trail;* and the chapter on Campbell County in *HCV.* Howe also provided fascinating reading on New London and on the origin of the Lynch Law, the latter of which I trimmed from the text on the grounds that it didn't fit comfortably in the narrative. (But now that I've brought it up: yes, "Lynchburg" and "lynching" refer to the same surname, though not the same person. During the Revolution, John Lynch's brother, Charles, lived on the far side of Campbell County, along what's now called the Roanoke River. Charles didn't much care for the lawlessness he observed in those parts, particularly the lawbreaking perpetrated by Tories. The quick and simple solution was to have the hooligans rounded up and flogged against a tree, sparing everyone the fuss of a trial. Charles Lynch meted out his punishment with a whip; hanging the accused was a later refinement of the practice.)

97–98. The section on the *John Marshall* comes courtesy of Trout, *Batteau Festival Trail;* WPA, *Virginia;* and Richard B. Loyd and Bernard K. Mundy's *Lynchburg, A Pictorial History* (Virginia Beach: Donning Co., 1975). The boat's placement in the park is described, and a photo of it reproduced, in the *Lynchburg News,* sesquicentennial edition, October 11, 1936.

DAY 12 (BENT CREEK TO HOWARDSVILLE)

The bulk of this chapter, concerning Hurricane Camille, originally appeared in longer form as an eight-part *VP* series called "When the Rain Came." It was published daily from August 15 through August 22, 1999, and reprinted as a slick thirty-two-page magazine later in the year. I wrote the stories; Ian took the pictures.

Among my sources were contemporary accounts of the flooding in the *New York Times,* the *Washington Post, VP, Newsweek, U.S. News & World Report, Weatherwise,* the Charlottesville *Daily Progress* and the *Richmond Times-Dispatch;* and U.S. Army Corps of Engineers, *The Au-*

gust 1969 Storm. I also relied on more recent stories in the *Lynchburg News & Advance,* and on Paige Shoaf and Jerry H. Simpson Jr., *Torn Land* (Lynchburg: J. P. Bell Co., 1970). This last account of the disaster and recovery in Nelson County is told by several survivors, each accorded his own chapter and allowed to deliver his recollections in a free-form monologue. On the one hand it suffers from the approach, because most of its subjects dwell far more on the recovery of bodies in the days after the disaster than they do on the rain or flooding. On the other, the book's raw, unedited feel is electrifying in places, and fascinating throughout—not everyone in the cast comes off looking good.

The stories of Tommy and Adelaide Huffman and Warren Raines are the product of detailed interviews with each. Warren Raines and I, in particular, spent long hours on the phone over several weeks in the spring and summer of 1999, in addition to meeting in person on three of my trips to Nelson County. I came away from those interviews confident that these survivors were among the most courageous people I would ever meet.

DAY 13 (HOWARDSVILLE TO BREMO BLUFF)

Most of this chapter is based on Ian's and my observations while journeying along this stretch of the James on Monday, September 21, 1998. Otherwise:

122. I've had the good fortune to ride with David Haney and crew twice; in summer 1999, I floated the section from Wingina to Howardsville while on assignment for *Chesapeake Bay* magazine.

122–125. Much of the material on batteaux originally appeared under my byline in *Chesapeake Bay* magazine's June 2000 edition. Robert Rose's invention and the later rise of the batteau is detailed wonderfully in the James River Batteau Festival's website at <http://www.batteau.org>. Other sources on batteaux include Trout, *Batteau Festival Trail;* Tompkins and Davis, *Natural Bridge;* and *Virginia Explorer* 11, no. 3 (summer 1995).

127. Moore, *Scottsville on the James*. The 1835 gazetteer quoted by Moore is Joseph Martin, *A New and Comprehensive Gazetteer of Virginia* (Charlottesville: Moseley and Thompkins, 1835).

The cave legend is described by Moore.

DAY 14 (BREMO BLUFF TO WEST VIEW)

The greater part of this chapter is based on Ian's and my experiences on the river on Tuesday, September 22, 1998. Otherwise:

128–129. The passages on Bremo and Gen. John Hartwell Cocke rely on Calder Loth, *Virginia Landmarks of Black History* (Charlottesville: University Press of Virginia, 1995).

130. Parke Rouse Jr., *Below the James Lies Dixie* (Richmond: Dietz Press, 1968).

131. The Monacan village is located at Point of Fork by David I. Bushnell Jr. in "The Native Tribes of Virginia," *VMHB* 30, no. 2 (April 1922). I've used his spelling for the place. The loss of American ammo to the British here is detailed in *HV,* and in the section on Fluvanna County in *HCV.*

131–132. Burial mounds, their locations and their fates are described in Tompkins, *Rockbridge County;* Bushnell, "Native Tribes"; Lindsey S. Weilbacher, "What's Happened to the Hays

Creek Indian Mound," *Rockbridge Weekly,* October 6, 1986; James W. McClung, *Historical Significance of Rockbridge County, Virginia* (Staunton, VA: McClure Co. Inc., 1939); and in *The Virginia Historical Register and Literary Note Book for the Year 1850,* edited by William Maxwell and included in photocopied form in the collection of the Rockbridge County Library in Lexington. It is in this last source that "Montanus" appears. I also encountered a remarkable pamphlet in the Rockbridge library that was produced by the Valentine Museum shortly after the Hayes Creek burial mound was excavated. Its photos of unearthed skeletons are troubling to behold.

DAY 15 (WEST VIEW TO WATKINS LANDING)

Most of this chapter is the product of our travels on the James on Wednesday, September 23, 1998. Otherwise:

138–139. The detail about the canal traffic's use of the river on this five-mile stretch is included in Trout, *Batteau Festival Trail.*

140. The origin of "Maidens" is from Trout and from WPA, *Virginia.*

143–145. The French settlement in Powhatan County is detailed in Robert L. Scribner, "Manakintowne in Virginia," *Virginia Cavalcade* 3, no. 3 (winter 1953); James L. Bugg Jr., "The French Huguenot Frontier Settlement of Manakin Town," *VMHB* 61, no. 4 (October 1953); and G. MacLaren Brydon, "The Huguenots of Manakin Town and Their Times," *VMHB* 42, no. 4 (October 1934). Earlier Huguenot settlement in Virginia is described by Patricia Holbert Menk in "Notes on Some Early Huguenot Settlements in Virginia," *VMHB* 52, no. 3 (July 1944).

DAY 16 (WATKINS LANDING TO RICHMOND)

Most of this chapter is based on our experiences of Thursday, September 24, 1998. Otherwise:

148–149. The mines are the subject of numerous articles and histories, among them Ronald L. Lewis, "The Darkest Abode of Man," *VMHB* 87, no. 2 (April 1979), a study of black miners and their working conditions that also details several of the bigger methane explosions to rock the shafts; Bettie W. Weaver, "The Mines of Midlothian," *Virginia Cavalcade* 11, no. 3 (winter 1961–62); and *HCV,* whose section on Chesterfield County includes a firsthand account of Howe's visit to the mines, as well as an account of an accident in which it was clear that many miners had "survived the explosion of the inflammable gas, and were destroyed by inhaling the carbonic acid gas which succeeds it," a death "said to be very pleasant; fairy visions float around the sufferer, and he drops into the sleep of eternity like one passing into delightful dreams."

149. The detail about the fire is from Lewis, "Darkest Abode." The descriptions of explosions are from *HCV* and Lewis, respectively. The remarkable information on mules, including the quote, is from *HCV.* The development of rail lines at the mines is described in "Forerunner of Virginia's First Railway," *Virginia Cavalcade* 4, no. 3 (winter 1954), and in Edward F. Heite, "Narrow Gauge to Farmville," *Virginia Cavalcade* 16, no. 3 (winter 1967).

150. The ladder's construction is described by Ben Cleary, "Rediscovering the James," *Style Weekly* (Richmond), March 1, 1997. Its design is detailed in Alan Weaver, "If We Build Them, They Will Come," *Virginia Wildlife* 56, no. 1 (January 1995).

The bulk of this chapter is based on Ian's and my experiences on the river in Richmond on Friday, September 25, 1998. Throughout the day we relied on William E. Trout III, James Moore III, and George D. Rawls, *Falls of the James Atlas* (Richmond: Virginia Canals & Navigations Society, 1995), another in the remarkable series of river guides produced by the society. Otherwise:

151. The council's instructions are included in Edward Wright Haile, ed., *Jamestown Narratives: Eyewitness Accounts of the Virginia Colony* (Champlain, VA: RoundHouse, 1998). The first visit of whites to the Falls is described by Virginius Dabney in *Richmond: The Story of a City* (Charlottesville: University Press of Virginia, 1990); by Philip L. Barbour, "The First Reconnaissance of the James," *Virginia Cavalcade* 17, no. 2 (Autumn 1967); and in a collection Barbour edited, *The Complete Works of Captain John Smith (1580–1631)*, vol. 1 (Chapel Hill: University of North Carolina Press, 1986).

153. A statistical description of the city's bridges can be found in "Richmond's Eleven Major Bridges: Some Facts and Figures," an unsigned article in *The Richmond Quarterly* 3, no. 4 (spring 1981).

154–155. The story of the POW stockade at Belle Isle's eastern end is related in detail in Robert L. Scribner, "Belle Isle: Time Was When Thousands Thought That the Island Had Been Misnamed," *Virginia Cavalcade* 5, no. 3 (winter 1955).

155–156. The passages on Hollywood Cemetery are based on our visit of September 1998; on a subsequent trip to the burial ground I made in May 1999; and on Mary H. Mitchell, *Hollywood Cemetery: The History of a Southern Shrine* (Richmond: The Library of Virginia, 1999). Much of the section first appeared as "Final Resting Place of the Old South," a *VP* story published under my byline on May 29, 1999.

157. The Arthur Ashe statue was the subject of a huge flap in Richmond in 1995 and 1996, between activists who demanded that the tennis star and Richmond native be memorialized on the avenue, and traditionalists who argued that his likeness was out of step with statuary of the South's Civil War heroes. The former prevailed, and the oddly proportioned rendition of Ashe took its place among the grander Confederate monuments.

157–158. The militia's abandonment of the fight is related by Col. John G. Simcoe of the Redcoat army in *HCV*'s section on Henrico County. The governor's actions are detailed in *HV*, the source of the quotes here.

158. *HV* and *HCV* provide accounts of Jefferson's movements; "liquor ran in streams . . ." is from *HV*.

The articles of impeachment are reported in *HV*.

158. A good description of James River Park can be found in Jan Robertson, "The Wild Heart of Richmond: James River Park," *Virginia Wildlife* 42, no. 4 (April 1981). Since our visit, the park has been augmented with the June 1999 opening of the Canal Walk, part of a $38 million project that combined fixing the city's problem with sewerage overflow in heavy rain, and a park-straddled restoration of downtown canals. The project is detailed in "Richmond's Canal Walk: Reopening the Riverfront," a special section in the June 1, 1999, *Richmond Times-Dispatch*.

159. The volcanic origins of the riverbed rock is detailed by James S. Beard, "Volcanoes in

Virginia," *Virginia Explorer* 10, no. 2 (spring 1994), and in Beard's "Riverbed Potholes of Richmond," *Virginia Explorer* 11, no. 3 (summer 1995).

DAY 18 (RICHMOND TO THE CURLS OF THE JAMES)

The bulk of this chapter is based on our experiences of Saturday, September 26, 1998. Otherwise:

164–166. The first upriver exploration is described by Charles E. Hatch Jr., *The First Seventeen Years: Virginia, 1607–1624* (Williamsburg: Virginia 350th Anniversary Celebration Corp., 1957), a site-by-site history of the lower James, terse but informative; in Haile's *Jamestown Narratives;* in Barbour, "First Reconnaissance of the James"; by Barbour in "Captain Newport Meets Opechancanough," *Virginia Cavalcade* 17, no. 3 (winter 1968); in Barbour, *Complete Works of Captain John Smith;* and in Dabney, *Richmond.* The expedition's speedy return to Jamestown is related in Barbour's *Virginia Cavalcade* articles, and by J. Frederick Fausz in "An 'Abundance of Blood Shed on Both Sides': England's First Indian War, 1609–1614," *VMHB* 98, no. 1 (January 1990).

166. The thickness of sediments in the coastal plain is described by Joseph K. Roberts in "The Triassic and Coastal Plain," a chapter in *The James River Basin.*

166–167. The fort at Drewry's Bluff and the battle there are described in Ralph W. Donnelly, "The Confederate Marines at Drewry's Bluff," *Virginia Cavalcade* 16, no. 2 (Autumn 1966); by Carvel Hall Blair and Willits Dyer Ansel in *Chesapeake Bay Notes & Sketches* (Cambridge, MD: Tidewater Publishers, 1970); in G. Melvin Herndon, "The Confederate States Naval Academy," *VMHB* 69, no. 3 (July 1961); and in William Kennon Kay, "Drewry's Bluff or Fort Darling?" *VMHB* 77, no. 2 (April 1969). Quotes from Blackford, Chestnut, and the Richmond newspaper are from Kay, "Drewry's Bluff or Fort Darling?"

168. The passages on the Confederate academy draw from Herndon, "Confederate States Naval Academy."

169. The origins of the Dutch Gap ditch are related in *HCV.*

169–170. The Ben Butler fiasco is detailed in "'A Bottle Strongly Corked,'" *Virginia Cavalcade* 4, no. 3 (winter 1954).

171. Dale's managerial style is discussed in William H. Gaines Jr., "The Discipline of Sir Thomas Dale," *Virginia Cavalcade* 3, no. 4 (spring 1954).

171. Jamestown's disease is the subject of Gordon W. Jones's fascinating "The First Epidemic in English America," *VMHB* 71, no. 1 (January 1963). Death by the flux is also related in Barbour's *Complete Works of Captain John Smith.*

172. Disney's liberties with reality are reported in "Disney vs. History . . . Again" and "Separating the Facts from Movie Fiction," both by movie critic Mal Vincent, *VPLS,* June 20, 1995. Smith's capture and travels are found in a multitude of sources, among them Barbour's *Complete Works of Captain John Smith,* Haile's *Jamestown Narratives,* and William Randel's "Captain John Smith's Attitudes toward the Indians," *VMHB,* Vol 47, no. 3 (July 1939).

172. Smith's own account of the Pocahontas incident is explored in Barbour, *Complete Works of Captain John Smith.* Further discussion is found in Kevin J. Hayes, "Defining the Ideal Colonist," *VMHB* 99, no. 2 (April 1991). Smith's believability is explored in Jennifer Robin Goodman, "The Captain's Self-Portrait: John Smith as Chivalric Biographer," *VMHB* 89, no. 1 (Jan-

uary 1981); Jay B. Hubbell, "The Smith-Pocahontas Story in Literature," *VMHB* 65, no. 3 (July 1957); J. Franz Pichler, "Captain John Smith in the Light of Styrian Sources," *VMHB* 65, no. 3 (July 1957). The incident's place in American culture is recounted nicely by Hubbell in "Smith-Pocahontas Story," and discussed at length in J. A. Leo Lemay, *Did Pocahontas Save Captain John Smith?* (Athens, GA: University of Georgia Press, 1992).

172. The best explanation I've found of the decay in relations is Fausz's "An "Abundance of Blood Shed on Both Sides.'"

173. Ibid. Percy's own account of the ugliness with the Nansemonds is included in "A True Relation of the proceedings and occurrents of moment which have hap'ned in Virginia from the time Sir Thomas Gates was shipwrack'd upon the Bermudes, anno 1609, until my departure out of the country, which was in anno Domini 1612," in Haile's *Jamestown Narratives.* Of the messengers he reported that he "understood from the Indians themselves that they were sacrificed, and that their brains were cut and scraped out of their heads with mussel shells." The debacle at Powhatan village is also detailed by Fausz, as is the English retreat to Jamestown and Ratcliffe's fate. The latter, by the way, wouldn't have surprised Smith, who reported that when Powhatan punished "any notorious enemy or malefactor, he causeth him to be tyed to a tree, and with Mussell shels or reeds, the executioner cutteth off his joynts one after another, ever casting what they cut into the fire, then doth he proceed with shels and reeds to cas the skinne from his head and face, then doe they rip his belly and so burne him with the tree and all."

174. The starving time is described in Fausz, "'Abundance of Blood'"; in Niles, *The James;* and by George Percy in *Jamestown Narratives:* "Then having fed upon horses and other beasts as long as they lasted, we were glad to make shift with vermin, as dogs, cats, rats, and mice. All was fish that came to net to satisfy cruel hunger, as to eat boots, shoes, or any other leather some should come by. And those being spent and devoured, some were enforced to search the woods and to feed upon serpents and snakes and to dig the earth for wild and unknown roots, where many of our men were cut off and slain by the savages." It's Percy who mentions the licking and the case of spousal cannibalism.

Day 19 (The Curls to Upper Brandon)

Most of this chapter is based on our observations of Sunday, September 27, 1998. Otherwise:

175–176. Hopewell's exciting early days are described by Bates M. Stovall in *VP,* January 20, 1952. The road signs are described by Donna Weatherly, "A New Image: Hopewell Struggles against Stigma," *LS,* September 13, 1980.

176–177. The Kepone disaster is covered in Weatherly, "New Image."

178. The bridge's length is from "Monument to Progress," an editorial in the July 1, 1963, *VP.* Other background on the span is found in the August 17, 1956, *VP* and in the September 10 and 11, 1956, *LS.*

179. De La Warr's arrival and the English turnaround are described by Fausz, "'Abundance of Blood,'" and by De La Warr himself in a 1610 letter to the Earl of Salisbury, quoted in the *VMHB* 14, no. 3 (January 1907).

179–180. Percy's account is from *Jamestown Narratives,* from Fausz, and from David E. Stannard, *American Holocaust: Columbus and the Conquest of the New World* (New York: Oxford University Press, 1992).

180. Lt. Puttock's fate, and Dale's reinforcements, are detailed by Fausz.

181–182. A slew of guidebooks, pamphlets, and magazine pieces describe the James River plantations. I found some interesting reading in Frank and Cortelle Hutchins' *Virginia: The Old Dominion As Seen from Its Colonial Waterway, the Historic River James* (Boston: Page Co., 1910). This 299-page travelogue records a leisurely houseboat voyage from Norfolk to Richmond by Frank Hutchins, his wife and his mother-in-law. It offers a fascinating snapshot of Jamestown in decay—this was well before the Colonial National Historic Park came on the scene—and the plantations before their discovery by the tourism industry. The self-sufficiency of the estates is described in Martha P. Munger, "Hog Island in the James," *Virginia Cavalcade* 10, no. 4 (spring 1961).

183–184. Stuart's quote is from *Memoir of Indian Wars*.

DAY 20 (UPPER BRANDON TO CHIPPOKES PLANTATION)

Most of this chapter is based on Ian's and my observations while traveling the river on Monday, September 28, 1998, and on subsequent trips I made to Jamestown, Smith's Fort Plantation, and Bacon's Castle in the spring and summer of 1999. Otherwise:

189. The old fort on Gray's Creek is described by A. W. Bohannan, "Jamestown Island and 'The Surry Side,'" *VMHB* 55, no. 2 (April 1947).

The history of the Warren/Rolfe house is related by Bohannan, and by Elizabeth Valentine Huntley, *Peninsula Pilgrimage* (Richmond: Whittet & Shepperson, 1941). Bohannan counters longstanding tradition by arguing the property's name refers to John Rolfe, rather than Thomas. The underground passage was described to me by several members of the Association for the Preservation of Virginia Antiquities, who directed me to the shaft opening in a closet on the house's second floor.

189. Pocahontas's capture, conversion, and subsequent marriage to John Rolfe, are discussed by Fausz, "'Abundance of Blood'"; by Louise Durbin, "Pocahontas in England," *Virginia Cavalcade* 18, no. 3 (winter 1969), and by Walter L. Heilbronner, "The Earliest Printed Account of the Death of Pocahontas," *VMHB* 66, no. 3 (July 1958).

189–190. Pocahontas's visit to England is detailed by Durbin. Her death is described by Durbin and Heilbronner.

190–191. The U.S. Fish and Wildlife Service figures that in 1999, the Chesapeake Bay region's eagle population reached 513 nesting pairs, producing 706 eaglets, according to Scott Harper, "Bald Eagles Abound in Bay," *VP,* March 25, 2000. Nearly half of that population is located in the lower James. A June 27, 1999, Harper story in *VP* called the James between Hopewell and Newport News "the largest summer concentration of bald eagles on the East Coast."

192. The divergent views of the peace are wonderfully explained by Fausz. Opechancanough's ascension to leadership is described by James R. Short, "Exit Powhatan; Enter Opechancanough," *Virginia Cavalcade* 3, no. 2 (Autumn 1953).

192. Opechancanough's behind-the-scenes preparations for war are described by William S. Powell, "Aftermath of the Massacre," *VMHB* 66, no. 1 (January 1958).

192–193. The 1622 massacre is detailed by Powell; by Short; in WPA, *Virginia;* in Niles, *The James;* and in J. E. Davis, *Jamestown and Her Neighbors on Virginia's Historic Peninsula*

(Richmond: Garrett & Massie Inc., 1928). The detail about Indians sowing gunpowder is mentioned in a September 14, 1622, letter from Joseph Mead to Sir Martin Stuteville, and included in "The Indian Massacre of 1622," edited by Robert C. Johnson, *VMHB* 71, no. 4 (October 1963).

193. The Virginia Company's harsh directive is included in Powell. Opechancanough's death is described by Short.

195–197. Bacon's Rebellion is best described in Wilcomb E. Washburn's terrific *The Governor and the Rebel* (New York: W. W. Norton & Co., 1957), a most effective debunker of the Bacon-as-American-hero myth. Bacon's popular transformation from firebrand to farsighted rebel is also discussed by Bertha Monica Stearns, "The Literary Treatment of Bacon's Rebellion in Virginia," *VMHB* 52, no. 3 (July 1944).

197–198. The quote is from Hutchins and Hutchins, *Virginia.*

198. Jefferson, *Notes on the State of Virginia.*

DAY 21 (CHIPPOKES PLANTATION TO GOODWIN POINT)

The bulk of this chapter is based on our observations of Tuesday, September 29, 1998, and on subsequent visits I made to Surry and Isle of Wight counties in the summer and late fall of 1999. Otherwise:

200–203. The Surry Nuclear Power Station's troubled history is recounted in Tony Germanotta, "8 hurt in Surry Plant Steam Leak," *VP*, December 10, 1986; Cynthia Hanson, "Man Dies of Surry Injuries," *VP*, December 11, 1986; George Hebert, "Intense Review of Surry Plant Imperative," *LS*, December 12, 1986; Bob Geske and Cynthia Hanson, "Thin Pipe May Figure in Accident," *VP*, December 12, 1986; "Faulty Valve Inspected at Surry Plant, but Pipe Still Believed Accident Cause," *VPLS*, December 13, 1986; Anita Lee and Tony Germanotta, "Surry-like Problems Predicted: Industry Critics Warn of Aging Plants in Nation," *VPLS*, December 14, 1986; Gerri Willis, "After the Accident: Nuclear Plant Responded by the Book," (Norfolk) *Business Weekly,* December 15, 1986; a press advisory from the activist group Public Citizen, dated December 15, 1996, which is filed in the archives of the *Virginian-Pilot;* editorial, "The Surry Tragedy," and Anita Lee And Cynthia Hanson, "2 More Injured Surry Workers Die," *VP*, December 16, 1986; Geske and Hanson, "Congressional Panel Starts Probe of Surry Accident," *LS*, December 19, 1986; Geske, "Nuclear Plants Test Pipes in Wake of Surry Accident," *VPLS*, December 20, 1986; Hanson, "Survivor Relives Tragedy of Surry," *VP*, December 23, 1986; Hanson, "Grief over Surry Deaths Slow to Subside," *VPLS*, December 28, 1986; Geske, "About 60 Pipe Sections Found Faulty at Surry," *VP*, January 13, 1987; Associated Press report, "Surry Rupture May Indicate Aging Pipes Elsewhere," *VP*, January 16, 1987; Germanotta, "Va. Power to Brief N-plant Operators on Safety," *LS*, January 23, 1987; staff & wire, "Surry Accident Avoidable, Lawmaker Says," *LS*, February 3, 1987; Geske, "Va. Power Won't be Fined for Fatal Surry Accident," *LS*, February 11, 1987; AP, "Surry Burn Victim Leaves the Hospital," *VP*, February 16, 1987; AP, "Surry Nuclear Reactor to be at Full Power Today," *VPLS*, February 28, 1987; "Virginia Power to Restart 2nd Surry Nuclear Reactor," *VP*, March 18, 1987; Germanotta, "New Report Clears Utility in Surry Accident," *VP*, April 9, 1987; Geske, "Surry Accident: Families Live with Deaths, Grief," *VP*, December 15, 1987; Bill Byrd, "Troubles Mar 1988 at Surry," *VPLS*, October 2, 1988; Jon Frank, "Virginia Power Defends Safety of Nuclear Plants," *LS*, January

10, 1989; Frank, "The Trouble with Surry," *LS*, February 27, 1989; Byrd, "Va. Power Fined $500,000 for 12 Violations at Surry," *VPLS*, May 20, 1989; Frank, "NRC Puts Surry Plant on Problem List," *VP*, June 2, 1989; Frank, "Nuclear Plant in Surry Opens after Shutdown," *VPLS*, July 8, 1989; "Surry Officials Say Plant is Over Past Difficulties," *VP*, May 17, 1990; Frank, "Surry Nuclear Plant Taken off Problem List," *VP*, June 28, 1990; "Faulty Device Closes Both Surry Reactors," *VP*, Nov. 2, 1990; Frank, "Va. Power Fined for Clogged Cooling Pipes at Surry," *VP*, February 14, 1991; AP, "Surry Nuclear Plant Has Improved, NRC Report Says," *VP*, June 19, 1991; Tony Germanotta and Thomas Boyer, "Va. Power is Fined over Safety Gear at Surry Plant," *VP*, October 23, 1991; Germanotta and Boyer, "U.S. Sees Risk of Surry Meltdown: Danger If Water Pipe Should Break," *VP*, October 25, 1991; Germanotta, "Va. Power Ordered to Meet with NRC about Surry pipe," *VP*, October 31, 1991; Diane Tennant, "NRC Chief Says Surry Plant Safe," *VP*, Nov. 30, 1991; Mark Weaver, "Scores Up at Surry Nuke Station," *VP*, September 15, 1993; "Surry to Test Nuclear Emergency Plan," *VP*, December 7, 1993; Allison T. Williams, "A Test of the Unthinkable," *Isle of Wight Citizen,* a tabloid supplement to the *VP*, December 29, 1993; Scott Harper, "Surry's Unwelcome Guest: Hydroids—Animals Akin to Coral—Clog Power Plant Pipes, Reduce Water Flow," *VP*, April 3, 1995; editorial, "Surry Nuclear Plant Warning System Fails: Silent Sirens," *VP*, June 20, 1995; Harper, "NRC Orders Hearing on Surry Safety," *VP*, August 3, 1996; Akweli Parker, "Virginia Power Surry Plant Must Pay $55,000 for Late Paperwork," *VP*, September 3, 1997; and Parker, "Surry Power Plant Gets High Marks on Report," *VP*, May 1, 1998.

Further background on nuclear power can be found in Thomas Boyer and Joseph Cosco, "Virginia Experts Divided on Safety of U.S. Reactors," *VP*, April 30, 1986; and Parker, "Since Three-Mile Island: Twenty Years after the Near Disaster, the NRC Has Begun Scaling Back its Watchdog Efforts—and That Concerns Some Folks," and "For Outnumbered Inspectors of Nuclear Power Plants, Prying Is Just a Part of the Job," *VP*, March 28, 1999.

The explanation of a nuclear plant's internal workings can be found in the Public Citizen's press advisory of December 15, 1986.

203. Hog Island's colonial past is described in A. W. Bohannan, "Jamestown Island." My anecdotes on Hog Island wildlife and the dating of the holly come courtesy of a conversation with warden Mack Walls, during my visit to the management area on December 9, 1999. Further background on the refuge can be found in *A Guide to Virginia's Wildlife Management Areas,* a booklet produced by the Virginia Department of Game and Inland Fisheries, and revised in 1996. Munger, "Hog Island," provides details about the island's past.

204–207. Ian and I toured the idle fleet by speedboat in summer 1998, while preparing for the journey.

208–209. Information on the oyster can be found in Nelson Marshall, "Marine Fishes and Invertebrates," in *The James River Basin.*

209–210. Fort Boykin's past is recounted in an unpublished paper by Genie Cory, which I found in *The Virginian-Pilot's* files, and in Don Hill, "Rebel Shots Boomeranged," *VP*, February 23, 1964; Guy Friddell, "The Little Fort That Survived," *VP*, June 1, 1975; "Fort Boykins Turned Over to I. of W.," *VP*, April 10, 1976; Frank M. Roberts, "Fort Boykin: Lovely Historic Site Little Known," *Suffolk Sun* (*VP* tabloid), August 26, 1979; Carole Maguire, "Fort Boykin Water Well Yields Tale of History," *Suffolk Sun,* May 3, 1987; and Linda McNatt, "Fort Boykin a Site of Unspoiled Beauty," *Suffolk Sun,* July 9, 1989.

Day 22 (Goodwin Point to the mouth of the James)

Most of this chapter is based on our travels of Wednesday, September 30, 1998. Otherwise:

214. The quotes are from *Official Program for the Occasion of the Opening of the James River Bridge* (Richmond: Whittet & Shepperson, 1928). A copy is on file at Norfolk's Kirn Memorial Library.

215–216. Newport News's development, and Collis Huntington's legacy, are detailed in Parke Rouse Jr., *Endless Harbor: The Story of Newport News* (Newport News: Newport News Historical Committee, 1969), and in several articles from *Newport News' 325 Years* (Newport News: Newport News Golden Anniversary Corporation, 1946).

216. The Monitor-Merrimac Bridge-Tunnel is described and pictured in Scott M. Kozel, *Roads to the Future,* posted at <http://www.richmond.infi.net/~kozelsm/I664MMMBTMain.html>.

216–218. Information on the Newport News Middle Ground light is from the files of the National Archives; from files in the library of the Mariners Museum in Newport News, Virginia; and from Robert H. Burgess, "Pillars of Fire by Night—To Guide the Ships at Sea," *VP,* May 2, 1954.

ACKNOWLEDGMENTS

You'd not now be holding *Journey on the James* if not for the dozens of people who helped plan the trip, who paid for it, who edited and published its skeletal form in the *Virginian-Pilot,* who helped Ian and me on our long journey down the river, and who held my hand as I struggled to transform the story into a book. Were I to thank everyone who owns a piece of it, the list would run for pages—so I'll just mention a few of them, and hope that those not listed understand that they have my everlasting thanks.

At the *Pilot,* Dennis Hartig brought his boundless enthusiasm to the project from its infancy. Kay Addis, the paper's editor, not only gave the trip the thumbs up, but gave me permission to lift passages from several *Pilot* stories for this book. Maria Carrillo was as calm, confident, and encouraging a boss as any writer could hope for. Finally, Fred Kirsch, my spiritual advisor, shared the series' expert line editing with Maria, helped me over the river's rough spots in long phone conversations, and bought me beer when it was over.

At the University Press of Virginia, Boyd Zenner invited me to transform the series into a book, then coaxed me through the ensuing fourteen months of lonely torture, blown deadlines, and existential dread. David Sewell edited with grace.

Lillie Gilbert's advice helped keep me alive long enough to start writing. Dick Bayer and Laureen Rowland struggled through early drafts. Jay Livingston of *Chesapeake Bay* magazine gave me the nod to include some history I gathered first for that publication. Others helped me maintain a fingerhold on sanity during the book's preparation, among them Laura LaFay, Naomi Aoki, Robin Russ, Lori Denney, Jane Sherman, and my parents. My daughter, Saylor, accompanied me on several 1999 forays upriver and to the library, contented herself with coloring books and cartoons while I worked weekends at home, and grew so cheerfully accustomed to my schedule that she now has trouble falling asleep unless I'm typing in the next room.

I'm especially indebted to Mike D'Orso, my mentor, Scrabble partner, and sounding board, whose encouragement has propelled me on this odyssey.

And, of course, Ian Martin, without whom this story wouldn't have happened.

CPSIA information can be obtained
at www.ICGtesting.com
Printed in the USA
LVHW111605021121
702252LV00010B/1644

9 780813 921198